THE KITCHEN BOOK
THE COOK BOOK

Nicolas Freeling

THE KITCHEN BOOK
THE COOK BOOK

ILLUSTRATED BY
JOHN LAWRENCE

David R. Godine, Publisher
BOSTON

First edition published in 1991 by
David R. Godine, Publisher, Inc.
Horticultural Hall
300 Massachusetts Avenue
Boston, Massachusetts 02115

Library of Congress Cataloging in Publication Data
Freeling, Nicolas.
[Kitchen book]
The kitchen book & the cook book / by Nicolas Freeling ;
illustrations by John Lawrence. — 1st U.S. ed.
p.   cm.
Includes index.
ISBN 0-87923-862-3 (pbk. : alk. paper)
1. Cookery, English. 2. Gastronomy. 3. Freeling, Nicolas.
I. Lawrence, John, 1933–   . II. Freeling, Nicolas. Cook book.
III. Title. IV. Title: Kitchen book and the cook book.
TX717.F86   1991
641.5—dc20   90-55279   CIP

First edition
Printed in the United States of America

CONTENTS

The Kitchen Book

The Cook Book

THE KITCHEN BOOK

LOVE FROM FATFINGER

I saw you in the old Vél d'Hiv, the bicycle stadium in Paris where, with that peculiar sense of fitness, and order, and logic that some people had, the Jews were once rounded up. If they got cold—but the French themselves called it the Winter Stadium, didn't they? Well then, let them go round and round in it. And if they want to be six-day riders, eating and drinking too much isn't going to improve them either.

It was going to be knocked down, because the French found six-day bicycle races old-fashioned, and you were tasting it for the last time; tasting that particular stink of beer and sweat, the tinny music turned up to maximum, the riders going round and round, the banners waving for Pschitt and Pernod and all around you the hermetic mystique. You were sitting comfortably at a little metal table, actually smoking a cigar, enjoying yourself, hearing sad cello music. Good evening, Monsieur Bemelmans.

But listen, Ludwig, how is it that I never met you in New York?

Going drinking with you in Bemelmans country, in Paris or Amalfi or the Tirol, is fine, but New York would have been special. I shall never cease to regret that. Why did you have to go and die? So this is a clumsy sort of effort to make up; really this is for you. Because, damn it, we're unique after all. Cook books and cookery books and cuisine books (since some of them are pretty fancy)—there isn't a year, there isn't a publisher's autumn list without a few. And as for all the people who are knowing about food, we're inundated with them. The perfected colour-photography, those luscious dishes; exquisite torture to read in bed when on a diet, though they make us long for a piece of stale bread and a few olives. You wrote a restaurant book, and it is the only one. So here is a kitchen book for you. I am sitting in Alsace, in a powerful reek of ham-hocks and sauerkraut, drinking this year's wine which has only just fermented and has not yet clarified; sour-sweet and clouded-yellow, and I'm eating bread and walnuts to go with it. Come and sit down; share my table.

This is about the dull and sickening smells of burnt fat and boiling stock, and the pungent reek of freshly strewn sawdust. Very like the smell of the Vélodrome d'Hiver. This is about kitchens, and about cooks, those cooks about whom you wrote a phrase of marvellous poetry: fat fingers, sliding round the insides of pots, buttering them, fat fingers sitting on top of a carrot, feeding it slowly to the chopping knife. Here, have a look: yes, I know that my fingers are thin. But the thumb is thickened with the scar tissue of a million tiny cuts—the tiny knife, that, with which vegetables are trimmed. Called a turning knife. And the thick callus at the root of the first finger there—there is where the base of a chopping knife fits into a cook's hand. The permanently misshapen nail is in memory of a lobster, and that thick scarred knuckle that can no longer bend properly: it was poisoned, that cut, and for a fortnight I thought I would lose the finger.

It is all different now. Kitchens, and restaurants, changed finally the day they got the accountant in, and now a kitchen is an air-conditioned caravanserai, with closed-circuit television to see that nobody pinches a sausage. But I worked in the old kitchen, the one that is the same as yours, for fifteen years, and that unmistakable air got into my lungs, my bloodstream and my heart, so that I will never be rid of it. Any more than you. At home, where I work, I write upon a table that is a big oblong slab of pine. It was originally varnished, and was the table of a French country bistrot. I took off the varnish, scrubbed the pine with Marseille soap, and it was a kitchen table. I wanted a table to eat from, so I took it again, and painted it with layer on layer of red, and white, and brown paint. Between the layers I dribbled and smeared, rubbed it with the heel of my hand and with fine sandpaper. At the end it had taken on a veined and knotted appearance with scars like the cuts and burns upon a cook's hands, and I was happy with it. My children spoiled it by digging in the surface with their forks while the leisurely adults finished eating, and I took another similar table, but of hardwood, to eat off, and because it was hardwood I left it bare and scrubbed, and the painted one I took for work. Above this table on the wall hangs a drawing you made, of the cooks the clochard saw when he looked through the kitchen window of the Restaurant La Pérouse in Paris. All this is woven into my texture.

1 NOTES ON A KITCHEN BOOK

Professor Sainsbury, a scholarly gentleman of Edwardian times, a person of eminence, wrote a book about wine in the discursive anecdotal style of the era and called it *Notes on a Cellar Book*: the title could not be bettered and I cribbed it. These cellar books were a typically Victorian invention, telling one that in the first five dozen there was one smelly cork and that the Dow 1908 settled down admirably after a peculiar flavour of liquorice at the start. Sprinkled with little tags and illustrations from Catullus and Rabelais, they were also diaries, telling what one had drunk upon what occasion, who the guests were, what the grub was, and what the conversation had been about—nostalgia mostly, about pre-phylloxera days in the Bordelais.

A good nose for claret was a tremendous social asset; in fact you were not a gentleman, remarks Mr. Mason in one of his marvellous Hanaud stories, unless the principal growths of the Médoc were tabled upon your heart. It must be a remnant of this tradition that provokes all the claptrap in restaurants; having a taste poured out and looking stern, as though you might send the bottle back, even if it is a half bottle of Sauternes in the dining-room at Liverpool Street. A French waiter pulls the cork and smells it: you know from his face whether the bottle is right. That is what he is for; by definition he knows more about it than you do and if he doesn't you have walked into the wrong restaurant.

The Victorians really were great wine experts, and all the best stuff on the market came to Saint James's Street, but their food was often odd, and they did guzzle, as we see in Dickens.

'Polly, three marrow puddings,' says Tony Jobling, dining in the city with that other eminent man of the world Mr. Guppy.

What is marrow pudding? Could it really be bone marrow, used instead of kidney suet? Sounds rather splendid and delicious —the best kinds of Sauce Bordelaise use marrow instead of butter, and indeed the Victorians had a great thing about marrow: a devilled bone and a bottle of claret for breakfast, and one viewed the day with equanimity. 'Throw physic to the dogs,' said Duff Cooper's father, viewing his ten-year-old son with slight disgust; anaemia was unmanly—'What the boy needs is a pint of champagne and a mutton chop.'

Such robust aphorisms were much admired and copied into cellar books. I cannot resist doing the same, for that is the right place for aphorisms. I think that my first one would be 'Don't go to a restaurant for something you can do better at home.' Like Elmer Gantry's clerical acquaintance I drink and I am shaky about Jonah, but I am sound on food, and so I ought to be after fifteen years a professional cook and ten more a professional customer in restaurants.

Food for pleasure, and not just nourishment, is best cooked in one's own kitchen and eaten with the feet under one's own table. Still, in good restaurants there are things unthought-of at home as being too much time and trouble, or simply needing more skill and imagination than one possesses.

A narrowminded person told my mother that he disliked restaurants; so dear and so snobbish—being both cheated and high-hatted was more than the poor man could bear. My mother replied sensibly that she went to restaurants 'to be treated like a princess'. She was not greatly interested in food, but she did love the clean tablecloth, episcopal waiters (the more Anglican High Church the better) the little pink lamps and the antique panelling. She liked them all the more for being dear and snobbish, and the bigger the bill the more she overtipped, permitting herself a few raps on the knuckles in return. 'My soup could have done with a little less pepper, and that boy over there—yes, the one picking his nose—his apron is what I would call dubious.'

Aphorism number two: this is not a cookery book because such things are whited sepulchres, that tickle but do not satisfy. They appear each year in swarms, burgeoning in spring like horse-chestnut buds, and about as much use—decorative, gentlemen, purely decorative. Nothing wrong with that, no, but the bad cook who buys a bundle of recipes thinking it will turn him into a tolerable cook is in for disillusion and so are all his friends. The worst cookery books are the ones that give formal recipes. The least bad are the coffee-table books, glamorous affairs that waffle on about the little place on the banks of the Loire: the illustrations are lovely and there are historical, archaeological and botanical interests. Most wicked are the dogmatic ones which give quantities and times, peremptory stuff about giving your chop seven minutes each side. The inexperienced cook, starting confident in his mentor, becomes flustered by strange gaps in the information, is confused, irritated and finally exasperated—what should have been a nice meal turns out spoilt and it's the wretched book's fault, not the cook's. You cannot teach cooking out of a book any more than you can carpentry. No two stoves, fryingpans, ovens—come to that no two cooks—are the same. No good writer on food gives formal recipes. 'A recipe has a hidden side, like the moon,' remarks James de Coquet tolerantly.

The lowest of the low are the womens' page recipes in newspapers and magazines, which appeal only to the showoff—'Startle your guests' or the seducer— 'Surprise your husband', which give neither value or pleasure and whose premise, coyly stated, is that cooking is easy and is such fun.

Classic cookery books are collects of tradition, with brief instructions to the professional, as in Marcel Boulestin. They are kitchen books, full of wise saws, herb lore and country medicine, scraps of philosophy and poetry and often of an innocent snobbery—'the sound old snobbery of sterling and strawberry leaves'—reminiscences of dukes and diplomats, crown princes and sopranos and who was whose mistress. The interest in medicine is implicit in Brillat-Savarin's title: The Physiology of Taste. The literary side is noticeable in a good writer of our time, Raymond Oliver who owns le Grand Véfour, cooks and talks on the French television and wrote a lyrical book once entirely about noodles. A story tells that he met a distinguished man of letters in the Kafka-flavoured corridors of the Maison de la Radio in Passy, held his hand warmly out, said how pleased he was, he had long wished to meet, and so on, casually identifying himself as 'the cook here': humble man, since he is as well-known a personality as any in Paris.

'Very good of you,' replied the great man, polite but puzzled, 'I'm sorry I didn't recognize you but the truth is I never eat in the canteen.' Véfour, one of France's twelve three-star restaurants, was known as the canteen for some weeks. I must add that I do not have any idea of pushing myself into all this illustrious company. . . .

It is obvious of course that my own favourite kitchen book is Bemelmans' *Hotel Splendide* and this, with my love, is for Monsieur Louis, who dressed up a humble old platewasher who once long ago had been a Marchese in the headwaiter's spare evening clothes and sat him down at the banquet that was being given for the Italian Ambassador. Just as my favourite picture is the little gouache of the old clochard who holds a child by the hand and gazes with unenvious affection and admiration through the window of a very splendid restaurant that might have been le Grand Véfour. . . .

There is poetry in the fat fingers of cooks, said my principal aphorism, quoting *Life Class*. Poetry, and a lot more, for a recipe can tell you what ingredients go into a dish but—James de Coquet again and another aphorism— 'C'est le tour de main qui compte', translatable as 'It's all in the wrist'.

'Yesterday,' remarks the grandiose hotel-school instructor in an old Humphrey Bogart comedy, 'we learned how to boil water. Today we will learn how to crack an egg.' James de Coquet writes a food column in the weekly *Figaro*, and in the daily he becomes the chief crime reporter. The two interests often go together, as though there were a strange alliance between gastronomy and criminology, and Monsieur de Coquet is the scourge of both toque and toga, the cook's hat and the lawyer's robe.

Cook's hands. . . . Mine are both awkward and nervous. Though he is scarcely ever without a knife in his hand the cook is trained not to cut himself: a burn is more common than a cut in the kitchen. But I was always a clumsy fellow, and my kitchen years are written on my hands. I should have liked to use my handprints as endpapers for this book, but alas, Osbert Sitwell thought of it first.

The thumb, there—early days, that one; breaking up lobster claws with a steak bat I did not know how to use. The middle knuckle of my forefinger—boning a turkey in a bad light, hurriedly; we were badly understaffed. I wound the hand in a rag; it became infected and I was out of work for six weeks, got the sack, and nearly lost the finger. Now how can that be? asks the union-minded reader—getting the sack for an industrial injury, received too under dangerous working conditions? For we were overcrowded as well; I had had to take my turkeys (five or six, for a party) into an ill-lit vegetable cellar. But cooks had no union—still have none, for all I know; cooks are a cranky, non-conformist crowd, more so even than waiters, though both are unstable, irresponsible, and often downright infamous. A cook then could get sacked for anything, such as having the cheek to ask for pay while still unable to work. No wonder that in England so many 'catering managers' are unsuccessful army officers, with a hankering for the orderly-room and a wish to put insubordinate cooks on a charge.

A deep cut—I sliced the tip off a finger and half the nail with it: I was shredding mushrooms with another cook's knife. Most cuts are had that way; under the pressure of orders against time you may suddenly be called to help another cook, you need a knife and snatch one of his, a thing not to be recommended. A knife only obeys its owner and with your own knife, a thing so integrally part of your hand that it seems to breathe with you, things can be done that cannot be risked with another's.

Even without cuts a cook's hands are unmistakable. The fingertips are flattened and ironed by the touch of hot silver dishes and copper serving-pans; for a pot you automatically take your ovencloth. The side of the forefinger becomes corrugated by the peeler, and the ball of one's thumb ploughed by a mass of tiny cuts that have not severed the toughened skin. Turning cuts these—to 'turn' or shape a piece of carrot into a small regular cylinder you hold it thumb and forefinger, thumb down. The other hand holds a little knife by the blade, and makes six tiny shaving movements (the holding hand revolves the carrot or whatever in six regular turns). It is done fast—it must be—the eye can hardly follow—toctoctoc, toctoctoc and splash, into a bowl of water, a hundred, two hundred, five hundred times. Cooks' knitting, it was called, and the blade nicked down, each time, into the ball of the thumb. It is no longer done; cooks were cheaper then.

Last mark, but characteristic, of a cook's hands was the chopping mark. He holds the heavy chopping knife in a kind of golfer's grip, thumb and forefinger forked over the join between the knife's blade and its base: as with the golfer this gives precision of force and direction. At each blow the knife, flattened and squared at this point, jumps against the hand and the cook acquires a heavy callus at the base of his forefinger which would have puzzled Sherlock Holmes, who knew no cooks.

Why the emphasis on hands? Because the cook is a handcraftsman, very much like a smith or a potter. The tools of cooking have not altered in essence since Louis XV and the invention of the fork, any more than those of the cabinet-maker.

A few details, such as the invention of stainless steel, itself unused for long by cook or carpenter because it did not hold a sharp edge.

Cooking is not an art, the snobs to the contrary. Art implies a noble end. That is not to say cooking is ignoble, but it is both impermanent and frivolous; scarcely ever will the cook be called upon to work for someone who is not already overfed. If handed a bowl of raw rice, and told that there was a hungry Indian waiting, he could permit himself, perhaps, to speak of his art.

A hand craft—machines are constantly tried out in the kitchen and quickly discarded. The only contrivances which during my time found acceptance were thermostatic controls for electric fryers, which at least stopped the overheating of the classic and odious fat-pot of my apprenticeships, and the electric mixer, which allowed the pastry-cook to get on with other, less undemanding chores. Neither helped to cook any better: the one, since oil heated more evenly, was an economy in material; the other an economy of effort. But innumerable gadgets were thrown out after a day's trial; this was not obstinate conservatism. The old method served better, simply. Of all the jobs a cook does daily, none is repeated more than chopping onions, a fairly complex chore needing practice, a really sharp knife, and three consecutive movements or processes before the shiny globe crumbles into a pile of tiny grey dice. Every newcomer complains at this minuscular labour but no machine can be made to do it: the onion is a sensitive object and must not be bruised, or it goes an unappetising black and loses its juice.

Even in the matter of fuel our century has offered the kitchen no advance. There are electronic, ultrasonic, and nuclear stoves; there is a glitter of chrome and enamel. There is improvement in efficiency and asepsis; the cook gets less dirty, breathes fresher air, his personal and professional hygiene are much assisted— but the cooking is if anything worse. The weight of metal in stoves—as in cars—has been reduced, and the light, thin-walled cookers hold the heat inefficiently and distribute it irregularly. The old coal or wood-fired oven still to be seen in French country bakeries makes better bread; as simple as that. Nothing of course could be more stupid than an electric barbecue. The principle of a grill is that food should meet smoke as well as heat. On this subject the talking and writing about pine-needles or vine-clippings, apple- or olive-wood, which sounds such affectation, is in fact good sense: each has a special flavour that impregnates—each is in fact a herb.

The blackened old nineteenth-century stoves are the special secret of many classic restaurants. Such a cooker is painful to work at; heavy to stoke and tiresome to polish, but only on this stove, at the dirt-encrusted back, will the stew really simmer slowly. Only in the echoing tomb of this oven will a chicken or a tart really go crisp and gold without drying or toughening. One of the many paradoxes of good restaurants is that the unsophisticated visitor who caught sight of the smudged and sweaty Cinderella in the back would stamp out in indignation against such filthy conditions.

Left hand, right hand. For myself as for Osbert Sitwell the phrase has a special meaning. I hold a knife, which is to say that I cook, with my left hand—this clumsiness, backhandedness, marked my character profoundly. My left hand is my action hand, and earned my living for many years. But I hold a pen right-handed—hand of imagination and of silence. 'All power springs from the back of the neck,' remarks the old pike in *The Sword in the Stone* and this is where the two hands meet.

I have not worked as a cook, now, for ten years: my right hand, throughout my life the weaker, strengthens slowly since I have earned my living from writing and comes to balance the left which has lost the special skills and sensitivity of a cook, the rapidity and dexterity (or right-handed skill) it once had. It is now truly the sinister hand, humble servant of the other—I use it to type with. The right hand had to be apprenticed like the left, and learned that writing like cooking is a trade painfully acquired. The two seem so different, and are so strangely the same. The very phrase 'cooking the book' which has in English a simple, pejorative, financial meaning, is in French more literary and much more respectable; a careful and craftsmanly hammering and shaping of phrase, quite opposed to the spontaneous, but crude and clumsy throwing of raw words upon paper: the first jet as it is called, metaphor of geyser or volcano, now so fashionable among painters, writers or sculptors who imagine it to be more 'genuine' somehow to work with their stomach rather than with the back of the neck.

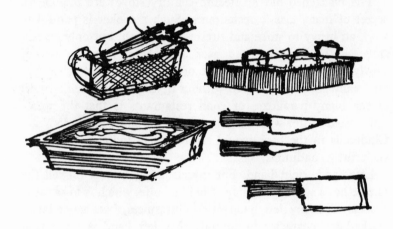

2 MORE NOTES AND SOME NOTABLES

Lord knows why I became a cook; it seemed pure chance. My childhood, in Le Croisic on the Loire estuary, and later in Saint Malo, and later still in the town of Southampton—in the thirties a pleasant town, and homely—may have given me an interest in food. A feeling for food?—one cannot know how much weight to give to heredity. My father loved eating and since my mother, an aristocratic personage who like Jessica Mitford thought that electricity was a gift of God and needed no payment, was unable to boil an egg, he turned himself into an amateur cook of much originality. This may have influenced me more than I know, since he died when I was twelve and I admired him immensely.

He was a countryman, from a landowning squirearchy kind of family, dull people he had little interest in, but he never lost a taste for pigeon pie—'Oh God why is mine always full of shot?'—devilled kidneys or country pâté. He loved devilling things and never enjoyed himself more than when setting to with smashed peppercorns and Dijon mustard.

A neighbouring farmer, who had loomed large in his own childhood, had much influence over mine, and stories about Mr. Betts were numerous: this is the one I remember first.

'What is for breakfast?' asked Mr. Betts, coming in with boots and gaiters—up of course since dawn. Mrs. Betts produced a mighty steak of salmon.

'What's a pound of salmon to a man like me?' There were several variations to the end of this phrase, my father's favourite being—'Bring me six boiled eggs.'

Mr. Betts was no peasant; he was a country gentleman on the lines of Oliver Cromwell. He liked a massive roast, a great rib of beef which he would carve himself since women did not understand such things, and being a gentleman he served his numerous family first—a peasant would eat himself first while the women stood—and my father loved telling how he would always get into a rage.

'Everybody eating, and me not begun yet.'

Papa overdid hanging game, believing that a pheasant should be properly 'faisandé', while most French people think it best still warm from the gamebag. We lived by the sea, far from hills and woods, and Papa in a homesick moment told the butcher to get him a haunch of venison. This was duly hung for weeks in the cellar to get it nice and tender but when the fête, announced with trumpets, arrived it was found to be too gamey even for Papa's palate; it stank the house out and what could one do to get rid of it? It was thrown in the sea, where it floated with horrid phosphorescent buoyancy. Seagulls swooped upon it shrieking, and recoiled in horror. Do seagulls ever recoil in horror?—I doubt it, but Mama, who made a jewelled piece of embroidery of this tale, claimed that they did.

'The tide will take it away,' said Papa hopefully. It didn't: the thing receded, revolved uncertainly, came slowly back. . . . There is a legend that mackerel eat corpses but they failed to come up to scratch. No helpful sharks or dogfish appeared; why were there no piranha in the Atlantic, asked Papa pettishly.

'We cast our bread upon the waters,' intoned Mama in a whining, nasally parsonical voice, cruelly imitating my father's accent, which was that of King's College, Cambridge— 'and lo, it returned unto us after MANY days.'

Mama's cooking was haphazard; since she had been brought up to be a lady this was not her fault. She was moreover the kind of admirable person that reads romantic poetry in the kitchen oblivious to a smell of burning. At the age of eleven my elder sister composed rhyming couplets for everybody we knew in the neighbourhood.

> 'Déclame les vers du cher Milord
> Mais—zut, alors—le lait déborde.'

Or, roughly—

> 'Byronic heroes lie in clover
> But hark! the milk is boiling over.'

(Another went: 'Les jumelles stink and I know why:
> They leave their washing till by and by.')

While I was small things went well enough. There was a great family prop, bonne, nurse, and cook, called Jeanne. Jeanne's husband, Maurice-the-gardener, who had a wooden leg from the Chemin des Dames ('No more tipsy Maurice walk/But a swing, a swagger, and a stately stalk') had been a cook in his day, and was always called upon for guests. One day my parents gave a very grand dinner for Monsieur le Sous-Préfet and all the local notables, and Maurice dressed up in whites and a toque, and great castles of Châteaux-de-la-Loire food were borne in; quenelles with white butter and sweetbread with nantua sauce, all a great change from grilled sardines and mutton, a wild success and Maurice was called in for congratulations, pretty tipsy by this time but so was everyone else. Mama claimed that all the guests took turns to repay this hospitality and served, every one of them, exactly the same meal so that by the third time she was hysterical with giggles throughout dinner, charitably put down to too much porto, the invariable bourgeois apéritif—this was before the invention of whisky. I have doubted this tale, yet when one thinks of the mentality of a sous-préfecture around 1930. . . .

Alas, things went wrong with finance, and my mother's jewellery was all sold. Papa went, very businesslike, to several jewellers in Paris to Get an Offer, left the jewels at the most promising, and when due to go back next day to get his offer was quite unable to remember the address. This is certainly hereditary; whenever I wish to be Businesslike the same thing happens to me. We moved to a pokier house and there was no more Jeanne.

'What shall we have for supper?' Mama would ask. A long pause and then 'I know—a lightly boiled egg.' Just the thing. Papa, remembering his youth, after torments of hankering went out and bought a cookery book. I have it still—one of the dogmatic ones. Opposite the command 'Cucumbers must always be sliced from the thick end' a pencil in the margin has crossly written 'WHY?'. One morning he hustled all the women out of the kitchen, much to their relief no doubt: my sister, a student by this time, was good at making chocolate fudge, but little else. Tart, filled with chicken vol-au-vent, appeared instead of the lightly boiled egg and the air was loud with praise. Things that simmered were Papa's chief strength; pot-au-feu, sow-belly with lentils or cassoulet: simple and delicious food that stuck to the ribs. He was good at English suet pudding, for which he had a passion, and at jam: I remember with affection his vegetable-marrow-and-ginger.

Like all countrymen he was a good shot: thus, one summer in Sussex when we were poor—it must have been around 1935—we ate, as far as my memory serves, nothing but rabbit. He was also a fisherman and the Test, near Southampton, held both trout and salmon. Papa was acquainted with an old gentleman called Lord Swaythling, and brought back goodies from the

Private Reach. He found a little shop in the slums where they sold bloaters, and when I was with him would buy me un-hygienic sweets which scandalized my fastidious mother and were known in the family as Twopennurth of Touched.

And then he died. It was 1939, everything seemed to fall to pieces all at once, and there was nothing fit to eat for many years. Perhaps it was natural that when I came out of the army I thought of being a cook.

He left me several cookery books which I used to read in bed, where they are all right if one has plenty of peanuts—read them in the kitchen and trouble starts right away; ounces of this, gills of that, and one rod, pole, or perch of nonsense every time. The dashing ones, which enquire whether you've ever thought of putting whisky in the tinned baked beans, did not exist then, and they were all very precise and tetchy, tyrannizing the reader who is too frightened to disobey.

Not long ago I read a piece by one of the 'women experts' complaining that professional cooks were no good at giving instructions because they never gave 'definite times or proper quantities'. Just so; even things like flour or potatoes fluctuate in the quantity of water they hold, a piece of meat a week old from one butcher is not at all like another piece eleven days old from another butcher, and sorry but the success of a dish is not following the book. It's having done the dish often enough to get it right.

A story about Somerset Maugham will illustrate. A famous host, he had been lent a house (during the war, in America) with Negro servants whose cooking reached as far as buckwheat cakes. Friends were surprised at being invited to dinner and getting a sophisticated meal. Pressed to explain the miracle, Willy said that it had been simple really: he had eaten the same meal, with the servants, every day till they got it right.

Only training can tell you when there is enough flour or if the roast needs another ten minutes. The books, especially those by women, tend to start brightly, 'Tell your butcher . . .' and avoid the truth, unpalatable in both the literal and metaphorical sense, that the butcher probably doesn't know and quite possibly will fiddle you.

The same 'expert' had another piece about bouillabaisse, the Mediterranean fish stew which is so simple—but not to these people. Back in Birmingham, she said, you didn't get the right fish; fair enough till you got to her suggestions, which included plaice and trout. Whoever has eaten the dish knows that it is a salt-water meal, best cooked and shovelled down in the open air, made with coarse saltwater fish, round and firm-fleshed, for the pot is boiled for twenty minutes. Trout of course is a delicate freshwater fish: plaice is flat, highly fragile, and full of bones. Recipes for this dish invariably tell one to use herbs, such as thyme, sage, fennel—even all three! One does not, of course, use any herbs at all. The stew is flavoured with garlic and saffron, the mayonnaise with paprika and a point of cayenne.

Amateurs always put in too many herbs, and too much. The phenomenon can best be studied in rich people making salad: they put in everything and the result is a medieval cure for snakebite. These people can be squashed by telling them they forgot the dragon's blood and had better start afresh. Simplicity is an axiom in good cooking.

Suitability is another: it means not serving asparagus with chile con carne.

Good taste is the third. Everybody has it, but nobody else. The most important thing is practice. Renoir put this well. He had to draw something—an apple—every day, or he would forget how to draw. After I became a writer it was understood between my wife and myself that I was the writer in the family and she was the cook. I have sometimes made the stupid mistake of going into the kitchen, generally to show off. Invariably there was a fiasco. I had quite simply lost my hand. I was always in a hurry too, and impatient, and this is fatal; one must take time and pains. Food needs thought, careful handling, close watching. Popping out for drinks leads to disaster. It is no good to forget the vinegar and slop in a bit at the last second muttering that no one will notice; they do notice.

There are schools that teach one to cook; cordon bleu and such like. They are all right, I suppose. Generally they give you a diploma after you have made a meal from three classic recipes after Escoffier—a soup perhaps, and a casseroled chicken, and a soufflé probably—and a jury has gravely eaten your effort and pronounced it up to scratch. I think that this method lacks reality.

I would leave the aspirant in a kitchen with a cooker which did not work very well, a few beaten-up pots, and some slightly hairy leftovers. In the fridge two grilled pork chops, three eggs and some cold boiled potatoes, a dried-out piece of cheese and half a packet of butter. In the rack half a cabbage, two wilted carrots and an apple: in the cupboard a tin of sardines, a packet of spaghetti and a few tins of herbs that have lost their labels, so that one can no longer be quite sure what they are. In other words, the conditions are those of your kitchen or mine on a Monday morning.

The cook is asked to make a meal: he may do as he pleases, one course or three. He would be judged on ingenuity, skill, imagination and presentation. I believe that there are schools which do something like this, and the results would be a lot more interesting than all that Escoffier stuff, which is best left to Nero Wolfe, an endearing tyrant who when I last saw him was arguing his head off about how many juniper berries ought to go in the venison marinade—impossible to argue with Nero, who just drinks beer and goes Pfui at you (is this Montenegrin for phooey?).

Being a professional cook is a narrow life, and a dreary one. You do not get enough fresh air, you no longer enjoy food yourself, you lose a sense of proportion. It is a sorry sight to watch a row of supposedly intelligent supposed adults being fervent, for instance, about beating last year's target with the frozen fish fingers, but it is just as sorry a sight to watch a cook worrying about some way to tart them up, his ambition being to get Nero to eat them.

This reminds me—Nero quite often bawls 'Fritz!' and that terrible fellow—he has busts of Escoffier *and* Brillat-Savarin in his room—is always standing there at attention by the desk quicker than that. He never says 'Hold on a sec, the milk's boiling over.' But Fritz of course is a fantasy, a dream of Nero's about the Ideal Cook. He belongs with the cook on Captain Nemo's—how nearly one said Captain Nero's—submarine, who could imitate any terrestrial dish with what he found in the sea, and all one can say is that they were a lot better organized than those poor boys who get shut up in sputniks and shot off with instructions to mix their bite-size capsule of steak or cornflakes into a paste, with just enough water to stop it floating off the spoon. . . .

If one made an anthology of all the cooks in literature, from 'Trimalchio's feast' down to Fritz, it would be important to distinguish between the fantasy cooks and the real ones, like Brother Eusebius in Dumas, whose eels swallowed a whole chicken at a gulp. Dumas was as imaginative a cook as he was a writer—he wrote a marvellous kitchen book and heredity, strangely, passed his talent for food, but not for writing, to his son who invented chrysanthemum salad (one nearly said camellia salad, which sounds disgusting). He is perhaps so extremely readable and credible because his characters love food, eat and drink a great deal, and talk about it all the time. One has only to compare, say, Porthos with the poor wretched James Bond pressing down that ghastly ham sandwich. Then we learn afterwards that Ian Fleming was quite uninterested in food himself, and we understand immediately.

When Brother Gorenflot tastes the burgundy, says 'It's from La Romanée, give me a little more,' takes another swig, says '1556' and has it dead right, we know at once that he hasn't cheated. And when the spy gets away because the FBI who are hidden behind the curtain belch noisily at the wrong moment (they overdid the spaghetti back there in Joe's Diner) we feel increased interest automatically; now that is a thing that might have happened to any of us.

Food is an inexhaustible subject, it is well known, and the temptation great to go on and on, getting duller and more dog-

matic every minute, about aluminium saucepans (one of the
greatest enemies of good food), or how to make mashed potatoes;
a great deal of you must do this and you mustn't do that and it
would be exactly like all the exasperating people I have spent
much time complaining about. In this book are no recipes,
absolutely no useful hints, and above all no damned instructions;
they do not give one an appetite. In the old rule of the classic
restaurant 'they may not be happy at the end; see to it they're
hungry at the start' a kitchen book should create an appetite.
Really the most sensible remark made about food in fiction is in
'Astérix and Cleopatra'. That impetuous lady is fond of getting
rid of tiresome people by feeding them to the sacred crocodiles,
and there comes a really touch-and-go moment when Astérix
is accused of trying to poison her with scrumptious cyanide cake.
She bellows for the high priest, and tells him in a most menacing
way, 'Serve the apéritif to the crocodiles.'

3 POOR LITTLE TROUT

When I decided that I wanted to work in a hotel I was a boy, shy and inexperienced. I knew nothing, but I was quick and energetic, I spoke two or three languages, I thought it should be a fine thing, and interesting, to work in a good hotel. I picked the best hotel I knew of, which even though this was just after the war had very quickly regained its haughtiness and splendour. The gilding was freshly touched up, the velvet upholstery new and unstained, the wood and marble floors polished and gleaming.

I was very frightened, because the employees were indifferent and contemptuous, but I stood straight, with freshly cut hair and well polished shoes. I persevered and asked for the manager, and very much to my surprise the manager himself came to me, quickly, walking very lightly, humming to himself like a bee. He was a type of Frenchman more commonly met with than is thought, heavily built but rapid and supple. All day he walked with that quick light step through his hotel, humming, giving plenty of warning to anybody who might be standing idle. But if he caught you he became terrible. Because of this severity he was greatly feared, but he was respected because he had given fair warning, and he was also greatly liked, for he was fair and just, and very kind. He was called Monsieur Hector.

He listened to me politely, and although I stammered and was stupid he understood. He looked at my polished shoes and my clean fingernails, and agreed to employ me. He explained kindly that hotel employees began in the kitchen, since that was the first and most essential step in their training, that I would be paid very little, but that I would be fed and lodged, and that if I was intelligent I could learn quickly. To all this I agreed eagerly. He nodded, and said he would not forget and would keep an eye on me, and that I should come to see him next morning at eight, and be ready for what would be a long hard day's work which would make my head swim and all my muscles ache.

I ran to a shop where they sold overalls, and bought the blue and white checked cotton trousers, and the heavy double-breasted jackets with their deep cuffs and cloth buttons, and the strange-shaped cotton toque or bonnet that is a cook's hat. These were not starched, but the man showed me how to double it in and punch it down so that this did not matter. He told me that I would be a 'commis' or help-cook, and that as such I should not wear a tall hat. I did not know what to do about shoes, and took a pair of tennis shoes, white canvas with rubber soles, which I thought would be suitable.

When I presented myself to Monsieur Hector he hardly looked at me, but snapped his fingers for a page, and told him to take this young man to the chef. Like all pages he was a horrid child, who sniggered at me in the passage, dark and dingy, which led to the kitchens, and chanted 'You'll be Sor-ry' in an insolent whisper of song, and rudely opened the office door saying 'Victim' before running away quickly, whistling. The chef, a tall, cold and handsome man of only forty, which was very young for a chef in a first-class house, looked at me for hardly longer than

Monsieur Hector had. He came to the door, turned me with one polished fingernail and pointed with another.

'Larder,' he said, and went back to his desk. I was dispirited, because this seemed very curt. I did not know how lucky I was. The larder is high in the hierarchy of kitchen departments, and is cool, and quieter than the others. A good place for a beginner.

I might easily have been sent to the potatoes or the spinach. I think too that this must have been because—like you, Ludwig— I was a 'young man of good family, recommended by le patron'.

I was very lucky too in my first chief. The larder-chef, Fred Roblin from Annecy, was one of the nicest men I have ever met. Without him I would not have lasted long in the kitchen. In my life as far as it had gone, he was the first person who taught me anything.

Fred had come from Algeria, where he had been a soldier, but of course he had been a cook before the war, or he would not have been a chef in as important a place as the larder. He was young still, square and springy, with amused brown eyes and the

dented nose of a boxer. Boxing was his passion; he spoke often
of a comrade in Algeria, also a boxer, of whom, he said, we
would hear more, much more. He was right, for Marcel Cerdan,
the best boxer I have ever seen, became world middleweight
champion, and Edith Piaf's lover, and an extraordinary hero
before his tragic early death. But then he was just 'le copain de
Fred'.

Fred's other passion was bicycling, and he came to work on
an old racing-bike. When changed into his cook's jacket he
would do a little dance to loosen his muscles, shake his big
shoulders down, and take deep breaths by the opened larder
window. He had something of Cerdan's grace as well as agility,
and when I think of one, I see, as well, the other. In the larder
he would talk of boxing, and the great bicycle champions, but
only when we had finished work, and when everything was tidy
before time, on slack days.

Fred looked at my hat and punched it still further in, the way
he had his own, with scarcely any top to it. It would do, he said,
but the tennis shoes would not. They would be sweaty and smell
bad; the rubber soles would overheat on the hot kitchen floor,
and they would be bad for my feet.

'Always wear leather on your feet.' He himself wore sandals on
bare feet, and I copied him, and through all my years in the
kitchen wore nothing else. In the heat, and by the stove where a
boiling sauce or soup can easily splash your feet, most cooks
wear boots, but as a sort of souvenir of Fred I disregarded this
sensible idea. I learned to move my feet very fast instead.

The hotel was not a large one, and in the larder beside the
chef were only two senior commis, one for meat and one for fish,
as well as little Danny, a kind of tiny *piccolo*, a little slum urchin
who must have been fifteen but looked ten or eleven from the
undernourishment of the war years. I made the fourth, but of
course I was little use to anyone. Although not big, it was a
busy hotel and served a very large variety of the most complicated and elaborate food in the classical repertory, for it was
what is still called 'restaurant classique et élégant' in the Michelin

guide, and had stars. This made it a good place in which to learn. At first, of course, all I did was to scrub and tidy, learning how to pick up a knife and clean it and put it away. I had no knives. Every cook has his own; they do not go with the kitchen like pots or plates or table silver. They become part of you, and if you are so imprudent as to use another man's knife it will cut you. Not, naturally, for any whimsical reason. It is only an object. But each knife has its character, its especial feel and balance. Once used it bends to the owner, to the way he holds it and sharpens it. If you pick it up all unity and movement is at once gone, the hand is stiff and awkward, and a cut is as good as inevitable. Fred, a good cook, was meticulous with knives and in the morning he would stand by the butcher's block, for in all but the largest hotels the larder-chef is the head butcher as well, and lay knives out like a theatre sister preparing an operation. He would lay a piece of meat on the block, arrange it to his satisfaction, take his already bitter-sharp boning knife and lay a fine edge to it with a butchers' steel, standing up on his toes lightly, a boxer, always in balance.

Even a large, stiff side of beef did not alter his style; he never fought it or worried it; never coarse or brutal his knife stitched with small easy movements that hardly bunched the muscles of his bare forearm. It was as if the monster, greasy, bloody and obscene, slid apart and dissolved into beautifully shaped and balanced morsels.

As soon as he saw that I was bright, and anxious to learn, Fred disregarded all tradition, for a boy with less than three years' experience would never be allowed before the war to touch anything as sacred as meat. He taught me the anatomy of the bones and muscles, and when I overcame my natural extreme clumsiness he stood me in front of a piece of meat, gripped my hand from behind, and showed how to handle the knife. Thus I learned that for beef the knife must be held like a dagger. One must not be afraid to cut into the meat, which is firm and solid, but the wrist must be very controlled and very flexible. For the knife to jump off a bone or a nerve, and dig into the meat, would be a crime. But for veal, which is lighter-textured, without heavy fat or muscle, and whose clean meat is separated by fine white nerves in clear lines, easy to follow, the knife is held forehand, and one works with the very tip in light neat movements like a series of little flicks. Lamb or mutton must be scraped off the bone, to which the meat clings, whereas pork holds much looser and can often be boned with no more than a piece of string.

All this, however, was a technical fascination, and looked at from this distance what I find more unexpected is the way I was educated during my two years with Fred. There was nothing so vulgar as a fixed-price menu in this hotel. Everything was à la carte, and the fifty or so items in this carte were changed daily, top to toe. The staples of every restaurant—steaks, soles or chickens—were evidently always there, but the manner of serving them was varied. Many of the classic dishes have the names of the old French nobility—Rohan, Montmorency or Montpensier—others the great names of the Empire, Murat, Suchet, Masséna, and the most recent are named for Third Republic bigwigs. As these were ordered Fred would embellish them with a history lesson. It was part of the job to learn that a 'Talleyrand' was macaroni and foie gras, but one wished to know why. When one knew that Otéro and La Paiva were notable whores was that all there was to know about them? Had Napoleon's cook really invented veal Marengo on the battlefield or was this just a stupid legend like King Alfred and burnt cakes? For Fred took history seriously. It was part of the fabric of the kitchen and of life generally, and should not be a series of tales for tiny tots. 'In Paris' indistinctly because of a chicken wishbone between his teeth 'is a very funny palace' and while I peeled a lobster for 'Poincaré' Fred would tell me about Boni de Castellane. At the time, being very young, I was astonished at this erudition in an ex-boxer. Later I was to work with more sophisticated cooks from Paris, and would see Fred as being in reality decidedly provincial.

This is the biggest difference, I think, between French cooks and those of other nationalities. There are of course countless ruffians and savages in French kitchens, but there are also many men who would have made teachers, doctors, or magistrates.

It would be wrong to give an impression of the larder as a place where leisurely historical speculation went on all day. This was when we were quiet, when there were few customers, and we had time for difficult and delicate work, like boning and stuffing little birds, that needed a lot of care and concentration and grouped us all round the big table. But far more frequent were times when customers came raining in relentlessly, and one got more and more behind because the dish being 'pushed' by the headwaiters to clear an excess stock was often something tiresomely slow and difficult to prepare. The trout, for instance. They lived in a tank in the larder, and were always a pest, to be counted and cosseted and fed on finely-chopped liver. When ordered they had to be fished out with a wire basket, knocked on the head, and cleaned most carefully for if their natural slime is lost they do not turn blue. One day we ran right out of trout and Fred looked around, picked on me because my jacket was clean, and sent me to get some from the display tank in the restaurant lobby. These trout were old and cunning, splendidly fed by headwaiters. They could hide behind ornamental rockeries and waving flowers; the tank was high and awkward. I stood upon a banquette and dipped my basket to no purpose. Waiters made insolent comments on my presence; I became sweaty and fumbling, and my hat fell into the tank. 'Is it for today, this trout?' the chef would ask '—or for tomorrow?'

Customers waiting for tables gathered round exhilarated. A man poured a large dry martini into the tank to slow, he said, their reactions. 'Poor little trout' said one horrible woman. Being thus in the spotlight I had become extremely awkward, and when I finally did catch a huge one and manoeuvred him to the surface he felt the contact of the hostile air and jack-knifed into the audience to slither along a pretty girl's long white skirt. She gave a horrible great scream, I scrambled along the floor upon my hands and knees, and Monsieur Maurice the restaurant manager appeared in the doorway, looked at me with infinite disgust, and told me that unless I disappeared instantly like the cockroach I was he would chop my liver and feed it to his trout. I scuttled back to the larder hoping for sympathy and Fred asked crossly whether the trout were for today or tomorrow, and I felt ready to cry.

4 'OUR UNIFORM IS BLUE AND WHITE'

Cooks have to buy—or had, at least, in my day to buy—their
own clothes and a very expensive business it was. Since we were
expected to be spotlessly white at all times, since kitchens were
cramped and filthy, since we worked with earthy vegetables,
burnt fat, and a million things that splashed and spattered, and
since most stoves then were still old coal-fired ranges, one had
logically to change clothes daily. This was impossible. Cooks
had four, five or six jackets in various stages of disrepair, and
commis had often only two or three. They took a long time
coming back from the laundry, and when they came they were
often torn and then stuck together with too much starch. One
pulled them apart with squeaking and glugging noises like a
gumboot coming out of deep mud, until one reached a lamentable
frayed edge.

As a result kitchens were full of most unhygienic sights; lowly boys on the spinach or the roast with cuffs black and shiny, girdled with old sacks, and the chef often the only clean cook in the kitchen, in an expensive feather-light muslin toque from Messrs. Dupont Malgat in the Rue Coquillère, while we wore cheap jackets of coarse tropical weave, and much-patched trousers. The kitchens were often wickedly hot, and it was wisest to buy your jackets big and long, and wrap yourself up like a Bedouin. The elegantly rolled and knotted napkin cooks wear as a necktie has a squalid origin as a sweat-rag.

These napkins, and a few rough oven-cloths, were often the only linen provided in restaurants. Hotels were better, since they had their own linen room and often their own laundry, and a cook might easily take a job in a house where they were generous with free aprons and the laundry was back in three days rather than one where pay or other conditions might be better.

One day a cleaning woman brought up a pile of linen including several new oven-cloths bought by the housekeeper in some sale; vulgar affairs with broad red stripes. The sous-chef picked one up disdainfully. 'I'm not using these skivvy-cloths. When I went into the kitchen my old dad told me my uniform was blue and white.'

Once, with all my trousers torn, I put on a pair of blue jeans. The weave is thicker and coarser, but otherwise there is very little difference. The chef made faces every time he passed for three or four hours, then sent for me, and in the peculiar pidgin he spoke (this hotel was more wildly cosmopolitan even than most and he had relearned his native tongue from Czech and Greek waiters)—'Manager saw you and say to me "Who that man is? Is a cook, or an ingénieur?" '

These anecdotes show the intense conservatism of cooks. They live, of course, in an enclosed and narrow world, and have the utmost hatred and contempt for such people as waiters and room-clerks, who are idle, dishonest, and disreputable to a man. Even inside the kitchen there is a sectarian snobbery. The sauce-cooks and larder-cooks are the aristocracy of the kitchen. Pastry-cooks loathe all the others, and are in turn loathed. Grill and soup cooks are low, a cunning and debased lot, probably dirty and certainly suspect. The tournant or rotation chef (restaurants have generally a closing day but hotels by their nature have not, and this cook serves for the free days of all the others) is a déclassé, who has lost status.

My first kitchen had all these aspects highly developed. Vain, conservative, isolationist and snobbish: everyone there was French, of course. I had not been there a week before realizing how very lucky I was in my own chef, Fred, who never lost his temper, never blamed his boys for a fault or negligence of his own, never screamed or threw things (almost all cooks do; the heat and the haste acts as a constant irritant to their naturally nervous temperament), and took pains to be just, calm or as they say in the navy to take an even strain.

The sauce-cook was fat Bernard, a Lyonnais. He was a good cook; Lyon is famous for cooks, but he was hysterical, and a coward. With him worked the fish-cook, a dyspeptic, rather sad Breton, and two commis, whom they shared. Whenever anything went wrong it was the fault of these three, privatim et seriatim— never never never does anything go wrong in Lyon and such is the force of suggestion that I have never cared for the place since.

When as happens often in smaller kitchens the sauce-cook and the fish-cook work together, sharing the same bench and stoves, there is an operation of great importance taking place there the whole time, which is the dosing of dishes with various kinds of alcohol, known to cooks as 'Vitamina'. Nearly anything gets cooked in red or white wine some time, and there is always a jug or a bottle on the bench. The commis take surreptitious swigs whenever they can but wine is cheap and the sin venial. Alcohol is quite another matter. Fish dishes are often flavoured with apéritifs—a sole Noilly Prat and a sole Cinzano are both classic dishes—and nearly any distillation can be and is used for flavouring food by setting it on fire. Madeira and Marsala are used for a great number of dishes made with white meat, such as veal or chicken.

Even in France these things are dear, and French chefs are by
nature very economical. The vitamina is always kept in a locked
cupboard in the chef's office, and gets doled out for each order,
a tiny glass at a time. But when the chef himself supervises all
the service, which was the case here, and the orders are coming
in fast, discipline gets relaxed. Fat Bernard had a most ingratia-
ting manner, and that air of trustworthiness possessed by the
superior villain. (As I write how clearly I see his meek face and
features stamped with sweaty sanctity.) Bottles collected on the
bench and Bernard would suddenly drop a mushroom or his
palette knife, bend the knee and fold the stomach with holy
agility, and under cover of the bench take a quick swig, wiping
the mouth of the bottle with his hairy palm. Drinking in the
kitchen was punished by the sack, instant, without notice, and
although the chef could not fail to know about this, he never took
any action, I have no idea why. We loathed Bernard and pretended he stank, which he did, but he was a wonderful cook, and
perhaps the chef held on to him for fear that another cruder
sauce-cook would lose the kitchen one or more of its precious
stars.

René the entremettier, which is the technical term for the
soup-and-vegetable cook, was very different. He was young, thin
and pallid; he came from the Paris district of Aubervilliers and
had an undernourished look. He was illiterate, softhearted, and
frantically conscientious. He would often stay behind and work
all afternoon on a consommé that was not bright enough. His job
included egg dishes, which he loved and was good at, and
potatoes which he hated and did badly. This threw him in
despair and he would scream at sticky mashed potato or a
scorched pomme sautée, throw his hat on the floor and jump on
it. He was terrified of the chef, who bullied him mercilessly. He
had many boys, for this corner, though in theory the least skilled,
is complex and the work is lengthy, but they were oafs and
imbeciles, good for nothing but washing spinach, and poor
René would always try to do everything himself, trembling and
muttering behind his castle of high stock pots. It was, of course,

the insistence on doing everything that led to the pomme sautée getting scorched. In the kitchen he was known as Bang-Bang, from the neurotic way pots got banged on the floor and with pettish violence sent skidding across the floor to the potwash. There was also in the town a perfectly harmless person who spent his days leaping on the back platforms of buses, where he would hang on the rail till he saw a policeman. When he did he pointed two fingers, shrieked 'Mort aux vaches—Boum-Boum' and leapt off the moving bus into traffic, in order to avoid the submachine-gun fire that would certainly rain down. He was much beloved by all, never charged bus fares, never run over, and even policemen went indulgently 'Boum-Boum' back, which sometimes startled tourists who wondered what France was coming to.

René, who would dearly have loved to shoot the chef, the headwaiters, and nearly all the customers (who kept eating potatoes), felt deep sympathy with this character, and when he was in a good mood because the consommé was nice and clear he would hide behind his biggest stockpot and go 'Bang-Bang' at cooks.

His commis had a simple trick, which never failed. Réne spent hours knitting, which to a cook means turning vegetables to small regular shapes, and he did this with one leg cocked up on the bar of his bench, so that he looked very like a pale, rather dirty Parisian flamingo. His commis would fill a large pot with cold water and push it quietly into position beside his leg; he was too busy working, twitching, and muttering ever to notice this. They would then give a sudden shriek. 'René the soup's burning!' He would start and put his foot in the water, signal for horrid pandemonium, so that the chef would step out of the office and say icily—'Monsieur Valdenaire are you incapable of keeping order among that riffraff?'

The roast-cook, Louis, was a nasty person; roast-cooks generally are because the work is vile and turns everyone nasty. Everything is greasy and the heat from the big grill is colossal. Oil and salt is the leitmotif; you never get the feel from your hands or the taste from your mouth. It is simple if dirty work, and is really less skilled than that of the soup-cook, but further up the hierarchy because you are Handling Meat.

Louis came from rugby country, from Dax or Tarbes, but anyone less like d'Artagnan would be hard to imagine. One can like rugby—I do; so skilful, rapid and dramatic—and down in Pau they are very good at it. One can like Pau—a beautiful town, among the nicest in France or Navarre. But fanatics are a bore anywhere. Louis was sour and sullen, always suspicious, paralysingly mean. To make him human one had to talk rugby to him all day, every day, and be regaled with the statistics of the score Dax made against Mont-de-Marsan in nineteen thirty-five. There wasn't a commis in the kitchen who could keep this up, so a boy had been found who being Italian possessed a vanity and vitality that survived Louis. He was called Benzino because no Frenchman could remember his name. He was a colossal tumbler of girls, guitar-player, hair-comber; he took his hat off all day to arrange his coiffure. I liked him very much; he was so innocent, so funny, and so lively. He was always spotless. The roast-cook's drawer was full of nail-files and orange-sticks, and Louis could do nothing about it. He was perfumed too, with an expensive swooning scent from Schiaparelli, because, he said when we objected, the girls did not like a boy whose hair smelt of fried fish. Meaning looks at the dirtier of the spinach-washers. Above the grill, fixed to a butcher's hook, was a large carrot carved in a deathshead and the legend 'Pericolo di Morte'.

We had in this house no patisserie, thank heaven. There are of course lots of sympathetic pastry-cooks, though I have often missed meeting them, but the pastry kitchen itself, a nauseating bland smell of sugar and vanilla, is an unreal world and those who work in it find it difficult to resist. Taking on the character and colour of one's surroundings is as platitudinous in the kitchen as anywhere else, and inevitably sauce-cooks become tricky and buttery, larder cooks become hearty and meaty with loud echoing voices, grill-cooks pungent and spluttering—and vegetable cooks become vegetable, one is tempted to add unfairly. Just so are pastry-cooks too often false and sugary, with an over-gentle fluffy style. There is often an atmosphere of spite-fulness and gossip around the pastry. The chef of the pastry kitchen is independent of the general kitchen routine, and left largely alone, and his staff become more withdrawn and snobbish than any of the others. I have never worked in this corner, because I never wished to.

In this hotel it was, I think, simply a question of space, or perhaps design. Or it may have been economy, because kitchens of this standard by definition make no profit if they are not run with great skill and care. In the larder we made fruit dishes and soufflés which the sauce-cook baked, and a few simple tarts and cakes. The restaurant made things like pancakes and rum omelettes, and that was all.

I have mentioned the chef several times; it is difficult to write about him because I never fully understood him. A good general is not necessarily liked by the troops; perhaps that is why he is good. Monsieur Le Page was not a likeable man, but he was a

good cook and an excellent chef. He was young for his job, and like most chefs was a sauce-cook, from a very large splendid house, intensely fashionable and snobbish, on the Cote d'Azur. He was tall, dark and dry; he never raised his voice. He had the cutting intelligence and icy sarcasm that frequently goes with being unlikeable and knowing it. These people are distant and solitary, and often become unbalanced. This one was very balanced; he was a good administrator and an excellent technician, whose kitchen ran like silk off a spool and who made a consistent profit, a thing always difficult. His menus and his 'party pieces' which he would do for favoured customers were works of art, balanced, fashioned with mastery, invariably successful. He was one of those people who are never in the wrong but who have a horrid talent for putting others in the wrong with minor-key snubs. One day when I was in the kitchen warming aspic over the sauce-cook's stove he became irritated at my gossiping with the commis there. I was in favour just then, I have no idea why, so he waited till Bobby presented the next dish to be ready, something on a silver dish masked in sauce, which Bobby, obedient to training, wiped carefully round with his dishcloth, to be sure there were no spatters or smears. Monsieur Le Page regarded the dish with dislike and turned it around with his finger, long, black and as though of polished metal—he was now that I think of it a bit like Doctor No. Then he looked at Bobby as though seeing him for the first time.

'You trail that noxious rag of yours through every sauce, Monsieur Robert. Do you imagine that it adds to the flavour?'

This was typical of his style.

In the larder we were gay and uninhibited. For a cook there are only two conditions; one is either 'en place', which is cook's heaven and comes from the expression 'mise en place' meaning a ready reserve—or one is 'dans la merde', a phrase even more obviously expressive of what is happening. Since Fred was energetic, meticulous and nice to work for as well as highly skilled we were generally en place. We would tease Anny, the fat, pretty cleaning-woman (she had two missing front teeth, which gave piquancy) by putting live lobsters on the floor to lurch about after her, at which she shrieked. She was kind-hearted, and would often chop parsley, shell almonds or whip cream when we were flustered. The larder commis were raffish and sophisticated, with a casual suggestion of debauchery that irritated Monsieur Le Page, but they were all good at their work.

Then suddenly we disintegrated. William the fishmonger got a job at the Savoy in London, from where he wrote exuberant postcards saying that the English were lunatic, that he was paid vast sums, that life was lovely, and that he sincerely hoped we were all in the merde. We were. It was in a very busy season, and we were shorthanded. Fred invented the system Alcool pour la Machine—a bottle of red vino to inspire us at difficult moments; he himself was partial to mint tea which Anny had been trained to make. Despite being inspired I got a rheumatic chill from

spending too long checking stock in the cold-room after I had been soaked in sweat doing some job on the grill, where I was quite unused to the temperature. Unable to move next day I was not at work. I telephoned, and Fred accepted the news without a fuss. Two days after I was well, and went to the chef's office to say so. Monsieur Le Page looked at me bleakly, and said 'Sack.'

'But I was ill—I really could not work.'

'Sack. Now. Straight away. I have never been ill. One has not the right to be ill.'

I went away very puzzled. Had I worked badly? Had I been insolent, stolen truffles or raped Anny? What was the real reason? Whatever it was there was nothing I could do about it. In those days such things happened frequently. Quite possibly just a way of tightening up discipline among the spinach-washers. I went to Monsieur Hector, who said politely that he could not interfere with the chef's affairs. He gave me a recommendation, and Fred gave me messages for old pals. I went to Paris.

5 'UPON THAT NAME A STAIN OF CREAM'

The nicest cook in literature is the one in *Cyrano de Bergerac*, who writes poetry in his spare time and is pestered by his wife, who keeps the shop and in consequence despises poetry. She has a crass soul, and instead of tearing up or burning the manuscripts like an honest poetry-hater she is economical, and uses them to wrap up cake. He revenges himself by allowing hungry poets to eat cake free, and there is a splendid cry of despair when he presses choux à la crème into somebody's hand and finds it sitting on the 'Sonnet for Phyllis'.

'Phyllis', he cries with theatrical passion—'Phyllis—upon that name a stain of cream!' This was told me by Paul, the literary sauce-cook, while I made the day's bowlful of hollandaise sauce and he was busy as usual (he never worked if he could help it) carving a block of salt, hardened by a few days in the hotplate, into the likeness of two pigeons drinking out of a birdbath.

Since I knew nothing but larderwork I was put in the office to be inspected by the chef, who was old and decrepit and never learned to recognize me in three years, and then sent immediately to the larder by Adrien the sous-chef, who was an old friend of Fred's. The larder-chef had heard about my misfortunes and gave me a good reception—he was nowhere near as nice as Fred, but reasonable to work for. For the rest of the staff I had indeed quite a glamorous aura; I came from one of the most gilt-edged houses in France, and in comparison this was a scruffy place.

It was to be sure an expensive good-class hotel in central Paris with a luxurious tourist trade, a pompous Haussmanesque façade and a medieval kitchen entrance through tumbledown fourteenth-century courtyards, but there was something a bit cheap about it—they did Rotary banquets, which definitely lack class, and the public rooms were always full of shady businessmen looking just like Rotarians but more fly-by-night, always munching peanuts, drinking huge amounts of whisky, and speculating in 'futures'.

As a consequence I was entrusted with more delicate work. I looked after fish and did some butchery, I made terrines and pâtés, and though I felt uneasily a bit of a fraud I was sensible enough to confess ignorance rather than make any horrible fiascos.

It was a large house—we thought nothing of two hundred lunches—and like most large second-class city houses we had a huge consumption of hors-d'oeuvres, of sandwiches, of cold meat and salad because so many people are in a hurry. There is a railway-terminus atmosphere, a lot of floating and temporary—sometimes very temporary—staff, and one never gets to know half the waiters. The grillroom was full of waitresses, and the larder full too of these tough, serious married women; hard, muscular, and disillusioned about sex. They do not give a damn about their looks, but are swift tireless workers. These larder women are in Germany entrancingly called 'Kalt-Mamzells'.

René the larder-chef was big, strong, goodlooking, like a tenor in operette, and played the tenor assiduously. He sang, indeed, a great deal, his voice helped by the larder roof which was glass, twenty metres high (railway architecture was a strong influence throughout the hotel) and gave a powerful echo. He was a good craftsman, a serious cook, but not a serious person. He hardly spoke to the rest of us except on business, and always kept up a barrier. The larder walls were dotted with loudspeakers, and on the butcher's table we had a mike and a keyboard to call any kitchen department. The loudspeakers quacked and echoed all day like René's voice across the dim, dirty roof through which no daylight filtered.

I was very provincial, accustomed to knowing everybody, talking to anybody. It took me many months to become 'Parisien', used to curtness, anonymity, and being quite uninterested in anyone else. You were there to work, and that was all there was to it. The chilly 'railway' feeling of the larder, after the decidedly cosy atmosphere I was used to with Fred, put me off, and after six months I asked Adrien for a change; I wanted, I said, to learn kitchen work. He agreed, and made me commis 'tournant' working on a different corner each day. In this way, he said, I would get a generalized experience that would be valuable.

This was quite true; after thirty months in the larder I was a competent commis, a useful butcher, fishmonger or buffet man, but this experience was narrow, for in the kitchen, 'on the stove' as cooks say, I was useless, and mocked at: I hardly knew how to cut 'frites', turn carrots, or make an omelette. But in this kind of house everything was looser, less formalized and departmentalized than with Monsieur Le Page. Commis came and went, a party or a banquet threw a sudden strain upon a particular corner, and the organization had to be fluid and improvised in order to work. Besides Christophe, the chef tournant, there were three or four 'demi-chefs', cooks of skill and experience but not yet to be trusted with a corner of their own, and as many junior commis; I joined this floating brigade, who would go each morning to Adrien as they tied aprons and knotted their neckties and said 'Where today boss?' The day before a big party one might be back in the larder, filleting soles or boning saddles of mutton; the day of the party one might be sent to the banqueting kitchen or to any corner that was shorthanded. In this way I got a great deal of hard, rough experience over about a year, learning to be quickwitted—at any second one might be peacefully turning potatoes in the dim recesses of the 'veg', only to be seized by the fish-cook and told to put that lobster under the grill and look sharp about it. This is all very useful as long as it does not go on too long; one learns to do everything, but nothing particularly well. I learned to be 'Parisien'—to talk the jargon, to know all the corners and crannies of the big hotel, to scrounge cups of coffee from the stillroom, to butch up a steak or a cutlet on late-night guard duty, and steal one too for a luxurious supper.

I was lucky. I had learned to like the sauce-cook's corner the best, which is natural, for it is the most complex, interesting, and sophisticated in the kitchen. Paul was the most intelligent cook there; he took a fancy to me, and when he wanted a commis on the corner he asked for me, and I worked with him for eighteen months. Like Fred he was a good professor and enjoyed teaching, with the result that after only five years in the kitchen I would be a really useful cook, well trained and able to hold my own anywhere. I only left this hotel because it became impossible to get further promotion or earn a better wage. I was by then 'demi-chef', an in-between sort of position in which one has quite a lot of responsibility but is paid no more than a first commis.

Paul was lazy, clever, and oversophisticated; he had spent his whole life on or around the 'grands boulevards' between the Madeleine and the Opera, and had views to match. He enjoyed the theatre and the cinema more than books, politics more than history; he was a mine of information about ministers and music-hall stars, and who was whose mistress. He had been trained in Matignon, the hôtel particulier that is the official residence of France's first minister, the President of the Council as he was then known. He had gone on to work in the big boulevard restaurants, Lido and Capucines, always full of rastaquouère millionaires and characters out of Balzac. He was bald, slow-moving, very neat, a delicate and fine sauce-cook. In and around 'the corner' he was as great a fusspot as Fred; everything had to be emery-papered, even the poker. To make the fire up—for these were huge ancient coalstoves, immensely thick and heavy—he made us put big lumps of coal on by hand, one at a time, building and packing carefully, and there must never be dirt or dust. Up on the high glass canopy hung rows of Paul's 'own' little copper pots, highly polished (by us) and never to be used by others; we scrubbed and burnished everything, and all this was in the highest tradition of plain Parisian cooking. His style was much simpler than that of, say, fat Bernard the Lyonnais; far less cream and butter, and 'not so much chopped parsley; you're not on the farm now'. He used herbs in minuscule apothecary's pinches, loved beef-marrow, light clear sauces and little, neat steaks, and loathed exaggeration.

'Provincial cooks,' he snorted, 'putting a glass of cognac and a half-litre of cream in everything, imagining that on this account it should be good.' In this he was quite right. Good Parisian cooking is light and crisp, very simple, and never gives one liver attacks. He also loathed 'mucky food'—quenelles and little bits of foie gras, dressy stews and chicken sauté with a dozen different ingredients. Paul wanted everything plain and recognizable, and his best dishes were things like liver with onions, a Liégeoise style kidney, a steak au poivre with hardly any pepper at all. His favourite phrase was 'too much' and he taught me that the over-elaborate, over decorative food of the provinces is often very bad.

'. . . And calvados, And cider, And cream.' I can hear his sarcastic voice—'They may love that down in the backwoods but here we call that Chicken Cirrhosis.'

Paul's greatest enemy was Christophe, the tournant, who took his place once a week, and was the other kind of Parisian cook, quiet, indifferent, detached, and infernally negligent. French cooks are in general extremely clean or excessively dirty, and Christophe was staggeringly dirty. Paul's white scrubbed table would be soiled and raped in five minutes by Christophe throw-

ing liver about while we stood aghast. He had the awful trick
of spitting in the friture to see if it were hot enough; he let the
brown sauce go cloudy because it was too much bother to skim
it; he scorched and smudged; he was a master of the short cut,
the easy way out, the system D. D stands for dé as in débrouiller
or démerder—to extricate, and I suppose that in English it is
'I'm all right, Jack'. To a hair, Christophe knew how to stay out
of trouble. He was a very skilful cook, and a very bad one.

Much more fun was Hervé the soup-cook, Hervé 'Patate', a
barrel-chested unshaved bear who looked like an executioner's
assistant and who while ruffianly in dress, behaviour and 'on the
table', 'on the stove' was of a lovely precision that came by
instinct. His omelettes were feathery, fluffy, tender as soufflé.
'Look at the carrots' he would grunt, and invariably they would
be exactly right. Since he had to cook his potatoes, rice, or
noodles on a colossal scale one would expect them to be heavy and
soggy, not very appetising, but his never were, and spaghetti for
a hundred done by Hervé was as beautifully cooked 'al dente' or
with a bite still in it, as the half dozen sticks of macaroni done by
Paul for a Talleyrand.

In return for being such a beautiful cook Hervé was allowed
many liberties. He was a fearful satyr, disdaining no prey, and
would push some stringy and decidedly desiccated vegetable
woman across the potato sacks with the same zest as a sixteen-
year-old chambermaid from Brittany who wandered innocently
into the kitchen asking for something to eat.

'I'll fix you up, dear,' Hervé would say in fatherly tones, and
invariably did.

Hervé's name, to say the least of it, was stained with a good
deal more than cream. But his mashed potatoes were unfor-
gettable.

Women in the kitchen were too tough for him—any of the
larder 'girls' would pick up a fillet of sole knife if he appeared and
say 'One step more' in icy tones—but we had one who was his
master. Joséphine-Anne, 'dite' Joanne, had the build for it, the
character, and the tongue for it too. She was the head vegetable-

woman, who weighed a hundred kilos and could carry two sacks of potatoes without it stopping her breath.

'Joanne—where's my carrots?' Hervé would bellow.

'I'll give you carrots you syphilitic old sodomite,' she bellowed back. Archetype of the market-quarter 'strong man' she had a thick Dickensian smell of beer, tobacco and onions, and a vocabulary to put Henry Miller to flight. Not unexpectedly she had a kind heart and was generally followed by a flock of plucked-chicken country girls who were under her protection. She was in her own phrase 'staunch' and went to five o'clock Mass every morning. She looked after sad little commis too, and lent them money. One such, a wretched boy who could do no right and had his bottom kicked by everybody, sidled up to me and whispered 'I'm going to run away.'

'But where will you run away to?'

He thought for a long time. Plainly the Foreign Legion was no good. He was too young, and it would anyway be just like the kitchen (this boy had more sense of reality than Beau Geste).

'Meaux,' he said at last. It is a little town only just outside Paris but was then still thoroughly provincial.

I found this a pathetic answer and said as much to Adrien the sous-chef, who put his head on one side and smiled.

'Il n'est pas fainéant de vice,' he said cheerfully, 'seulement de bêtise.' Not lazy out of vice but only from stupidity. Adrien took hold of the boy, made him wash, gave him two old jackets, and put him in the larder, where he was happy and the women looked after him.

Adrien was small and thin, with a Vietnamese look. He came from Issy les Moulineaux. Although tiny he was tough and wiry: he had also humour. Wanting melon one day—a crate of them had been shoved on the cold-room roof—he jumped on Hervé's shoulders, scrambled up, seized a melon, turned, went 'Oo-Oo-Oo' in a shrill soprano, beat his chest, yelled 'Tarzan' and leapt off the edge, apron flying. He was a good sauce-cook too, and an admirable decorator of buffet food, which he did with great rapidity, a slapdash impressionist style, and a taste for indecency; his favourite trick was to mask a baron of lamb, which is the two haunches joined at the loin, in smooth cream sauce, decorate all this with flowers, and model it into a young girl's bare behind, invariably greeted with guffaws in the restaurant and eaten with appetite.

The chef was, as I have said, old and decrepit. He did nothing. Once a day he would totter out to the service hotplate and ask for a plate of soup, which he would complain of. For ten minutes he would stand there, unseeing. He detested whistling—which was severely punished in all old-fashioned French kitchens, and invariably Hervé would purse his lips gently over the beans and send a ghost of melody wavering into the steam.

'Who's that, who's that?' the poor old boy would shout.

'Hearing things again,' Hervé would say audibly. The young

are cruel. But the old man had been, I was told, a dreadful bully in his day, an Attila among cooks, sabring and sacking right and left.

Opposite the service hotplate, and next to the chef's office, was the pastry kitchen, a small, square, rather hot place. When there was a complaint about cream or fondant the pastry-cooks always blamed this heat, and always got away with it.

There were two of them, with a commis who arranged trolleys, made fruit salad, and whipped the cream. Both were Swiss but one was from Basle and the other from Zürich: they detested one another.

'Fat Baslois pig.'

'Stupid Zürichois toadstool.' This went on all day, but against any French manifestation of hostility the Swiss presented a united front. Both were pale and greasy, both had expensive cars, both liked Guinness of which they drank a lot. They are now indistinguishable to me and even then had much the same features, bland, smooth and watchful, features half effaced by plenty of pastry which (as it did to young Wackford Squeers) made their skin shine.

The door to the pastry kitchen was in two halves: when the lower half alone was closed a flap could be let down on top of it, enclosing the Pastryswiss in their fortress, which now resembled a bank or a post office, with a counter and a window where clients could come and make applications. Here, during the service, commis waiters in their ankle-length white aprons came for ice-cream and sponge fingers, little saucers of petit-fours, or refills for the trolley. For anything taken, as was of course the case with all the corners of the kitchen, the waiter had to bring or write a check on a perforated pad, the top copies of which were kept in the pastry, the larder, or by Adrien at the service hotplate, while the duplicates went back to the restaurant cash desk or the liftman for the floors. Twice a day a girl from the accounts office came to collect all these checks and 'marry' the carbons to their originals. This paperwork, called 'the control', is of great importance.

It did not take long, however, to see that the paperwork in the pastry was unusually sophisticated, and not all on the waiters' side. The Pastryswiss were forever doing sums on pieces of paper and holding conferences with waiters, but also with porters, pages—with in fact the whole staff of the hotel, for here the wide passage past the kitchen was a main road to stillroom, linen room, the shops of carpenters and engineers, and many other places. Curious, I asked Hervé what all this scribbling meant.

'Bleeding moneylenders,' he replied indifferently. I understood. The sugary cavern was the Basle and Zurich Bank, with plenty of security too—the Pastryswiss had massive padlocks for everything, even whisks and wooden spoons. No wonder they had expensive cars. An elaborate fantasy grew and danced before my eyes—I was to learn it was no fantasy—of waiters' duplicate checks, white for the restaurant, pink for floors, green for the grillroom—converted into bankers' jargon, of Virements and Versements and Domiciliations, Bons de Compte and Bons de Trésor, lists of names, hundreds of names—even chambermaids came to borrow from the Pastryswiss—names of half the staff in the hotel, and on every single name a stain of cream.

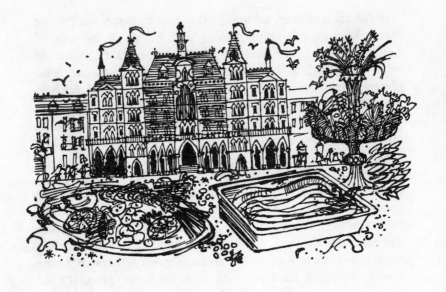

6 GRAND HOTEL THERMES ET BAINS DE MER

Hotels, like governments, will pin a medal on you any time; it costs nothing. I was a good cook, I did responsible work, but when I asked for more money I was told that I had little experience and they really could not see ... and so on. I had now two recommendations from very good houses; I walked out. Paul the sauce-cook said he did not blame me.

'Do a couple of seasons in the provinces,' he said, 'and get a good screw—then you have a minimum wage below which you don't go wherever you are. But don't stay away too long or you'll spoil your hand—and don't take any jobs in dumps where they pay high just because nobody will stay.' This was good advice; I did not listen to any of it. I ran off to an agency which specialized in hotel staff and asked whether anyone was looking for a sauce-cook. They looked at me dubiously; I was very young. But my recommendations were good. Then the man said slowly that the Hotel Atlantic in Belleplage wanted a second sauce-cook. The wage was double what the Pyramides had paid me. I could live in the hotel. Visions of sugar plums danced in my head. I said yes, eagerly. He picked up his telephone and told somebody all about me, with more emphasis on where I had worked than how long I had been there. Then he hung up and asked politely whether I would accept a week's trial—during which I could walk out too, if I felt so inclined, and there would be no hard feelings. I took the next train.

Belleplage is what you would get if you put together Le Touquet, Deauville, La Baule, Royan, and Biarritz, and then divided by the number you last thought of. As for the Atlantic Hotel—Thermes, et Bains de Mer—there is one in any of these places, and a hundred more besides. In England, the Low Countries, Germany and Austria, there are—or were—hundreds more, at every seaside resort, in every spa town. Some stand derelict, some have been knocked down—no easy job. A few have been modernized and are still running. They are the memorials to la Belle Epoque, and to the System. I have not been to Belleplage in twenty years, but I imagine that the Atlantic still stands. It was singularly immovable, and must be a great embarrassment to the municipality.

Really all hotels were an invention of the Belle Epoque, that is if we agree to date the Belle Epoque back from 1900 to the highwater mark of the railway age. Hotels, like railways, were a monument to the exuberance of Victorian energy and imagination. Before, large towns had inns and coffee-houses, the country had staging posts for chaise and diligence, everywhere had auberges and bistrots. But the Victorians, the third Napoleon and the third Republic, imagined something on a far larger scale, a place of public repose and nourishment that would equal in grandeur and in luxury any palace, and instead of being a 'hôtel particulier' it would be public. Any little bourgeois with a banknote in his pocket would be able to enjoy the standards of eating, sleeping and lounging about hitherto reserved for dukes and princes. Louis Philippe, the first bourgeois monarch, with his umbrella looked like any businessman of his kingdom: the hotel would be a Tuileries for businessmen.

The Victorians worked with astonishing speed. The Great Western Railway was driven clear across England, bounding over obstacles, in a matter of months (it startles us today, when motorways are built inch by painful inch, costing meaninglessly huge sums). France, so much larger and with less industrial development, poorer in coal and iron, was slower, but contributed climate, the seaside, and the genius of Viollet le Duc for monstrous gothic buildings. Railways whizzed across the countryside, and where they touched a spa or health resort, or reached a pleasant seaside fishing village, hotels jumped up, using the railway architecture; riots of lavish gothic in granite and bold ironwork. This gothic revival is not surprising when one looks at Reims Cathedral and notices that it is exactly like a huge Victorian railway engine.

The sky was the limit in luxury and gigantism; Versailles and Chambord were the models. Tiny hamlets near a sandy beach woke up to find a palace, in the approved cathedral-Carcassonne style, towering over them, and Cannes or Dinard, Bournemouth or Torquay found themselves born. I do not know if exactly the same pattern existed in America, but the railway kings, Vanderbilts and so on, certainly built houses just like these hotels all to themselves, and Hearst's San Simeon is still there to show us what they were like.

Around 1900, when the hotel idea produced its indisputable genius, Ritz, and King Edward had invented Biarritz, it seemed that the fantastic welter could go no further. Arched entrance halls, springing fifty feet and crowned with crockets, pinnacles and battlements, were by now a commonplace, the great triumphal arch at Euston Station showed that there was no limit to money, confidence, and prosperity, and people were wondering what to do next. The Hotel Ruhl at Nice was showing that one could combine a splendid fortress with standards of comfort, pleasure and luxury in an almost tropically romantic scene of sunsets and palm-trees. With another marvellous jet of imagination someone put out a hand, pushed the Ruhl over the edge into the sea, and the floating Hotel, the transatlantic liner, was already there.

As a boy in Southampton around 1934 I recall seeing the 'Aquitania' and the 'Berengaria' being lifted above the water in the floating dock. When the 'Queen Mary' came, and stuck on the mudbank outside Cowes, we looked, and jeered at the ugly great cow. The earlier liners had been as fantastic as hotels, but they had been beautiful. How can we be sorry for the squalid end of the 'Queen' liners, we who saw the Aquitania sent to the breakers' yard? But I never saw the Titanic. The sinking of the Titanic, I cannot help thinking, killed the Belle Epoque with one thrust. Never glad confident morning again. . . .

Inside these hotels, ashore and afloat, the passion for detail reached the same vertiginous heights. It is ironic that Ritz, whose name should be so closely associated with hotels, had completely different ideas. His hotels—as we can see even now—have simplicity and lightness, an eighteenth-century balance and elegance. They survive because Ritz tools, whether architecture, furniture or decoration, were so good, so simple, and so suitable that they cannot be bettered. . . . The Ruhl survived as long as it did because everything in it was well made, down to the last mustard pot, and because everything had been ordered originally by the thousand. The less well made of these hotels vanished long before.

If one could dredge up the Titanic what treasures one would find. A Spanish plate-galleon could not equal it.

My name is Ozymandias. . . .

The menus of the time reflect the hotel. Everything is staggeringly rich and detailed; the humblest dish, calves' lungs or ox-liver, appeared larded, truffled and cockscombed, castellated in leafy pastry, for the cooking copied the architecture faithfully. How did they do it? One must imagine cooks, moustached and indestructible, with the energy and fecundity of Victor Hugo and Jules Verne, working hour after hour, and driving crowds of pale little boys. It is exactly the world of the great country house, the rigid pyramids of valets and footmen, down to the tweeny staggering under the coalbuckets. Iron discipline, ruthless code— but the marshal's baton waiting as reward for absolute loyalty and application.

The wealth, the lavishness—this did not lead to waste: far from it. The Victorians were extremely frugal and parsimonious, watching every halfpenny. The staggering waste of anything and everything which we see today was the exact contrary to their world. It was because of this parsimony that they could afford to buy a thousand solid silver fishknives—and pay in gold napoleons—and get something that would be polished daily for fifty years without wearing out. For this they had a system; in the kitchen called *the* System. Its exact French title—for the French were the most frugal of all Victorians—is 'Rien se Perd' which is translatable as 'Waste does not Exist'.

Even today French kitchens are run on this principle. When I was in the kitchen the System was still at its height. Monsieur Le Page could never have made a profit without it, high as were the prices he charged. Without it the Hotel des Pyramides (excellent example as it was of a Victorian city hotel) could not have carried on. We will see that only a very talented man pressing the System beyond its accepted limits saved the Atlantic Hotel.

We are accustomed to thinking of the pig as an economical animal because nothing is lost—nose, ears, tail, blood, intestines: all is used. The System consisted of treating everything in this way. For example, a chicken, and not a roasting chicken but a 'poule', an old granny that has made herself useful already throughout a busy life with eggs and chicks, eggs and chicks. . . .

It was carefully cleaned; everything was saved. It went in the pot and was simmered for stock, base of a hundred soups and sauces. Cooked, the white meat of the bird went to the restaurant in many forms, while the dark meat of thigh and legs would be sliced, chopped minced or pounded for as many more. As for the carcass, and the carefully saved skin, and the giblets, it was picked over by the pale little boys. Every scrap of meat was saved;

it made pâté, and stuffing, and it fed the staff. Finally the 'bouquet'—the carrot and onion, and the celery used to flavour the stock—was neatly sliced, decorated with the bayleaf and served for hors-d'oeuvres. Good too; discoloured but impregnated with chicken juices. . . .

Hors-d'oeuvres were never the expensive Scandinavian 'cold table' they are today; rule dictated that they be leftovers, and to make them appetising—why, that was what a cook was for. Any cleaning woman could slice sausage. Leftovers were indeed the kingpin of the system, and the chefs' favourite dishes those which could be 'served twice' or in which there was a lot of debris, such as trimmings, outside slices, tail-ends, awkwardly shaped or 'nervy' bits; all these were collected, chopped, mixed with a good sauce, trimmed up and enriched with such things as mushrooms, gherkins, or tomatoes, and served up in a gratin, or wrapped in a pancake, as a croquette or a crépinette. Falsche häse, as the Germans say.

The depression, followed by the war, destroyed the old 'luxury' notion of hotels, and the System became no more than an economy campaign with a smell of rationing, with inventions like acorn coffee, carrot tart, swede jam and Woolton Pie (which took the place of roast beef as the English national dish for ten years) being taken in their stride along with False Hare and bitocks. In this way, with boys doing men's work, darned tablecloths and a dim light to draw no attention to the carpet, some provincial hotels limped on almost to the nineteen-sixties. But when governments began at last to frame laws about safety, hygiene, minimum wages and tourism, these places collapsed overnight. They lie now on the beaches like stranded whales, the tide lapping among their bones, and serve them right.

They were hurried downhill, of course, by moral as well as economic reasons. In 1945 cooks no longer cared for loyalty and authority. One was no longer sacked for the slightest breach of discipline; if it did happen—as it did to me—there were plenty of other places. With this went a failure of trust. Cooks were no longer allowed even to control their own materials and as a foreseeable result they stole. The shell of the System, tight, exact, complete, was broken and by the time I moved to the Atlantic daylight was showing through the roof in more senses than one.

The owners tried to rescue their hotels by 'rationalizing'. An army of accountants and stocktakers appeared. They were a lamentable failure. There was nothing for it but to scrap everything and start again on factory lines, with mechanized production lines, continuous flow, and a merciless control upon both customer and servant. This is very dull, and working in a hotel now is to be an efficient, hygienic moving part; I am glad to have been spared that.

Except for the introduction of labour-saving machinery the new hotels show no advance over the old: rather the contrary, in fact. It is all there in Bemelmans' *Life Class,* not only in the affectionate portrait of the System in its last palmy days before the crash of the New York stockmarket, but in the emphasis on how extremely well the public rooms of the 'Splendide' were designed. The Victorians would see our architecture as sadly feebleminded as well as hideous; the restaurants mean, ugly and awkward, the kitchens crammed with machinery but incompetent. The Hotel Atlantic, preposterous place as it was, had the best and simplest kitchen and service layout I have seen, and could easily have been built by the designer of the Aquitania.

These are some of the tasks I was given as a boy in the kitchen. Wearing an old overcoat, to go with the larder-chef, every night, through all the pantries and cold-rooms. He carried a clipboard on which was listed every item of food the kitchen stocked. Every tray and crate had to be lifted down for him to inspect, count and note. Since he was a highly-skilled man, he noted, too, the degree of ripeness everything had reached. We did not serve melting cheese, tough steak or rotted tomatoes; all had been written down and allowed for.

To divide all the butchers' trimmings into meat and fat, and chop them both fine. Meat was for consommé, fat for the roast-cook's fryers (one for meat, one for fish, one for potatoes). Smash lobstershells for Américaine Sauce. They were pounded to fine paste in a marble mortar fixed, with masonry, at waist height. The pestle was the size of a baby's head, with a long handle held upright by an iron ring, so that one could work with both hands. The fish-cook's commis tied a sack around his waist and another round his neck, and washed his face afterwards. At other times this mortar was filled with crushed ice, in which was fitted a bowl of steel. Certain kinds of pâté and stuffing were worked in this with cream; the ice was to stop them separating into an oily mess.

To trim vegetables to regular shapes; wheels, stars, cubes or matchsticks. One might have to 'turn' potatoes to the shape of artichoke bottoms. For little balls there were special cutters; the fifty or so others were done by hand. It sounds terrible but with practice all cooks became skilful and rapid.

To rub blocks of hard salt through a sieve. To rub meat, fish or vegetable purée through a finer sieve. To polish the stoves with emery-paper wrapped round an iron weight. To lift the fish out of the icebox, hose the ice down, replace the fish, and crack and pack fresh ice over and around. To crush ice to a powder, for serving caviare and oysters. To hand-pick the tiny membranes out of calves' brains. To stir a sauce over the stove for an hour with a wooden paddle, that it might reduce without sticking to the pot. To make old sacks into little cushions, using string and a trussing needle, for cleaning the bars of the grill. To, draw, wash, singe, trim and truss poultry. To 'channel' mushroom heads with a little knife, producing a spiral wavy pattern. To skin and seed tomatoes, to skin and trim chicken gizzards, to make 'mimosa' of chopped hardboiled egg and parsley, to pick all the little quills from the skins of ducks and geese.... Once launched, one could extend the list indefinitely.

Most of these jobs were long and wearying; all were painstaking. Some were fiercely hot or cruelly cold. Not a few were painful. A boy's clumsy hands were quickly cut and scarred. Grating cheese or potatoes took the skin off palm and knuckle. Many fish had spines that gave poisoned wounds. One learned to use the many different knives. For a bad cut you went to the

chef, who kept bandage, sticking plaster, and a bottle of anti-
septic in his office, and of course for a serious accident there was
the hotel nurse and the hotel doctor. But in general you went to
your own chef, who in his experience had learned an efficient
homoeopathic pharmacy, and a widespread nature cure. In cellars
and pantries cobwebs could always be found, and so could penicillin mould, which cooks knew long ago. For bandages were used
slips of carrot for a cut, the transparent membranes of onion
for a burn, lemon juice for disinfectant. A scorch was dipped in
melted butter and dusted with flour to exclude air.

The boys were often ill as well as wounded. Cooks could treat
this, too, with thyme and lemon for a cold, garlic for bronchitis,
carrots for the intestines. I have seen nasty boils cured with a
cabbage poultice, and boys wormed with garlic. . . . It sounds
crude; it was in fact extremely efficient. The kitchen could be a
dangerous place, with live steam and smoking oil waiting for a
false move, but part of the training—and not the smallest—was
in self-discipline. The kitchen was a school of fortitude.

It is a surprise to me now to realize this, but my eight years in
French hotels were happy.

Impossible to recall the Atlantic, a really spendid example of
Grand Hotel Thermes et Bains de Mer, without a sensation of
just having drunk three strong apéritifs in quick succession. The
building is awestriking, like a meal of jugged hare, Christmas
pudding and port. I felt drunk when I first went in; I was I think
slightly drunk when I left. I can't have been drunk the whole
time since I was there nearly three years, but it seems like it now,
so strong is the flavour of farce.

It is of course by the seaside and just as pompous as the name
suggests. It ought to be tumbling down but cannot because it was
so solidly built. A really concentrated aerial attack, as with
Monte Cassino (there is a resemblance) might do it. The great
central façade stares out to sea like Winston Churchill; impressive
despite everything. On top there are many pinnacles, eccentri-
cally floodlit at night, when they acquire fantasy and even
grace, and remind one of Prague. Within the bulky block are

courtyards deserted and silent, so abandoned that their existence seems forgotten. One day while trying to open a smeary window in the staff quarters I discovered a little clocktower in Victorian gothic that nobody but me, surely, knew existed.

The staff quarters are seven storeys high, under the slates, alarming on windy nights, for there are decayed spots and the corridor carpet, inherited like everything on this floor after being worn out on a floor below, humps itself and groans, and raps loudly with its tail upon the straining floorboards. Red-painted fire-buckets stand about everywhere to receive rain with thick plops. I used a bathroom in a corner for some time; when in the bath, by holding my head at an angle I could see the night sky, racing troubled clouds. This gave a feeling of vertigo, like being in a lighthouse. Together with the loud groaning of wind and the clanks of the plumbing, to wash needed strong nerves; one glanced at the door, where Boris Karloff would come in at any minute.

On a corridor with twenty rooms four of us live; the whole place is like this. At the height of the summer season with the Casino going, and in successive weeks the races, the big golf tournament, bridge, chess and tennis the Atlantic is even then only half full. The other half has not been shut. It has been abandoned, but is all still there. I notice myself using a present tense, which shows the grip the place had on me. But I feel sure that the building at least still *is* there.

When really running it must have been quite a sight, with two hundred staff in each wing (men east, women west) and room above the central block for two hundred more; the maids, valets, and chauffeurs brought by guests. For these, in the basement, there was a special dining-room, a sitting-room, and a bar, all served by hotel staff. In the basement was a strong Sleeping Beauty feel, so that at first I went on tiptoe, afraid of being caught and ejected. Confidence came as I learned short cuts to everywhere and found that only two or three others used these passages. They had assignations, perhaps, but I had a taste for bathrooms and tried them all in turn. On the forgotten staircases were little nooks where sometimes chamber-maids and floor-waiters had gone to earth and left greasy plates, empty bottles, and packs of cards.

The main arteries of the basement were like the Moscow Underground, as lavish as the floors above with tiled corridors three metres broad and flights of marble steps—marble in the basement. . . . Exploring an unknown passage I reached a long flight leading to a scene of hallucination—the Thermes et Bains de Mer! Long-abandoned, with the turkish baths and the gentlemen's barber-saloon. Moonlight filtered, I opened doors and peered round dusty screens, and was astonished to recognize the Palm Court, which I had only seen from the other end. It was still used, for it was intimate despite its size, and made a good room for smaller, family parties, when the huge public rooms became too chill and desolate for guests except the big 'convention' parties who were hearty and noisy, generating a special fervour from contemplating their gods, which might be ballbearings or transformers.

Bits of the basement hummed to be sure with activity, such as the linen-room where pallid girls patched and darned the sheets and tablecloths, or the engineers' workshop, full of huge metal objects of unguessable purpose but that were in fact dismantled remnants of ingenious Victorian devices for air-conditioning the restaurant or supplying bathrooms with warm seawater. Here machines still in use were mended simply by cannibalizing others that were not.

But most of the sousterrain was a drowned Atlantis of hollow ringing corridors long and wide enough to drive a car along them. The ceilings were lined with piping that bristled with stopcocks, with tubing and trunking—air, gas, steam, water for every purpose—could there I wondered be one or two old men who still knew how to make the fountains play? On every side loomed rows of doors; the paint shop, the upholsterers' shop surrounded by piles of stagings and awnings, curtains and carpets and broken furniture. Other doors were shelved cupboards piled with china, glass and silver. The huge black and white squares of marble were still true and level; it was an impressive monument to folie de grandeur.

For cooks the best-known stretch led to the 'banqueting kitchen', used for the largest parties. It was not a kitchen but was filled with hot-cupboards and waterbaths where party dishes for up to five hundred persons could be stored, reheated and served. Next door was a suite of pantries with huge wooden sinks for washing it all up. But one day the chef brought me along a maze of tunnels into just such another party suite but far smaller, designed for a maximum of forty persons. It was in miniature, which had something touching about it. Dust lay thick here; the Sleeping Beauty feeling was very strong. We drew buckets of water and scrubbed everywhere; the stopcocks yielded grudgingly in slow clogged movements and the long-disused steampipes shook and groaned.

The main kitchen was naturally an active place still, part of the central service block which, admirably designed, worked perfectly and always would. The centre of this block was a vast oblong lobby, whose long sides had two pairs of swinging doors leading to the kitchen and the restaurant, respectively. In this lobby was stacked the china, glass, and silver. The short sides were occupied by the glass and silver pantries, and the plate-room, where china was put on conveyor-belts and passed through canvas tunnels where boiling water squirted on it. In the middle of the lobby was a square fort full of plated silver machinery, and this was the stillroom, where waiters got tea or coffee. On the other side of the glass-pantry was another service lobby, reached only from the restaurant, and here was the dispense bar and the wine cellars, and here was served bread, butter and little things such as olives or potato chips.

When a waiter entered the kitchen he found the long service-counter of heated stainless steel in front of him. He could pass along the sides to the far end, where on one side he would find the larder, and on the other the pastry. Completely ludicrous as the Atlantic was, it had the simplest service area I have known, where things worked without strain. The kitchen proper, a large square, was itself divided by three rows of gas ranges, and between them by long wooden work-benches. All food and all movement flowed naturally up the passages thus formed to the service counter at the top. The two outside ranges were the 'corners' of the sauce-cook and the soup-cook. In the middle worked the fish- and roast-cooks.

Along the side walls, beyond the open space used by waiters, are ranged more stoves, big coalfired things. These are used for parties and for any extra, inferior work (the breakfast and staff cooks, melting fat or boiling up old stock). On each side, too, is a steam oven with a big steel wheel to screw the door tight.

Along the back wall is a row of galvanized sinks with wooden tops. In the middle of this wall is a door to the pantry where the 'plongeur' scrubs the great copper pots, and where the 'casserolier' polishes them with salt and lemon rinds. At the corners of this back wall are the doorways to larder and pastry.

The swing doors take half the space on the lobby side, but in the middle hangs a large noticeboard full of menus, memos and regulations—the tours of late duty and days off, and exasperated notices from the management saying that if breakage passes a certain point the cost will be deducted from wages. In the corners on this side are two wooden desks, where the sous-chef and the kitchen clerk do their paperwork.

The entrance to the whole kitchen area is from a yard at the back of the hotel, generally gritty from the coal that is poured in daily floods down a chute to the stokeholds beneath. Here in a kind of box sits an old man, who checks all materials delivered, and the coming and going of the staff, and asks any stranger who he is and what he wants. Passages lead from here to all the service areas of the hotel; the kitchen passage leads past the cooks' changing-rooms to a small paved yard full of dustbins. The cooks call this yard 'Our Garden'. A double door here leads to a lobby, quite like that on the restaurant side of the kitchen, but flagged, dark, draughty, and smelling of musty sacking and damp earth. On one side of this lobby is the larder and the way through to the kitchen past the chef's office. The other two sides form a warren of cellarage, much of it disused and forgotten, like the old hotel bakery; huge ovens scaled and rusting, great marbletopped tables—all just left to moulder away gently. In other cellars fitted with sinks are kept vegetables, salads, potatoes, and in one dark cool corner the florist has staked a claim. In this lobby cooks gossip and lounge and take quick drags at cigarettes before going back to work.

The chef's office is small and dark. A cupboard for his clothes, another for special things like foie gras kept well under his eye, two cupboards full of files and bundles of paper—there is barely room for an old-fashioned desk with many drawers and pigeonholes and a swivel chair to go with it.

The chef was called Monsieur Bonvalet and was a most interesting man. He had taken over the Hotel Atlantic immediately after the revolution of 1939–45, and as First Consul had been both ruthless and efficient.

First stabilize the currency. It had been Monsieur Bonvalet who had closed the bakery—or kept it closed, rather—who had pared away everything luxurious and lavish, had cut the staff to an absolute minimum, reduced the staggering System to plain statements of austerity, and brought Carefulness, Circumspection and Economy along a glorious success-studded road.

The cooks called him 'Dad' precisely because he was not at all like a father-figure. He was neither old nor young; a thick, compact little Savoyard with a bullet head, a suspicious circular face, a soft voice, and iron self-control, Monsieur Bonvalet was like no other chef I have known, and had a strong character. Nothing was too much trouble for him, no detail too small. He was the first cook in the kitchen of a morning, and the last to leave. His finger was on everything, and no corner was too dark, smelly, untidy or obscure.

His economies were startling. He had reduced the 'carte' to proportions so small as to discourage the boldest tourist; a believer in fixed menus, he had many of these, from 'touristique' to 'gastronomique' scattered round the dining-rooms: under different names they were all the same and with around eight basic dishes every meal-time he could make combinations to suit any price range. To the waiters' order he would add code-words. 'Make a bit rich' or more frequently 'Make not too poor' lifted anything into a higher price-bracket. . . .

These dishes, of good materials, were cooked in a classic style, and nicely served on the hotel's beautiful rococo silver, but one had to admit that Dad got away with things not ordinarily seen on hotel menus. Homely dishes of calves' head and pigs' trotters, ox-liver and sow-belly, figured daily. Mutton stew and braised beef appeared three times a week: as for meatballs of all kinds, fish kedgeree and chicken pojarski, a great deal of breadcrumb and plenty of chopped parsley, these of course were Dad's delights. His pet accompaniments to anything were carrots-and-turnips or stuffed tomatoes, guaranteed to make a decidedly small cutlet look twice its size. . . .

Similar economies applied to the staff. I saw at once why I had got this job so easily; all the cooks were, like me, too young for their jobs or else too old. The sous-chef was thirty, the larder-chef sixty. None of the boys had more than a year's experience. To save the strain this threw on the more experienced cooks, and to get out of paying higher wages, Dad was generous with time off. We got half holidays, a great luxury. Before every service we had a half hour to eat in peace, whereas most cooks then had to eat hurriedly after the service, in their own time. Since nearly all the cooks were quiet, settled married men they found these conditions agreeable.

Dad was pleasant to work for. He was neither self-important nor a fussy formalist. He was the greatest pragmatist possible, and hated even having to say 'Good morning,' a remark either unnecessary in his eyes or, more probably, untrue. He never shook hands with anyone. As economical with himself as with his kitchen he smoked two cigarettes a day, lighting them as he left each afternoon and each night from the pilot gas jet on the nearest stove to save matches. He arrived and left on foot, in the same brown suit and blue overcoat all the year round, by the kitchen entrance; he had no snobberies. He lived in a minuscule seaside villa five minutes walk away, intensely bourgeois and respectable, with pleated lace curtains covering all the windows. . . .

I had a lot to learn, it was plain, and it was at first a bewildering world, so utterly unlike that in which I had been trained. Still, I was being paid more than I had ever had, and at that age did not mind that I was being diddled. The responsibilities were in fact not heavy, for Dad's routine was so perfected that everything was cut and dried, so that life was nowhere near as nerve racking as even a commis', in Paris. Since nothing was too much trouble for Monsieur Bonvalet, when we wrote our indents for the daily stores, he would go carefully over the list with his blue pencil. He would halve the butter, cut down the tomato purée, put in another packet of macaroni, and murmur at the end 'I noticed too that you need more pepper.'

If one was economical, he cared no more for formal 'discipline' than he did for appearances. There was no concentration-camp atmosphere. The kitchen was decidedly tatty, enormous and lit by a glass roof like those of railway stations, strongly light-repellent but generous towards rain. I was used to white tiled walls, red-tiled floors—here, certainly, walls were glazed, but in the style of public lavatories in London, grey and covered in tiny cracks. The floor was patched concrete strewn with sawdust, with pools of water wherever the uneven surface impeded drainage. Much overhead space was taken up by a tangled bulbous tunnel of metal designed to remove fumes and smoke. It didn't, though it made a fine whining keening noise, but the draught removed the fumes anyway.

It was autumn, and quiet. Lunches busy still, but little work in the evening, though the parties would soon be beginning. I learned quickly about the carrots-and-turnips and applauded Dad's sagacity. I had time to study it all. Cooks no longer dodged nervously out for a quick smoke in the Garden, but sat peacefully in the staffroom behind the pot-wash, where a fire could be lit. Larder-cooks began to wear pullovers under their whites, and in the staffroom the potman installed a derelict armchair with the stuffing coming out and the decayed leg propped on an orange box. It was full of fleas, but that was the last thing to worry him. In the kitchen cooks cleaned their stoves, polished their knives, and turned all the year's rubbish out of the drawers in the benches. I was quickly happy. Outside mist came down over the little town, the grey sea snored on the shingle; everything was marvellously peaceful and the placid rhythm of the Atlantic rocked me upon waves of content. The hotel had in reality left its mooring upon the low chalk cliff and was drifting out to sea rapidly, but that I was seeing the last years of the Grand Hotel Thermes et Bains de Mer before the final shipwreck I had then no idea.

7 'EIN PISELLI APPARTEMENT'

Autumn in the Hotel Atlantic meant dried vegetables; they were
cheap, they did not go rotten, there was no waste: the stores were
full of sack upon sack of lentils, haricots, flageolets, and they
appeared daily masquerading under the grandiloquent names
of French racecourses (Longchamps, Saint Cloud, and Chantilly
were all variations on split-pea soup). This was cynicism on Dad's
part, since the names indicate that they were all in origin luxurious summer soups made of the early, fresh peas. . . . They
also accompanied the ox-breast and the sow-belly and suchlike
homely German dishes. Franz the sous-chef, who came from
Alsace, swore that Monsieur Bonvalet had spent his time as a
prisoner of war planning to get his own back on customers when
the war should be over by regaling them with lentils. I said that
the 'haricots de l'administration' were just as classic in the French

army, but we both agreed that in Monsieur Bonvalet's extremely lucid mind patriotism was one thing, but business altogether another.

Autumn meant, too, a great deal of cabbage, which got braised with different kinds of sausage and swaggered on to menus as Lorraine 'Potée' and Alsace choucroute. Indeed when a cheap vegetable came into season it stayed with us all day every day, and months in the Hotel Atlantic instead of being called February May or July became Artichoke or Marrow.

It was a foregone conclusion that Dad's chief mainstay was chicken: this of course is the case with every hotel. Chickens are cheap, easy, and there is no waste—an animal version of lentils. They can be cooked and served in a wonderfully large variety of ways, and by simply counting your chicken and multiplying by four you know exactly how many people they will feed. Dad got them from sources that were secretive, and probably squalid, even for him. Franz, for whom as for me Monsieur Bonvalet was a fascinating and richly comic study, had allowed his imagination to dwell on these terrible birds.

'Somewhere in Poland,' he told me, peering into a pot, 'there is a tiny wheelbarrow standing still with one turnip on it, lonely in the forest clearing.' Those chickens had worked for a living.

Dad was a Savoyard, with the legendary vices of avarice, obstinacy and distrust, but also with individualism, simplicity, and generosity. But one saw the vices first. He was a good chef, but a poor cook. Fish was his speciality, as it was of the hotel— we were by the coast, fish was cheaper than meat. When we had important customers, ministers, racehorse-owners and the like, he would choose sometimes to officiate at the fish-cook's stove, Marcellin watching impassively. He would then be madly extravagant, and not surprisingly he was no good at that, and would smash sauces by putting in too much butter or cooking the cream too long. It was at everyday drudgery that he shone.

He had a trick of hiding little treasures: a brace of woodcock for some special customer in the ice-cream cabinet, hidden under an old Nesselrode bomb—Dad invented deep-freeze before anyone else. In the obscurest corners of fridge and cold-room were always many little pots, but nothing ever went sour or grew penicillin; he was there first. An excellent judge of quantity, he could tell at a glance what a lump of anything weighed, cost, and would feed.

He very seldom showed anger, and even of the larder-chef, with whom he was at war, the furthest he would go was to say 'That one will never understand meat.' In any crisis he was level headed, and in my time with him I saw him handle a death, several accidents, and a fire. A rush of guests or a flu epidemic left him unperturbed. He was never ill, never raised his voice, and never used bad language.

Hotel staffs always are a ragbag lot, and the brigade here no more than most, really. Beside the usual French and Italians there were Germans and Poles picked up cheap, the larder-chef was English, the waiters all Turks or Czechs, and half these people spoke no French. To cope with them Monsieur Bonvalet had invented a strange language, which he used with great virtuosity; indeed he seemed to have forgotten French. It was made up of words from all languages. Since his character was so strong we all talked this language in the kitchen, and even the local tradesmen had all learned pidgin, or 'sabir' as it is called in French. Dad even spoke sabir on the telephone, unaware of doing so. He was fine on the phone: no chat, no good-mornings, no This-is-the-Captain-speaking or How's-your-wife's-cough. Telegraphese, as though thinking he would be charged by the word.

'Where my oysters, huh?' A long blah of excuse and explanation at the other end.

'No good, no good. Oyster no here on time I no pay.' Bang.

During the service he took charge himself, which few chefs do. He trusted Franz, but there were such opportunities for bargaining. Not of course in the restaurant, where there were headwaiters and a manager to deal with complaints, and he did not encroach upon the authority of others. . . . But living in the hotel, en pension, were innumerable rich old stinkers. They had lost their homes in the war, or could get no servants, or were shareholders, or simply lived there because it suited them best. They got everything at reduced prices, complained all the time, bargained bitterly, and were Dad's dearest enemies. Since this was the Norman coast a number were English, retired admirals and generals of the Indian Army who had lived here ever since the franc was cheap in the twenties, when France was full of English people making their incomes go further. Some did not talk French, but they all understood sabir. A few old biddies never left their rooms: we knew them only as names to be cursed, saltless diets or strange manias, but Dad was their match.

He would be tolerant for a while. Extra cheese waved on, nibbled fruit left benevolently uncharged. The enemy once softened up by this luxurious living, he would turn the screw, making helpings of everything day by day more skimpy. After a while the admirals saw the light, and came through with a little present, a bottle of brandy or a box of cigars. Dad did not drink, and sold these bribes back to the bar. Sometimes he would keep a cigar and sit in the office coughing, refusing to be beaten by the thing.

One of these 'appartement' dragons met him on equal terms. She was a horrible old woman; 'la guerre entre quatre murs' was her only pleasure. There is one like her in every hotel. War between four walls began with the liftman bringing down a check; this would be in vague terms. Melon; duck with nice (underlined) greens, a baked potato, a peach. Mrs. Finkle (her name in sabir): one five nine.

Monsieur Bonvalet studied this carefully, took his pencil and priced it, added mysterious annotations, rapped with the pencil on the counter. The larder cut melon, we cut duck. Dad called to the soup-cook, a rather nasty old Italian, for greens.

'Ein good porsione finkle.'

'Beans?—beans are freshest.'

'Well then send.' One haricots verts. Up went the lift. Minutes after the phone rang. We knew already—floor waiter on the line.

'Chef, she says the melon is overripe.'
'No overripe. Canteloupe is immer so.'
'She wants honeydew.'
'Got no honeydew. Good melone Spain, very expensive.'

'She says she'll leave it and have two peaches.'
'Write on check. Peach hundredtwenty franc on market.'
'But look chef. . . .'
'I no argue.' Bang and first round to Dad. The odious Finkle
now began a siege, and the liftman reappeared carrying the duck.
'Sent it down—says the breast is bone and the leg hard. Wants
a nice wing, nothing more.' This indirect trick of ringing the

liftman instead of that obtuse tiresome kitchen galvanised Dad,
who raced outraged for his telephone.

'Deuxième floor . . . waiter look, tell Madame Finkle in France
duck no grow without legs. Everyone want wing and leg I put
in dustbin, huh? How Finkle say leg tough—when she no cut
how she know?' A double shot, since the leg was untouched and
anyway, did Levantine ducks just balance on their tails?

The liftman reappeared with a patient expression. Like all
belowstairs staff he was a mutilated ex-serviceman, an excellent
worker with a quiet voice who like the rest of us had given up
French for Dad-language.

'She says she try, only because is nothing better. She say. But
want now peas.'

'Me too want now peace.'

'No no, piselli, petits pois. She say why send beans with duck?'

Dad was playing with the wooden batten that stopped checks
blowing off the counter; he banged it down hard but did not say
merde because he never did.

'Ein piselli, appartement,' he snapped. 'You liftman bring back
beans or she eat too.'

Restaurant waiters had a trick of inventing important customers in an effort to get a bigger helping and perhaps a bigger
tip in consequence. All waiters do this.

'I got the kitchen to make it specially nice,' they whisper, and
naïve customers glow with satisfaction. A clever waiter takes
pains to be polite to cooks, offer them cigarettes, give them
racing tips and can from time to time get something extra,
though this is rare. Our waiters, a cunning lot in many ways, were
oddly stupid with Dad and constantly tried to twist his arm with
non-existent celebrities. All this cry of wolf had the obvious
effect, that if there really was somebody influential in the
restaurant he was quite uninterested.

'Chef, chef—not enough,' they would wail.

'Basta basta,'—Dad imagining he was speaking Greek.

'This special, very.'

'Is always.'

'Make very special, headwaiter say, truly truly.'

'Ah. Who he is, this headwaiter? Where he is, huh?' And sure enough coat-tails flying, a headwaiter in an agony of self-importance.

'Chef—number seventeen—très très recommandé—Mr. Onassis.'

'And who he is, eh?' calm as a custard, playing with his batten, 'is a cook?' We stood transfixed. Could Monsieur Bonvalet have made a joke? He was well-known to be incapable of humour. . . . we argued about it in the changing-room. It must have been a joke.

'Nonsense,' said Franz stoutly, 'he meant it absolutely seriously. The one thing he's frightened of is a real cook arriving.'

As sous-chef, Franz saw more of him than the rest of us. He became the leader in a game of noticing new aspects of this intricate character, the gradual transformation from the stones and goats of the high Savoie to the prosperous businessman in a Norman coast resort: this is a long way in every sense. We began to collect and analyse mannerisms.

The umbrella, for example, perplexed us a long time. Monsieur Bonvalet carried it at all times; it was, too, splendid. This seemed misplaced; his clothes were well worn and he was not ostentatious.

'English businessmen carry them.' We knew all about English businessmen, who had already resumed the pre-war habit of popping over to Le Touquet. Many of the north coast resorts, like Dieppe or Dinard, have always been very English; extraordinary clothes and loud voices were familiar in every bar.

I disagreed.

'Doesn't pretend to be English businessman. He is cook.'

'He doesn't open it even when it rains.'

'Of course not. All that opening and shutting—get worn out.'

'Was very expensive.'

'You know when he went on holiday he took it with him.'

'Doesn't carry it around Chambéry, surely—people might laugh; that wouldn't do.'

'Well,' said Franz, 'he popped in to see if I were sitting at his desk, and he had it with him.'

'Maybe because nobody else has one? Local boy makes good—symbol of prosperity?'

'Who does have one anyway, back in the village?—the mayor, and the curé—his is all gone green like his soutane. . . .'

'And Monsieur Machin who was deputy and a minister once, for three weeks. . . .' We relapsed into silent enjoyment of Dad waddling down the street, raising his hat to Church and State, keeping the precious object well away from harsh stone and baked earth. Franz rubbed his jaw, grinning at the hat, for he always wore a hat, and only after a great rush, with complaints about tough steak, would he take his toque off for a second to push his hard short hand 'like a dachshund's paw' as Franz said, through his bootbrush hair while he loosened and regained concentration.

'Think of him as a child,' happily, 'hiking five kilometres to school with a big black beret pulled on right over his ears in the snow.'

'Carrying a big piece of bread.'

We constructed fantasies, like his apprenticeship in the Hotel Beau Rivage, where the specialities are little bits of goat on skewers, alternating of course with bits of goats' cheese, and supremes of flyingfish 'the wings left on to make the helpings look bigger'. In all this there was little malice; we were fond of him. Working the same hours as ourselves, leaving by the same door, umbrella over wrist and cigarette in the exact middle of his mouth—this we felt as a kind of loyalty to us.

He had very nice sides to his character. If anybody was ill or in domestic trouble he would listen with sympathy, give extra time off, even advance money. If someone brought a child into the kitchen he was delighted and one would see him walking gravely hand in hand with a tot towards the ice-cream cabinet. The same thing about him was both good and bad; he was always there, eye fixed on a hardboiled egg or a half-grapefruit, together with one of his special phrases, favourite being 'Un peu

poor'—this applicable to anything from overcooked spaghetti to
the filthy state of the larder floor.

So conditioned were we to these grooved ways that it came as a
thunderclap when he bought a car. It was black, small and sober,
but we looked for excitements, for we could see that it would be
fertile in incident. Its owner was uneasy; not the usual mastery.
The contrivance was too small and too flimsy, alien to the world
of Thermes et Bains de Mer where all the massive machinery
had been designed by Brunel. One saw him at the wheel, determined and rather red with enforced calm, but if objects entered
the field he became flustered; horns blew, lights flashed, and an
argument might start any moment so that we stood transfixed.
But gradually we saw the car less and less: we felt cheated.

'Afraid of wearing the tyres out.'

But when he went on holiday, and told Franz he was taking
the car, the air in the changing-room was thick with jeremiads.

'Fall in the ditch watching price-tickets instead of the road.'

'He'll blow the horn in Paris.'

'He'll meet a very large tanker in a very narrow roadway.'

'He'll be rolled by gangsters, and that'll learn him being a
bloody capitalist.'

October, slackest month of the year. Finkle had flitted to the
south, there to complain that the food was not what she was used
to, which was very true. Meanwhile her rooms were re-decorated
and several crates of empty gin and Vichy bottles removed. There
was little to do, but Franz's tread was heavy with responsibility.

Two Greek waiters, small but vicious, had a fight and were
separated by Franz covered in blood and gibbering. Another
won a large sum on horses—we were indignant; did they not
make enough money fawning on customers and selling their
sisters? We began a war out of boredom and the stillroom man
stopped the teas racket, which, basically means ordering 'tea
for two' with 'a large jug of water' and then selling it for four;
like all rackets it is capable of much refinement in experienced
hands.

The Greeks retaliated on the late-night sandwich racket, a

source of income to the larder, it was true, but also to themselves, so that it was a Pyrrhic victory. Authority, much against its will, was forced to take heed of these scandals, and two Greeks and a cook, pillars of the floating poker game in the headwaiters' changing-room, were sacked. These upheavals were sobering; there was hardly any comment when Dad came back from holiday with no car. None of us, at least, ever saw the car again.

8 CHRISTMAS PARADISO

Cooks get humiliated about being belowstairs. They have an uneasy feeling that smells, of fishstock, burnt oil or cabbage soup, hang about them no matter how much they wash, and they get complexes about being pushed out of sight and in general treated as cockroaches. There is nowadays a very bad tendency to put grills or other excuses for cooks to hang about right in the restaurant, but this was unheard of in my day, when cooks loved to infiltrate the public rooms, talking about art. In this they are abetted by women writing in magazines, who go on no end about art and illustrate it with pretty photographs. Bad cooks love this; they cut the pictures out, look at them with admiration, and resolve to outdo these over-decorated horrors at the earliest opportunity.

Of course it is important for food to be appetising; a good cook brings imagination and a colour-sense to his work. The delicate blend of scarlet, rust and cream that is a lobster Newburg would give anyone an appetite, even if they hated lobster. There is a very old tradition, too, of surprising the guest by food disguised as something else, to amuse and to please. All cooks like to show off virtuosity, and restaurants encourage them since it is good publicity. The horrors begin to creep in when all this art forgets about the nose and only clamours for the eye's attention.

All expensive restaurants decorated food as a matter of course. Cold dishes were the obvious choice because they could be done in advance and time spent on them. The sauce-cook did not bother; if his dishes were good they also looked good, and he had no time to fiddle. The roast-cook embellishes things because his slices of beef and grilled cutlets are the kitchen's simplest, barest dishes, and can stand a bit of tarting up. There is as well an economic reason—a steak from a roadside diner looks the same as one from a three-star snob-house, and something has to justify the difference in price. This accounts for all the rubbishy bits of fried bread and potato cut in fantasy shapes, for all the tomato flowers and watercress foliage. Cutting radishes into roses and waterlilies, stylising lemons and mushrooms, setting off the crisp, hot reds and browns with cool dewy greenery— the roast-cook's commis spends hours at this, and it is known in the kitchen as 'paradiso'.

For identical reasons the larder commis 'excites' the pale yellow of an egg mayonnaise—the haughtiest restaurants used to do this with a sprinkle of lobster coral and chopped truffle trimmings, always known as 'Stendhal' because it is scarlet and black.

So far, all this is fine and shows the cook is taking trouble. But in the heyday of the System cooks had often time on their hands. Bad weather, a slack season, a rival attraction—of a sudden there were too many cooks, and nobody thought of sending them home. Devices must be found to occupy them— paradiso in exaggerated and nonsensical forms. True to the great god Rien Se Perd the classic materials used were hot-water paste and mutton fat.

If you mix flour with a little melted fat and enough boiling water to make a plastic dough you have an agreeable toy. It does not stick; it can be pulled, moulded, bent and cut into funny shapes. It holds these, but distorts as it dries, and becomes fragile, so that little pieces of stick or wire are used as a base. A commis learns to plait, weave and twist strips of this into little boxes and baskets. When coloured with a brush dipped in egg or caramel these look attractive, and such things as plovers' eggs, little birds, or shrimps, bedded artfully on mustard-and-cress, and nestled in a sweet little basket, delight the restaurant. They break easily, but one simply makes more—that is the whole point.

There is always plenty of mutton fat. It is not used for cooking because it smells bad and burns easily. It is harder and whiter than other animal fats. It is firm, shiny, opaque. The larder-cook collects it and makes a little sculptors' studio in a pantry. When the masterpiece is ready it can go in the restaurant to crown a display of cold and smoked meat. Simplest subject is a sphinx or some such animal easily shaped from a block. Bricks of kitchen salt were also favourite sources for all kinds of flora and fauna.

Monsieur Bonvalet had no time at all for such toys, and the Hotel Atlantic was one house where there was no paradiso. Even in the larder decorating was discouraged; it needed little discouraging because it was not in the larder-chef's temperament ever to decorate anything. Sid was English; he had worked in a French hotel for thirty years but could not be bothered to learn French except for basic phrases like 'Box of matches' in a music-hall accent. He kept the flag flying, like Major Thompson. All Norman resorts swarm with English tearooms, and Sid could be found in one of these of an afternoon, quiet and neat in his grey tweed suit, eating scones and reading the *Daily Mail*. A startling sight for anyone who had seen Sid in the larder, where he was noisy, dirty, and extremely funny. Still, by extraordinary ways and means Sid was good at his job. The larder was bedlam all day, and it was a nightly surprise when we began to clear the kitchen and came in to find the larder scrubbed and tidy, and

Sid himself having a quiet cigarette in the garden. He was kind, friendly, cheerful and active; we all liked him, except Dad of course who afforded him a grudging respect. Sid and Dad talking sabir together was one of the kitchen's richest turns.

French larder-cooks are meticulous and oldmaidish to a man, and Sid was neither, and Dad's despair in consequence. He was sloppy, a shocking butcher, and had a trick of leaving every job half done; one came into the larder to find fish-heads all over the floor, blood dripping from an untidy heap of liver, and the electric mincer whining emptily with nothing to chew on. Right from the early morning farce predominated, when Sid arrived with a big jug of coffee, dragged dirty aprons out of his table-drawer, and rousted up his staff with the classic larder slogan.

'Come on boys, get the shit out.'

Sid always arrives early, and has a good breakfast, with porridge. After a cigarette he stumps off to his domain, clean and quiet, sinks scrubbed, fresh sawdust on the floor—Sid is now going to change all that. He collects things; a hat that might be cleaner than the one he has on; pencils, handkerchiefs, knives, his glasses which he cleans with his smeary apron—how does he ever see anything? All this time he bawls at his boys.

'Come on, jump about.' His staff is an odd collection; André the fish boy is dark, excitable, lazy, Provençal, and Ernst, a demure young German, is the opposite. Fat Robert the salad king is vegetable in thought, word and deed, and poor old Joe is a blurred Italian antique looking as though left out in the rain for the past hundred years but who makes wonderful quenelles of whiting to imitate sole, greatly treasured by Dad and on the menu nearly every day. Ernst was always spotlessly clean. I asked him once how he could survive Sid's lewd uproar; his answer was that as a boy he had worked in a sawmill.

Two or three other boys come and go in the larder but few hold out for long. There are generally a couple in one of the pantries next to where Robert makes hors-d'oeuvres, doing canapés and sandwiches for a reception, or filleting soles for a party. Everything goes smoothly, though one would never think so to see Sid trying to read the menu through his greasy glasses.

'Why can't the old man sharpen his bleeding pencil?'

The turnup of Sid's hat is full of pencils, and the hat itself is covered in blood. Larder-cooks keep an old overcoat and a beret for counting stock in the cold-rooms; Sid can't be bothered and gets his hat knocked off by a swinging side of beef.

The larder-porter arrives with his trolley, both squeaking dismally. The tradesmen brings things to the back door, where they are weighed, counted, and signed for by the old timekeeper. Crates of fish, fruit or poultry have to be ferried down to the larder where they stand till Sid has time to put them away, which is this evening some time. A stupid boy has put a tin high on a shelf; what can it be, this tin? Sid pulls it down and drowns himself in cooked beetroot; his face the same colour and his hat falling over his ear he stands fuming. In his hand is his dingdong knife, the largest chopping knife ever seen. Furious chopping has broken the wooden handle and Sid got the engineer to make one of cast metal. The rivets attaching this have worked loose, so that the contraption clanks like a cracked church-bell. Sid sharpens it on the concrete rim of the fish-box, with a fearful noise and showers of sparks.

Winter is the party season; biggest and messiest of all parties is Christmas, going on to the New Year, with the two big 'Reveillon' dinners after midnight and a feverish atmosphere to make the foggy Norman winter more festive. For the Christmas week we must have extra hands—apprentices, these, from a hotel school. They are anxious to do delicate and important work, such as stuffing quails or larding saddles of hare. Sid gets a couple.

'You go in there and start making breadcrumbs and don't you stop till I tell you which will be in five days from now, or I'll lard your saddle for you.' They are disgusted with the Hotel Atlantic. My boy is peeling chestnuts, and the fish-cook's, button onions; both are anxious to move to the larder.

Three days before Christmas arrive two very ancient retired cooks from Paris, known as Les Pères Noel. These wizened old gentlemen shake hands with Dad, get given a small vermouth, and retire to the old bakehouse where they are in nobody's way. Here they unroll plans, and sheaves of glossy cabinet photographs: the brigade of the 'Champagne' on the way to the New York Exhibition of 1911; many terrible baroque sugar palaces; naked women made of mutton fat, respectable and classical in feeling—Diane de Poitiers, or Pauline Bonaparte. They are going to make a Christmas Paradiso.

This is a cold buffet, a very grand one to be displayed in the public rooms, and photographed by the local papers with any celebrities who may be about; mayors, prefects, senators and the like. For this, a big effort is expected of the kitchen. Not us, thank heaven; we are much too busy. But the pastry-cook must bake a monstrous cake, and make bouquets of pulled-sugar flowers, and many thousand petits-fours of marzipan. Cross about this, he is sarcastic and says that Sid is going to make an Enormous Tower. What of? Well, of . . . but we have understood. Les Pères Noel, at peace in the bakehouse well away from Sid as well as his tower, will do all that is needed.

Back on the 'Champagne', of course, they were given great blocks of foie gras, mounds of caviare, the quails and the saddles of hare—but such ideas do not appeal at all to Monsieur Bon-valet. The only condition upon buffet work is that it should be constructed of—technically—eatable materials; les Pères Noel, being French, understand this perfectly and are quite happy to use swedes and semolina instead of that nasty foie gras. Of course the customers might be unhappy at being served beautifully carved helpings of swedes and muttonfat, so that various tradi-tional treats will also be provided. Franz has built a 'boar's head'; really a huge country pâté made from scraps of veal, liver, sow-belly, tongue, shaped into a kind of rhinoceros and lavishly painted with brown aspic. Two cutlet bones are scraped and inserted, for tusks. . . . There is also a sucking pig, rather large, that has not sucked anything for a good while. This beast is arranged crouching in a menacing way, strapped down to a board to prevent it kicking the oven door open, and roasted with its ears and tail protected by little hats of greaseproof paper, in which it looks like a tourist on the beach, sunbathing. Other bargain basement delicacies are a huge pie, Beauvais Cathedral with gilded angels blowing trumpets; a centenarian crayfish, 'Langouste en Bellevue' that is certainly too tough to eat, and a salmon, stranded upon a jetty of semolina, that may well be a basking shark in disguise.

Between the New Year and Easter is a bad time. There are no tourists, and there are never enough parties to satisfy Dad. Since the weather leaves few resources but eating and drinking, the hotel management and the mayor's office plot all sorts of grand-iose manifestations known to us as Folklore Feasts. At the Saint-Hubert, for instance, there is a hunting feast, with horns and dressing-up, torchlight, and some very naughty venison. The cooks were supposed to barbecue this, which would not have been very nice, so we cooked it secretly in our tall oven beforehand: it resisted this bitterly and although hung upon hooks kept on falling down with a crash. We smuggled it in a jeep to the picturesque local castle where the feast would be held, hidden under sacks, and built a great log fire in the courtyard. Much money is charged for these entertainments, which we enjoy very much, because a hilarious Chamber of Commerce gets lavish with drink on these occasions. All the local bigwigs and the Prefect are on parade; we baste our three-quarters cooked animal, set it on fire, and serve it with a great deal of poivrade sauce.

In the hotel itself more fantasies are enacted—Norman Menus, with cider and cream in everything and Dad keeping a sharp eye on the calvados bottle (more dressing-up, as Ancient Gauls this time) and as a grand climax we had an English week. It was discovered that we were 'jumelés' with somewhere in Shropshire, and English policemen came and stood about in the streets, a doubledecker bus trundled to and fro, there was an English pub with warm beer, and Sid was very cantankerous the whole time because he felt it was all aimed at him personally. The English certainly made fools of themselves, saying we should all eat Stilton instead of Camembert, but so did the French, and we could not see that anyone suffered.

For the last day there was a tremendous dinner with several mayors and the Ambassador; the management came excitedly down to Monsieur Bonvalet with sheaves of literature sent by the British Council, and we feared the worst, with good reason, because it was all about Olde Englishe food. Dad was dubious but the management overruled him and we had the Court of Camelot; swans, peacocks, porpoises and stargazy pie. Little nut trees decorated the tables, with silver apples and golden pears in marzipan and the Queen of Spain's Daughter in muttonfat. Sid refused pointblank to have anything to do with this, sensibly as it turned out because the stargazy pie was a fiasco and the fish-cook went on making coarse jokes about seagull stew for several weeks.

These jollities had enlivened the dreary February days and had been forgotten, spring was round the corner and the sauce-cook was on holiday. I was left in sole charge of the corner, and was nervous about a big party scheduled for a political conference of some kind. When the menu was posted I found I had a dish for several hundred described as Saltpit Mutton Grilled on wood charcoal, in Basque Style so please you. I rushed into the office in a flap. Had we not had enough folklore, phony barbecues, people playing bagpipes, Greek waiters pretending to be Sir Lancelot? I was alone with two idiot boys, remember the stargazy pie, and so forth.

Hush hush; Dad was very soothing and gave me some vermouth, rather heavily cut with water, left over from Christmas morning, when cooks all got a glass together with a limp handshake. I was not to worry. Was he not there? Did all not go, invariably, on velvet? This was indisputable. But what about this wood charcoal (beginning to quiver again)? What with Saint Hubert and the Ancient Gauls' wild boars we had really had enough wood charcoal to last the year.

Dad told me not to be distraught. There would be no charcoal, no saltpits, no bagpipes. It would be the most sober party imaginable. Ordinary roast lamb, with just a bit more garlic than was usual, done peacefully in the oven right here at home. A bit of rosemary, plenty of chopped parsley—all the rest would be in the eye of the beholder. As for the Basque style, it was none other than Dad's favourite dish, a few Spanish peppers and lashings of rice.

Monsieur Bonvalet had reached the logical conclusion that the best kind of paradiso was that which was totally imaginary.

9 CURRY AND THE LUCKY PEOPLE

Very strange people live in hotels. When you have said that a person lives in a hotel you are saying that he is a peculiar character. Of course I am not talking about Mrs. Finkle. People like that have no choice, and she was no more than an average and therefore typical example of the hordes of dotty wealthy old women who live in hotels because they have nowhere else. Their families, if they have any, would never let them in at the door, unwilling to have their lives poisoned from that moment on. Servants will not stay. They have no other recourse than to live in hotels—which have to put up with absolutely anybody—the whole year round.

This is why I stayed in the kitchen. It took little enough experience and observation to confirm that the kitchen is the only place in the hotel where you are safe from people who can make your life a continuous humiliation and do, because they have realized that you are a slave.

There are, though, other kinds of people living in hotels. Most of them do so because a house—meaning a home—has little interest for them. They generally concentrate upon making money to the exclusion of everything else, and are therefore indifferent to the extreme nastiness of living in a hotel, where you have no privacy, get no respect, and have not even the satisfaction of making a home which is something living and organic. They can only see that there is no need to buy or cook food, no need to make the bed or clean the bath, and that a fictitious luxury can be made to take the place of comfort. It is very sad to think that their wants, apparently, can be satisfied by porters, telephone girls, and pages. Their privacy is no more than a suite with a door they can lock, for hotel servants have no loyalty or discretion. Generally these customers, secure in the possession of much wealth, simply do not care.

Old mother Mizpash, the shipowner's wife, sat upon the pot in the middle of the sitting-room floor and went on doing so year in and year out without caring who knew it. The Mizpash couple were peculiar in eating only one thing, a carré of lamb unsalted: a carré is a little joint of four or six cutlets cut in one piece. This—nothing else—they ate morning and evening.

The ancient and wealthy Miss Whipple—she owned Ludgate Circus or Holborn Circus or some such squalid but fruitful piece of ground (the word fruitful seems ill-chosen)—dined from nothing but the contents of two little silver sauceboats. One was of cream, the other of the red juice which drips from roast beef. She spent all day, the chambermaids reported, writing very long, rude letters to lawyers (this is one example of lack of privacy). But the loudest, probably not richest, but certainly most entertaining of this type of customers had for us no name at all; throughout the hotel they were known simply as The Lucky People.

He was a man of about fifty, a millionaire speculator of sorts. He dealt in everything, house property, factories or businesses. He floated and dissolved companies, took them over when insufficiently liquid—strange, all these watery things that happen to business—reorganized them, and tossed them away when he got tired of them.

His wife, whom he called 'Daughter' like something out of Hemingway, was a very beautiful young woman. Was she a film star, or did she simply conform to her notion of being a film star?—I do not know. She walked about naked, threw things, wrote on the walls, kissed or slapped total strangers, and generally lived up to a busty reputation.

He was much the same, living all day in swimming shorts and throwing cigars about. On the hotel roof they had a private swimming pool, into which they pushed people. They were not, though, disliked in the hotel, though they certainly gave a great deal of trouble, and with the servants they showed a rough, familar gaiety. They launched insults with a smile, and topped them with an enormous tip, so that maids and waiters learned to smile too when pushed in the pool and wait for the twenty-dollar bill that came next. The man seemed relieved at escaping from care by these simple means, and the woman perhaps had no other way of avoiding the accusation she certainly dreaded of being 'stuck-up'. One is always surprised at the naïveté and crudity of the minds of successful businessmen.

The Lucky People were often away, to be sure, on their yacht, in New York or Palm Beach, or wherever, and while they were away we would think of them almost with affection. Their suite would be repaired and repainted; they were very destructive. When they got back we would curse them and their infernal dogs (as undisciplined as themselves) but we enjoyed, too, seeing what they would get up to next; the whole hotel began to effervesce.

They ate anything and everything, in any order, and were quite as likely to start with the chocolate cake as with the oysters. They were fondest of curry, and every second day the note would come down saying chicken, mutton, duck or lobster but with the word 'Curry' in underlined capitals. It was their habit to send a tip for the cook—which we shared—and a glass full of their favourite drink; a large glass—full—Gordon's Gin and Rose's Lime Juice, half and half. I found it a revolting mixture and gave mine away, but one day when making curry, this big crystal tumbler beside me on the bench, I remembered Paul the sauce-cook, who had trained me to put a little lime juice into curry. I picked up the glass, saw that nobody was looking, and added a good shot to my sauce, wondering what effect the gin would have. The curious and subtle flavour of nitroglycerine thus obtained was a great success. The Lucky People swore by my curry and would have no other. I kept my secret recipe in a little bottle, which quickly became a big bottle.

Curry was a restaurant favourite in those days—the present Coca-cola generation prefers food and drink to have the least flavour possible—and since it is a wonderful outlet for leftovers we made a massive pot full each week, which I duly drenched with gin. How long this might have gone on I have no idea, but I was caught gin-handed by the chef, an upright man of severe morals who was much scandalized, and did not sack me but punished me by putting me on the grill. I got no more gin, and threw what was left in the bottle over a skewer of kidneys which was grilling; delightful green flames danced for an instant, and what the customer thought I never knew, though I had an ec-static vision of a row of Lucky Pigs dancing happily with a gin bottle held to mouth.

Curry was a great favourite of Monsieur Bonvalet, who we know had elevated leftovers into a great art of often great complexity—how we suffered with those bits of meat mixed with sauce which had to be folded into a pancake, coated with more sauce, sprinkled with cheese. . . . Curry was a greater agony still, and on the day it was announced we would peel many 'button' onions, separate cauliflowers into nice bunches of bloom, and steal large potatoes from the roast-cook, to shape into little balls with a cutter, the size of a large marble. We then made a great deal of curry sauce with more onions, apples, a little coconut, thickening it slightly with flour.

The serving of this economical dish was ponderous and slow. For every amateur of curry—perhaps fifty—the service commis needed three timbales, which are round silver dishes, not too deep. One of these held meat in its sauce, another the vegetable mixture, which had been cooked separately and finished with more sauce (skill as well as pains were needed not to overcook it, but to keep it whole, a little crisp still and attractive), while the third dish held the rice which had been 'lifted' with a few almonds and raisins. All this was a very great pest.

Every evening Dad came trotting out with two pieces of paper. These were the menus for next day; the sous-chef made a dozen copies with his duplicator, one for every corner in the kitchen and the rest distributed through the hotel—printer, restaurant, front office, files. In this way we knew what to prepare and order from stores, and since our work for that day was already finished we started on the next, or what cooks call the 'mise en place'. During the day the chef would pin up other papers on the bulletin board, which were not duplicated for us, but the chef of every corner would note his own work down on a paper—these were forthcoming parties, the notices for which were posted a week or ten days beforehand. This system was identical in every hotel, and I should suppose still is, since it is foolproof. For parties that were very big cooks might have to be manoeuvred around, and days off changed, and this had to be settled in advance. For a daily menu, details were better left to the evening before, since then the kitchen got little notes from the reception office, figures on the number of guests staying and on restaurant bookings.

On big public holidays, such as Easter, Pentecost or Christmas, the lunchtime menus are much the same as usual, but the evenings are 'gala' which is hotel jargon for a fixed menu of a gaudy kind, balloons, a drunk orchestra, and letting the hair down. It is no great extra effort for us, since there is only one main dish, which must of course be showy and elaborate. These dishes are traditional and dull; the roast deer with chestnuts at Christmas and the spring lamb with baby vegetables at Easter. . .

Three weeks before one Christmas at the Hotel Atlantic, when Dad pinned up the week's menus, a ripple of interest ran through the kitchen and we crowded round. Had he made it easy, or were we going to be pestered with fancy variations on goose and turkey? Muttering, pencil-licking, relief at an easy dish with rice, a curse at a tiresome sauce with orangepeel, relief again at another kind of rice . . . there seemed to be an awful lot of rice. We had a Spanish one with peas in and prawns and bits of chicken liver, a Hawaiian thing with pineapple, the fish-cook had a Newburg—incredulity changed to certainty, the busiest day of all had curry for lunch, there was a mountain of rice on every single menu, and it dawned on us slowly that Dad had found the perfect formula for combining gaiety with economy, and that was to have a Chinese Christmas.

The fact was that by the rules of the System an easy gala dinner has to be paid for in blood on the days following, and the wreckage of the spring lamb, for example, comes back as Moussaka, a great Dad favourite—scraps padded with sauce and mushroom stalks, 'stretched' with slices of tomato and aubergine in a pattern, and dollied up with brown breadcrumbs and parsley. Delicious, says Monsieur Bonvalet, defiantly having some for his own lunch.

All this goose and turkey had to be sold twice, and the meaning of curry became clear. . . .

The service of gala dinners was mechanical, since there was only one dish. To serve five hundred in two and a half hours is hard work but needs no brains: have it ready, have it hot, arrange it on dishes by threes, fours and fives—make it fast and you cannot go wrong. Luncheons were a great deal more difficult, because Dad's love of fixed menus with a large variety makes prophecy difficult. How many people will there be exactly, and in what proportion will they choose the roast lamb, the stew, the turbot, the deplorable curry? Monsieur Bonvalet was very skilful at this. He looked at the weather, at his files for the last three years, added his instinct, and nearly always got it right.

We helped with the roast lamb; Nivernaise, one of Dad's vegetable loves—button onions to be sure, plenty of turnips! For two hundred, he said. We had curry for a hundred, plenty

of onions, and were pleasantly relaxed; the roast-cook, we sus-
pected had not done enough carrots.

For once Dad's oracles had let him down, and we sold two
hundred and thirty helpings of curry. At one-thirty his face was
no longer serene; he was congested and untidy, his hat was pushed
back leaving a red line upon his majestic forehead, and there was
a big smear of curry on his apron. I bellowed at him that there
was no more.

'You going to cut it off?'

'No no—make more—I help.' Might have known—the roast
lamb could always be sold again, but when would come another
day so golden for making a profit on scraps? Bonepickings were
scoured from every corner of the larder, cooks crowded round
to Dad's howls, and the soup-cook's reserves were raided.

'But I got no more onions.'

'Give more colly, va.' He was quartering boiled potatoes with
of all things a long ham knife.

'I got no more potatoes.'

'Give them rice,' screamed Dad. Two boys were sent staggering
to the sink with a big pot.

'Come lazy ones, fainéants, fesses d'huitres, no wash off, no
put kalt wasser, égouttez, drain and servir like so.'

Curry was served on flat dishes, in soup bowls, in cloche covers;
it was war, it was splendid. At three in the afternoon there was
rice all over the floor.

'We sell good,' said Dad, satisfied for once to his very depths, and bought us all a beer.

That evening we heard with joy of the goings-on in the restaurant. People had come in off the street in great numbers, been crammed in at extra tables, and this had left the waiters a good deal less space than usual; they had collided quite often. Greeks, excitable at the best of times, had got into a frenzy, and the Big Greek, a sinister bandit, had had words with a customer who had got up in a rage and started for him. The waiter balanced a timbale of boiling-hot curried cauliflower on a hairy hand and said 'One step more': prudently, the customer left. Presumably he had complained at the front office, but this kind of holiday was a time for drawing veils and the Big Greek had not been sacked; his station had not even been changed. A time of forgiveness, and curry must not alter that. Which we felt was justice.

The Lucky People, sending placidly down for curry at about two-thirty, had been told there wasn't any more and were most indignant.

I met Dad that evening in the larder. He was looking gleefully at a few day's collected débris of the fish-cook's: surplus trout, a grilled sole that got scorched, broken poached turbot and unused quenelles. The larder had added lobster wreckage and a tatty salmon tail.

'Fruit of Sea Thermidor,' Dad was saying happily, 'and what you get too much, put through hurdygurdy with old potato, make nice fishcake personnel supper'.

Not long afterwards the Eat More Rice slogan had a sequel, or perhaps a coda. The soup-cook had to go and have his flat feet mended, and the 'tournant' or ambulant cook who usually filled in on holidays had a poisoned finger. Nobody who understood the work could be spared and nobody wanted it anyway, despite Dad's artful appeals; it was a fearful penal colony. It happened that an extra cook, who had sometimes helped at big parties, turned up asking for a permanent place. Monsieur Bonvalet greatly disliked extras, lazy and unreliable people.

'If was any good,' he confided to Franz, 'would not be extra, huh?' But he was in a fix: the cook was hired on a week's trial and promptly posted to the soup corner.

Interested, we watched him make the 'mise en place' for his first evening's work; very nice and meticulous. Little pile of carrots nicely shaped, tray of endives folded and wrapped in a strip of bacon, little pot of boiled potatoes and little pot of mashed—we were accustomed to Giovanni's scruffy piles of rubbish, and were duly impressed: this character had anyway been properly trained.

Behind the corner was a kind of pantry for stock—soups à la carte, ready-cooked macaroni, and so on. Here, too, everything was spotlessly neat and here just before the service the new cook was observed with a bottle of beer, reposing from his labours. Dad, impressed by a corner looking really clean for once, had ceased to hover and was chatting amiably with a headwaiter. It was a quiet evening, with no parties, on which we would do sixty or seventy people.

Almost at once the new cook announced that he was running short of spaghetti, which was the night's alternative to soup.

'Give noodles,' said Dad unperturbed; such things often happened, and few customers would notice: with sauce on top and grated cheese it looked much the same.

A few minutes later the endive was gone; only twenty of the neatly prepared helpings had been made, and it took time to make afresh. Dad was still in a relaxed frame of mind, indulgent to someone unaccustomed to the routine.

'You got colly?—well, give colly.' But in less than no time there was no more colly, the beans had given out, there were no more noodles . . . and Dad had no patience left either.

'Give what you got—what you got?'

The cook had remained perfectly calm, sipping at beer and watching his supplies melt with no sign of unease.

'I got rice,' he bawled, and gave a loud weird laugh. 'Give the buggers rice.'

10 COUNTESS DRACULA AND THE DRUNKEN SAILORS

France in nineteen fifty-three or four was an uneasy and often depressed place. Money was much devalued, the cost of life high, and many people poorly paid. This provided some incentive towards looking for work elsewhere, but it was more a wander-lust that drove me to leave the Hotel Atlantic after three years. Monsieur Bonvalet's little ways appeared of a sudden unendurably tight and neat and over-careful. I wanted risk, I wanted to see the world.

I went first to England, where, we heard, cooks who knew their work would always find good jobs, well-paid ones too. While in England I got married, and thereafter for many years lived a vagrant and uncertain life, perpetually on the hunt for somewhere to live, some job that combined a tolerable wage with tolerable conditions, and never finding it. Those were the seven lean years, while we revolved restlessly about northern Europe, trying five different countries in turn and failing in all of them. I do not think I stayed in any one job more than six months, and for many I stayed much less. It was an unhappy existence, during which the three hotels of my beginnings came to look rosier and more peaceful every day. I went back to Belleplage, confident that kind Dad would give me my old job back—but the System had finally failed, the Grand Hotel Thermes et Bains de Mer would now forever stand empty and, crowning blow, Dad was gone to South America, too far for me to follow, there to teach sabir to the Spaniards and show them how to cook sow-belly with dried split peas.

A type of work which I came to know painfully well was that in the English countryside. The land is full of hotels which in origin were inns with a few rooms to let. They are solid places which have often been there for centuries, by right of their local importance in a market town, or perhaps a strategic place along a highway, an old staging post where coach horses were changed and travellers got out gratefully for a Dickensian meal. Their architecture is picturesque; they have gateways covered in wistaria, beamed and plastered fronts, cobbled courtyards and Shakespearian stables.

They were nice places as long as they kept the local character for which they were built—the local beer, the local cheese, the solid food for farmers come to market and travellers feeling lucky to get anything at all, after all those hours unable to feel their own feet. . . .

In the motorcar age their landlords discovered the tourist, and an ignoble tradition rose to block out the old, that of pretending to be a real hotel, serving a menu that was a parody of the pomposities of large-town restaurants and even of the great palaces, this at 'tourist prices' to attract custom. After the war, with food and petrol in short supply, they went bankrupt in droves, and were taken over by the breweries which owned the humbler 'pubs' of the district, and by large hotel companies which added the more attractive plums to their chains.

These were far away, centralized, and interested only in money.

They gave the decaying inns a financial injection—a dash of modernization to bathrooms, a splash of commercial 'decoration' to the bar, and installed paid managers, who could spend no money but were instructed on no account to let the services fall below the accepted level, which was still that of the pre-war generations; a voluminous choice of food, a wine list, a tailcoated headwaiter, and suchlike antiquated notions. Naturally, standards collapsed utterly. These places could neither attract nor afford proper staff. As a result they hired the failures, the misfits, and the desperate. I fitted all three definitions, and saw the insides of a dozen houses of this kind. A nice little place, called the Bull or the Bear or whatever, which had had a panelled coffee room for twenty persons in 1900, and a kitchen where a fat honest country woman made pigeon pie and suet rolypoly. By my time it had a restaurant for forty, a choice of table d'hôte menus in imitation French, a 'carte' with twenty items to order, a wine list of undrinkable pretentiousness, and an 'American Bar' —for the tourist with American Express cheques in his pocket was the imagined panacea to every hotel evil.

The kitchen, naturally, has been left in 1900. The customer does not see it. . . . A few modern gadgets have been found, an electric fryer, a deepfreeze, an infra-red grill. Small flimsy toys, useless to a cook, who is dignified with the name of 'Chef' even when he is the only one there is!

Places of this size have a manager and two reception girls— one is tempted to put inverted commas round all these portly functions—a porter, a headwaiter, two or three waiters, and a barman! Places that could be run, and in Europe still are run by a man, his wife, and two hired girls from the village, with an oddjob man. All this staff had to be lodged and fed. Idiot that I was, I took a place like this because I was offered a good wage. I found that I had to do a lunch and a dinner menu with three courses—and three choices to each—and have a carte of twenty-five items 'ready to order' as well as make cakes for tea. To help me I had a scrubwoman and a boy. . . .

Evidently, the only way to get through this mass of work was to make bad food. Before I was forced to the conclusion that this was the only way, I had to suffer. I had learned many ways of simplifying the flowery old-fashioned style of cooking I had been taught, but even Monsieur Bonvalet had never an instant departed from the one essential rule of any job—the man must have enough space and enough time. I grew tense and anxious trying to work properly. In England one must not keep customers waiting. They want it quick, and are indifferent to its being bad. I tried to train my headwaiter to give me the orders and keep people in the bar till I had things ready—I told my manager that such a system was that of all good restaurants and, since the bar made a profit, would help him too: they would not listen. It is a pity. One cannot blame the customers, who have been taught by the imbecile pretensions of these bad little hotels that a huge variety is theirs for the asking at the drop of a hat.

Even now I spend time thinking how good one can make a little country hotel. It is no wizardry; one begins by sacking all the staff—parasites the pack of them—and serving one really good dish in large quantities, and about six specialities that have to be waited for. A cook could make good soup, salad, and a cake, and still have time for accounts, the cellar, and lending a hand in the bar and the dining-room, which should anyway be in the same room.

In this sort of place, the cook's worst enemy was the manager, a poor devil forced by the terms of his employment to maintain illusions of luxury. He never dared refuse the whim of a customer wanting smoked salmon at the very moment that another was clamouring for his roast mutton. More direct and present enemies are the waiters who are underpaid and dependent on tips. Of course they grovelled before the customers and encouraged them in fantasies. By all means order sauté potatoes. Certainly you can have salad as well as beans. Naturally madam, the chef will have pleasure in making a soufflé.

My headwaiter, whom I saw, once I became neurotic from overwork, as a kind of fiend, was a sad shaky man really, terrified of my throwing things at him and as terrified of customers, thrusting salesmen these, who snarled at him the way the sales-manager trained them: be aggressive, penetrate. Why were there no kidneys? The chef said? Nonsense man; now bustle off and see that it's a proper mixed grill now.

Ground between a cook who might fling knives and yell, and a customer asserting masculinity, the headwaiter drank—but everybody in these hotels drinks. Waiters as well as cooks would never be in these places without a sense of things gone wrong and life passed by; they are all drunks by definition. I did not drink but often wondered why I didn't. All the waiters appeared at breakfast sipping glasses of cold Pilsener, just the thing to kill the worm and steady the hand. By about eleven they had wound themselves up to work and were fortifying with Guinness—and an hour later they were in a state of chronic anxiety, behind in their work and afraid of not pleasing, which meant gin.

Around this time a great many cooks and waiters in England had been in the merchant navy—the big companies were laying up ships and not building more. They are amusing to work with; I had enjoyed an otherwise detestable job outside London where all the waiters were straight off the P. and O. boats, Shipyard Sallys to a man except that their chosen names were more exotic—we had had a Sylvia and a Cindy pushing one another at the service counter, giving pettish little shrieks and plucking their eyebrows in classical 'tapette' style. Here in the country, of course, such things might be noticed, but a Shipyard Sally would not be seen, but definitely, dead in the provinces anyway. Our poor old George was a pathetically rather than comically marine landscape.

His three understrappers pretended to be sailors, though really they were the type known in the Cunard as 'cowboys' because they will probably jump ship in New York with dreams of ending up as a barman in Las Vegas, a dream lasting till the next Cunard ship sails. Our three had retired from this pastoral but exhausting profession. They now lived in the country, pursuing the female body and a likely racehorse. The second was easier than the first, since it was all in the newspaper, masses of print packed with instruction by backstairs experts, very knowing about what the trainer said, and such-a-one's fragile hocks and sensitive pasterns. Being in the country—nowhere near a race-course—did not hang heavy on any of the drunken sailors; the papers arrived just the same. Happy hours plotting tactics when they should have been cleaning the mustard pots.

Females took up as much discussion but cost less, since they were imaginary and could not even be betted on. To be sure there were days off, when one caught a train to London for fleshpotting, which came expensive—once a month was the best they could do. Most of the potting was a lecherous sigh over the imagined availability and suitability of a woman customer—or gallant pursuit of the hotel's available raw material, which was decidedly limited. Chambermaids, respectable middle-aged women of the most conventional kind; Dolly the scrubwoman's three teenage daughters—gay, but more promise than performance; the two reception girls.

These young women of petty-bourgeois family were unwilling and unable to soil their hands over anything resembling work. They came into hotels because it is even easier than being an air-stewardess, because one can be even stupider, and because they thought to find glamour, and troops of men like those in shirt or cigarette advertisements.

Miss Tomlinson and Miss Pym, without ever doing any work, reigned severally or together in the hall, where there was dim pink lighting, artistic flower arrangements, and a counter over which one could lean with slow elegance when 'receiving', allowing a fortunate man to inhale the fragrance of one's neck. They had a typewriter at which they picked languidly, a variety of charts and books for their receiving, and huge handbags stuffed with secrets, which they were always taking on interminable trips to the lavatory.

Miss Pym was the younger, the blonder, the better provided with flesh. She smelt quite nice in a Yardley way and was vaguely amiable. The drunken sailors brought her food and tea, and she thanked them with dim smiles. One could approach,

but it led to frustration and weariness because she had no enthusiasm; this puzzled all the sailors.

Miss Tomlinson was taller, older, meatless—she was conspicuous for never eating, and would take three drops of soup
before sending it back, and pick a minute morsel of meat before
tucking the rest under an untouched potato. She was pale and
dark, never spoke above a drifting whisper, and had ladylike
ways and long fingernails painted the colour of venous blood. A
foregone conclusion; the drunken sailors, of whom she took no
notice, called her Countess Dracula.

These two lived a privileged life, if one can talk of the slow
death in a country 'reception office' and use such terms. They
were boarded in the hotel, ate in the restaurant, stayed warm and
tranquil the entire day in their little fuggery—perfect parasites.

It astonished me that this should be tolerated but like so many other absurd features this 'prestige' was considered necessary.

The hotel was not owned by a company but by an elderly bonehead who imagined he was on a good thing—odd, for he prided himself on being a splendid financier, yet never saw that a brewing company could do anything he did at half the cost. He spent his days sour and withdrawn in a little office with a huge ledger, in which he wrote carefully. He had also a wife, a cantankerous old body who went about searching for economies, forever turning out lights, examining bathrooms for bits of soap to stick together, and rummaging in the fridge when my back was turned. She would have done quite well in a seaside boarding house.

This disgruntled pair had a son, a young man of my age who was officially 'the manager' who spent his days in the bar being cheery with the local notabilities. He came to me every morning with his pleasant brainless features arranged into artificial severity, and a list of complaints about my misdeeds. What had happened to old Colonel Withers' grilled tomato? I must use margarine and not butter. Customers did not like garlic; and so on.

It was exasperating, for one could not please such people. If I suggested plain English food I was reminded that I was supposed to be a high-class French cook. If I made French food it was too expensive and the customers disliked it. If I made genuine French food, like a cassoulet, it was even worse, at once plain and exotic, to their mind the worst combination. They wanted decorative flashy dishes like chicken maryland—a single-handed cook's nightmare. If I pleaded for a small menu I got knowing smiles, to show that they saw through my little game. When for economy's sake I suggested cheap things, paupiettes of veal or braised beef, I would be told that customers did not want 'cheap meat'. I saw no way out, but my wife put my wages in a biscuit tin and advised patience.

The Countess Dracula lived at the top of the house, next door to the drunken sailors but shrouded in modesty. I was told that when she came out on her fell quest at night she could be glimpsed in a chaste red bathrobe, but her doors were triple-barred. The sailors were driven into frenzy by a concession she had acquired, the right to be brought breakfast by whichever sailor was on early duty. They had to put the tray down, knock, and retire. After a careful interval her nose would peep out, she would grab her teacup, and vanish in a clatter of locks and bolts. The sailors pretended that her smell was unbearable and her pretensions intolerable. Poor girl, she did smell, and attempted to mask it with heavy sweetened perfumes, producing a deplorable effect. Nor was she trying to be horrid; anxiety at the rows of wonderful men who somehow never arrived was making her even more ladylike. It is classic that a prude surrounds herself with defences increased in direct proportion to the decreasing threat to her fading charms. As the girl saw her youth slip away to aridity she became primmer, and ate less.

When the explosion came it was, as often happens, a multiple explosion. The son of the house was discovered embracing Miss Pym in compromising circumstances, the poor old headwaiter was arrested for crimes concerning his car, which was as drunken and decrepit as himself, and the Countess Dracula had an attempt made upon her virtue by a sailor who must have been unusually far gone. She packed her bags in hysterics provoked I think more by the luck of her colleague, who was at least getting a wedding out of it, than by her own alarms. Exasperated by these calamities, and even more by losing money, the owner sacked me for insolence, rebellion, conspiracy and sloth. I was delighted and the village was in an ecstasy.

It seems so obvious with hindsight that the poor man had no notion what to do that it would labour the point to go telling him now. It would not be hard to think of twenty simple dishes, that would be satisfying, almost universally pleasing, unpretentious yet original, of materials easily found and not too expensive, fit to gain a country hotel a reputation for honest food at an honest price. I wonder whether even now somebody is actually doing this, or whether the whole of England still labours under the burden of a pile of unnecessary staff and silly 'menus' with the inevitable corollary of soup out of packets, salmon out of the deepfreeze, and that awful chicken maryland.

11 A BLACK ROSE FOR THE MATRON

There was a longish time, four or five years, in which I knew that I wanted to be a writer, and no longer wished to be a cook. I went about this with the incompetence that characterizes all young men who want to be writers: any job not actually in a kitchen seemed a step in the right direction. These efforts at not being a cook are squalid at the time, but exciting and often funny; danger lies in going on thinking them funny, especially to others. They are only threadbare commonplaces.

Since publishers like these episodes, and are fond of publicizing the flutterings of all their young geese, one comes across quantities of such stories, and they are all the same. Nancy Mitford once remarked that there was no sadder sight than a lettered beachcomber: she might have added, nor more tedious. No writer but has been courier for travel agents, door to door hawker of encyclopedias, composer of advertising copy.

I had intervals of sanity during this tomfool time, plunging back into hotels as a kind of rest cure. Always they seemed places of honesty and simplicity, with the self-respect of a job I could really do, the security of warmth and regular meals and a pay packet, the satisfaction of being again a real worker, with all my sympathies kept for ants, and none for the parasite cicada. And always after three weeks the restlessness crept in, the foggy muddled longing began to pinch, the cruel thirst for letters made me throw a knife down in disgust, my unformed mind only half realizing that my hands wanted a typewriter and not knives. Conrad has described the shadowline between a trade and the vocation for unhappiness that is writing so much better than anyone that it is useless to dwell on this point.

After a little while I had the two halves of my head, and my two feet pointing in opposite directions, sufficiently organized to be living out of two separate suitcases. One held the suit, the white shirt and bow-tie, several notebooks, proof sheets from trade magazines, and the mockup books with which 'educational publishers' seek to ensnare the simple-minded household. The other held my cooks' whites, my knives rolled in spare aprons, an envelope full of old references, a few packets of roll-your-own tobacco. It is important to hold out a fortnight without asking a new employer for money; this distinguishes the genuine if footloose craftsman from the mere sponger; more or less what the police call Visible Means of Support.

It has never been difficult to get work in hotels, though one is restricted to certain types of hotel. Experience enables one to distinguish quickly between the barely tolerable and the utterly impossible; one has been in many of both as an extra, and cooks' gossip has given one a huge file in the memory of places to avoid at all costs. When in London, for example, in those days, a morning spent in Old Compton Street would provide two or three handy addresses that could be sounded with reversed-charge phone calls; there would certainly be someone frantic for a skilled cook. One went down, to face a brief test by some manager full of self-importance about Portion Control, or with

luck a harassed chef who had known his job before being forced
into provincial pretend-cooking, was quick to see what one
could do, and more honest about what he could offer. Managers,
so often dullard products of minor public schools who have
been temporary lieutenants, love Authority, and give lectures
about What They Expect. But a real cook will say, 'So you've
worked for old Laplace—I was his sauce-cook for twenty years—
does he still put paprika in everything?'

In this way I often spent a couple of months in coast hotels,
faded minor key versions of the old Atlantic, and in one of these—
I recall it as a pleasant place, and I was sorry when the scribbling
Field pulled me by the elbow—I met the Matron.

Sauce-cook, to double as sous-chef. An easy job; thirty or forty
moribund residents who hardly ate anything, perhaps the same
number of walk-in customers ('chance' in hotel jargon) on a
winter day, parties for the Golf Club, the House Agents &
Auctioneers, and the East Wessex Cattle-dealers, a gloomy little
dinner dance on Saturdays and a sprinkling of businessmen on
expenses. I liked it at once—big basement kitchen that would
never be too hot, and an old chef with varicose veins. The staff
was good too—an elderly quiet pastry-cook called Stan or Ron,
a beery soup-cook called Harold, two Chinese larder-cooks,
possibly brothers, even twins, with striped pyjamas under their
whites—one was taller than the other, so they were known quite
naturally as Suzy Wong and Suzy Long—and a young jack-
about-shop with sweaty socks called Peter. Also, evidently, a
lunatic fringe of local old men and women employable only in
just this kind of place.

When I arrived it was eight in the evening, and quiet. I
unpacked my knives, at which the chef glanced. He warmed up,
seeing from them that I was a real cook. I looked at the menus,
the stove, and the sauce-cook's bench, and was invited for a quiet
beer in the office.

'Nothing to do tonight—be lucky to do forty-five—fifty.
Service upstairs—Suzy and Peter do it. Harold does breakfast,
stays nights if there's a party.' It was a life I knew perfectly,

familiar as my feet. I rolled a cigarette. 'Don't let the boss catch you smoking in the kitchen—keen type. You do soup, and roasts of course—I help with fish, any carte stuff. What you like for supper—nice bit of duck?' I was home.

The door opened and a young man came undulating in, with wavy fair hair, waiter's trousers, a white linen jacket and a black bow.

'Hallo Michael.'

'I just came down for a bite.'

'Apartments all served?'

'All the old bags are stuffing away quite happy.'

This was Shipyard Sally, the floor-waiter, and a useful source of information such as one needs in the basement, where cooks are isolated. The chef needs an ear and an eye that travels all over the hotel, a television set receiving 'above stairs'. A floor-waiter is good for this purpose. I realized that my old chef knew his job. The latest news would be brought three times a day, in return for a special meal and a few unimportant privileges, like sitting smoking in the office.

The old man seemed amused by the bright flow of chatter.

'I fancy a nice avocado pear,' combing the very clean hair and patting it.

'This is Nick the Greek, the new sauce-cook.'

'Pleased I'm sure.'

'What are the waiters like?' I asked, getting an avocado out of the box on the office floor. Expensive things are kept in the office in all kitchens; harder to steal, that way. There are always cupboards full of old menus and torn aprons, with space made for grapes, foie gras, and the cognac bottle as well as any other tempting 'vitamina'.

'Sodomites, catamites, and a few retired prostitutes. And of course the Matron.'

'Matron?'

'Oh you'll be meeting the Matron,' said the chef comfortably.

'Ask Suzy to give me some of that cold lamb and a bit of salad, Michael, will you, there's a good girl.'

Next morning was equally peaceful. As in most old-fashioned hotels the kitchen was in the basement, and all table d'hôte food had to be stored in a service pantry next the dining-room. It is transported by a pair of simple wooden rope-lifts, and communication assured by a two-way loudspeaker. Cooks shout obscenities over this intercom from above to get anything they need from the kitchen. At nine in the morning the only noise in the kitchen was the distorted and confused bellow from Harold, doing breakfasts above our heads. The occasional yell for more bacon or grapefruit sounded even more violent and profane than most cooks—breakfast is a universally loathed chore.

I was doing the morning's soup, stew, and roast pork in comfort. The chef was making pâté in the larder, and wondering whether the fillets of sole designed for lunch were after all too stale; rinsing them with vinegar might be an idea. The two Suzys were mincing scraps—shepherd's pie for the staff; Len—or was it Ron?—was humming contentedly in his floury corner: sweaty Pete was listlessly splitting carrots.

'Good morning, good morning,' came a voice behind me. I turned expecting a manager; the voice was plummy, soft, polished as a ballbearing. I saw a tall sprightly man in the tailcoat of a headwaiter.

'Ah, you'll be the new sous-chef. And I am Mr. Summers; how do you do?' Why did I know at once that this was the Matron? The voice? The clothes, from which maculae would flee? The face, rosy, healthy, overshaved? The pattering shiny feet?

'Have you by any chance seen O'Malley—the floor-waiter?'

'He was squeezing oranges here a little while ago.'

The Matron smiled pleasantly; his small black eyes gleamed like sunrise on the dark sea. He performed a conjuring trick, a plump little hand seizing his trouser-zipper, whisking it open and shut again in the same swift movement that recalled shiny false teeth opening and closing upon an oyster. He was pleased at startling me. 'I'll infiltrate that O'Malley,' darkly. He whisked round and was gone in sinuous oscillations of his tailcoat.

Shipyard Sally arrived soon after, biting his nails in early-morning petulance. 'Matron's looking for you.'

'Infiltrate the matron'—it sounded a joyless chore. 'That old brothelmadam hates me because I'm the only one with any intelligence around here.'

'Hands off your cocks and hit the deck,' bellowed Harold in the doorway. 'Breakfast is now over.'

Ageing cooks often become like this. Harold had his own house 'all paid off', an undemanding wife, a grown-up son. He no longer needed much money, nor responsibility. He had been chef here once; now he was breakfast-cook, and happy. He cared for nothing and this made him very happy. He spent the day in an uproar of lowerdeck language, with keen delight in pretending not to see the manager when that worried soul paid a shuddering visit to Below Stairs. He was full of horrid threats to infiltrate every female within the square mile, but these lecheries went no further than invective, whether on account of his wife or of incipient impotence I never did learn.

The first time I had an order à la carte to fill in the kitchen my old chef was behind me watching. A steak chasseur—simple dish of a shallot chopped and reduced in a little white wine with a pinch of tarragon, a sliced mushroom and a peeled seeded tomato.

'That's the peasant way of doing it.' I shrugged, and he lowered at me with tiny eyes.

'Oregano, oregano for cacciatore,' and I had no more trouble but for being told at least once a day that I was doing things a peasant way. 'Paysan de montagne' is the classic insult among cooks. It was his great word—he was a survivor of a once common Soho clan, the Cockney Italians, who speak Piedmontese dialect with an Old Compton Street accent. He trotted back to his flat there (thirty shillings a week—he had had it since 1923) every Sunday after lunch, reappearing for lunch on Tuesday. He cronied with other old cooks in the Club, collected his weekly bribes from the wholesalers in Covent Garden, looked the whores over, and came back gloomy, carrying a bottle of vermouth and a little packet of real Milanese salami. At this time he would complain most about south-coast peasants.

'What do these villagers know about food?'

He was a nice old boy but for being bad-tempered on Tuesdays, sitting in the office muttering and munching sausage and hating us all.

A large party was announced, a 'banquet' for the local stalwarts of the Conservative Party. Since there were a great many it was a considerable job: Harold stayed on, an old retired cook arrived to help out, all the cleaning women were impressed and I was sent to lend authority to these manoeuvres. Parties were served from a pantry next to the dance-floor. On the waiters' side there were all who could be spared, a dozen village women in black frocks and aprons, and the unhappy Michael, who had been bustled into serving the floors at twice the usual pace. This activity was supervised and coordinated by the Matron, a staunch Conservative.

After the dessert was served, and we were languidly clearing the pantry amid clatter, a Cabinet Minister or some such phenomenon had taken on himself to address the company, who hung breathless upon his words, as did the Matron. Disturbed by the racket in the pantry, which was provoking knitted brows, the man kept tiptoeing through the swing doors, placing an ostentatious finger on his little red lips, and going Ssshhh. After the third of these manifestations I was irritated enough to tell him to shut up.

'Sshh—the Minister!'

'Infiltrate the Minister.'

'Really! Insolence—silence there.'

'Who are you talking to? I'm a cook, you're a waiter—keep your mouth to yourself, peasant.'

The Matron became offensive: near me stood a pile of silver dishes used for parties, impossibly heavy. I pushed them till they toppled on the floor. It made a fine noise, followed by hysterical giggles from Shipyard Sally, at whom the Matron made a spiteful rush.

'Let me alone, bully.' Michael threw a squashy grapefruit and the Matron retired in a huff, to reappear next day with a monstrous cleaners' bill, which in solemn conclave was deducted from poor Sally's share of the 'trunk' (the week's collected tips from which everyone gets a percentage).

War entered an acute stage. Michael's strength was in the lubricious and picturesque phrase; he accused the matron of every strange sin. On the other side, when complaints of sloppy trays came down from the floors they were exaggerated at the front office to criminal proportions. I wondered why the wretched Michael did not leave—he may have been in trouble with the local police; the Matron often uttered nasty hints about depraved young criminals, probation officers and suspended sentences.

Finally he did walk out, stealing three pounds in silver from the chef's office and emptying half a bottle of vermouth for courage. The old man was nice about this, saying the boy had been hounded and victimized and generally infiltrated, and that the crime was forgiven. A week afterwards, we were sitting peaceably eating scrambled eggs in the office at breakfast time when the door burst open, and the Matron tumbled in. The cliché 'ashen-faced' had acquired a meaning at last; he clutched a small cardboard box.

'What's wrong with you then?' indistinctly, through bread dipped in coffee; the old boy's teeth were shaky. Inside the white box was a satin rose, as sold by milliners to brighten up some old hat. It had the usual shape, green leaves, and stem of swathed wire.

'Nice buttonhole.'

'But it's black,' howled the matron.

'E allora?'

'A black rose—misfortune is coming to me—perhaps death!' He was in a foul state of fear. Neither the old man nor myself had heard of such a thing, but we were just peasants. To a south-coast bourgeois it meant, apparently, Massacre.

We examined the rose, the red velvet skilfully stained with indian ink; I imagined Shipyard Sally's neat white fingers busy.

'No message?'

'None is needed,' hollowly.

From that moment he was a changed man, creeping about, shrieking at no one, forgetting his bullying ways. His suits became less pressed, his round rosy cheeks sank, his forehead took on a look of uncooked pastry. He bought a large Alsatian dog and walked behind it, secured by a thick leash which he played with nervously at all times. All this was real; I had been certain that the drama was no more than the usual striking of attitudes—it was no such thing, and I could almost believe the rumour that he had asked for police protection.

Certainly he saw the haggard shadow of Michael O'Malley, grasping the grapefruit knife, at every darkened corner.

Spring was almost upon us when a second black rose arrived, larger than the first, with the same London postmark and typed label. The Matron—I can hardly believe it—did not wait for the arrival of the third and presumed fatal rose. He fled. The man had property, a good situation. Prosperous, surrounded by comforts, a horde of serfs and peasants at his call—and yet he fled.

I have since thought much about this strange incident.

12 RIGHT BACK WHERE WE STARTED FROM

My first place in London was at a hotel like the old Carlton. The mentality was that of my earliest apprenticeship—right back where I started from—and I have called it the Hotel California in consequence. It is knocked down now. Like the old Carlton it was haunted by the ghost of Escoffier, for the chef was one of his last surviving pupils and a specimen I now see as perfect.

He lived still in the days of his greatness, hardly ever leaving his fortress next to the larder, for he was fat and infirm. He had spent the blitz there; the hotel had been hit, but not him. Sometimes, when he had had a good day with the horses, for he was a ferocious gambler, he would come out and sit on a chair and be talkative: discipline meant being a bully, as it did to most cooks then, but he was pathetically anxious to keep some contact with the new world and told the boys long stories. Of great times,

when royalty now so pathetic and moth-eaten—this was auto-
biography—reigned in huge schlossen, of how the lights were
lowered and soft violin music played when the sorbet was brought
on, to rest the digestion halfway through a feast of such extravagant dimensions that there really was a splendour about it. In
his day the basic brown sauce, then called 'Espagnole' was begun
according to the Escoffier recipe, with a fourteen-pound block of
butter. . . .

He was a Dickensian—Balzacien if you prefer—figure, and it
is in the style of these writers that one must try to see him. We
went into his office to serve his numerous and untidy meals.

The large table was covered with a white restaurant cloth,
pre-war damask, evident of ferocious bone-picking. On it stood
a bottle of vermouth, two or three of wine, several more of
patent medicine, and a pepper-mill as tall as a wine-bottle.
Under the minute barred window was a smaller table, holding a
large basket of flowers, both flowers and basket lovingly constructed many years before of lobster fins. The air, anything but
fresh, was perfumed with bunches of dried herbs and cough
lozenges leaking from a broken paper bag. It was very like Mr.
Venus' shop: the alligator, the African baby and the human
warious had all their equivalents, none looking the least out of
place.

On the bulbous mahogany desk (ministerial, with pigeonholes) stood a silver cloche cover, full of cigar butts. In another
corner was an oyster barrel, full of fruit débris fermenting
happily; all the old cooks made fearful drinks and some, despite
the atrocious smell, even distilled. On the walls were many glossy
photographs, showing a rotund, already venerable figure with
cold buffets, 'pièces montées' like dead camels embalmed and
impregnably armoured, beside which he stood in a dramatic attitude like the Duke of York going up the hill, finger pointing at the
sarcophagus of twice ten thousand quails.

The original sat in a wing armchair, chintz with faded purple
peonies, his head framed by diplomas signed in violet ink and a
spluttery pen, meritorious Orders, Palms, Cordons, and Gold

Medals. He was worthy of them: he wore the widest, tallest toque I have ever seen, his boots were high, and buttoned; his trousers were gingerbread serge, and the reverse of his cook's jacket folded back to display a striped flannel shirt, a separate starched collar, and a bow tie, mudcolour, with dots.

Looking at this cirrhosed, anchylosed monument—a diagnostician's dream—one was in the presence of the nineteenth century, high bourgeois époque, and at the bare mention of Jules Ferry's colonial policy, or the assassination of Sadi Carnot I see him.

The sous-chef ran the kitchen, an Englishman of middle age, system-trained before the war, a thin, stooped, bald man with flat feet, forever nervously sipping coffee from a silver soup-bowl. He managed the staff, the service, the buying; he did everything, a good administrator, much like Monsieur Bonvalet but quite lacking the character. The kitchen was not at all nice, and all the corners were occupied by cooks embodying the system's bad features, persons who had fought their way up to a little authority and clung to it, bullying, hidebound and formal. Unlike the Grand Hotel Thermes the kitchen was badly designed, a long terrible tunnel, crowded, redhot, and with rivers of dirty water that flowed past one's feet. The staff was aged, disabled and neurotic, the boys sullen and uninterested. It was not a happy place, but it was funny and abounded in crooked personalities.

After the war, the old hotels had got the System running again. No other way of doing things was known. To meet rising costs, few guests, and the universal climate of uncertainty the staff was cut down, wornout machinery was not replaced, and the hotel staggered on, along strictly traditional rails. This made for a calamitous situation; nobody of any intelligence or enterprise would have anything to do with this business and all standards of quality collapsed overnight, but not only the hotels were at fault.

The post-war generation of customers was also a new one. The food might not be good, the waiters had a newly aggressive servility, the furniture was stained and faded, the equipment insufficient and old-fashioned, but the new noblesse relished a still potent atmosphere of glamour, together with peculiar old fictions about spies and secret-service men, Hungarian countesses and the Lady on the Orient Express. The newly wealthy from the cinema and business world were raw and crude; they had tax-deductible expense accounts but few manners; they knew nothing about food, they were rude to servants, tipped badly and complained out of self-importance. They wore nice clothes but their table-manners betrayed them.

Waiters and cooks learned to cut corners and take fewer pains.

Economizers and troubleshooters got the top jobs. Managers became financial persons, more than ever faces—in the biting phrase of Ludwig Bemelmans—'like a towel on which everyone has wiped his hands'. They did not know the names of their employees.

Stealing and inefficiency broke out everywhere, combated by a new breed of vultures: accountants, efficiency experts, time-and-motion people. Under the System there had been no need for these. Stock was taken daily in the kitchen by the larder-chef: the books were balanced weekly, effortlessly, by a triumvirate of chef, restaurant manager, and control clerk; for a restaurant bill, showing every item of food ordered, and every penny paid, was always made in triplicate. Undermanagers now took over, trained in book-keeping to a conveyor-belt ideal, mechanical cheap catering with a thin veneer of vulgar luxury. Classical dishes were short-cut and cheapened; materials strung together with chemical reagents and synthetic fillers. The staff became increasingly unskilled, there was no permanency or stability, everyone was ill at ease and discontented.

The Hotel California exemplified the moment just before the final disintegration of the system. Another two years and it would be gone. My job was 'guard'. In old hotels one chef, with a boy or two, stayed on at night in turn, to handle late customers: this late work could be hard and was a perpetual grievance. Now, as part of economising, there was a special late-duty cook, and customers were not allowed in the restaurants after hours. They could get a meal if ordered beforehand, or they could have cold meat, soup, or things like club sandwiches. My work in consequence was easy. I had also to look after the night staff; managers who had no time to eat at a civilized time, and a wide variety of cockroaches who came creeping out of holes after everyone had gone to bed.

The first person I met who seemed interesting was the head night-porter, tall and distinguished in his goldbraided frock coat, grey-haired and dignified, but with a mad bloodshot look that bothered me. He complained about food, demanded steak, and when I refused threatened me with his influential contacts and once, in a great fury, picked up a long-pronged carving fork left lying around and desired to see the colour of my tripes. I took hold of a steak-knife, a thing like a cuirassier's sabre, and said that I could certainly move quicker than he did. I was puzzled. Why so violent, and why was the violence so incoherent? I did not get the chance to work it out because a few days later he was no more seen. An underporter came for the grub and I asked where old blood-and-guts had got to.

'Oh, didn't you know? He rang up the police this morning, suddenly, around three. Quite quiet and reasonable he sounded— asked them to come and take him away. I don't know why the Dee Tees didn't get him long ago—been asking for it long enough.'

This placidity in the face of drama was characteristic of the California. An old man in the silver pantry felled his workmate with a huge silver dish, and the poor old boy was already cooling by the time the manager appeared. The silver-room staff were not at all perturbed: they were however indignant—now they would have to work *two* short.

A little grey mouse, whose job was to wind the hotel clocks, fell off the roof. Since there were no clocks on the roof it seemed a fair question to ask what he could possibly have been doing, but nobody asked it. Life went on as before, except that all the clocks stopped.

A majestic individual appeared in the larder, where I was peacefully sitting smoking. He introduced himself—Mr. Black— shook hands politely, and asked for a sandwich. I soon learned new things about hotels, largely by being generous with smoked salmon, to which Blackie was partial. He was the head lounge waiter, and of more consequence than he seemed. Before long he was dropping in nightly, and would stay an hour chatting, while I pressed food on him and asked questions. He was intelligent; it was more a handicap in education and background which kept his thoughts simple and his inventions crude. He looked like a shady lawyer, and would have been one if he had been to a public school: his talent was for the borderlines of criminal offences. He knew just how to get out of a charge for drunk driving or seducing little girls.

He was brilliantined and persuasive, with a muffled confidential voice that sweated plausibility. He wanted an audience. Nobody appreciated him, so I did.

At first he was discreet, and his tales of exploits both false and boring: conquests of rich women in expensive flats. I told him that I was uninterested in his rackets, having no talent that way, and asked nothing but to be paid for extra work. After the first big party at night, with a running buffet, and consommé at three in the morning, he allowed himself to believe me: I countenanced all sorts of enormities, like extra olives, cheese, and fruit salad with no check, asked for, got and pocketed hush-money. It was then easier to get Blackie to boast. He had, as I have said, a simple mind, and did not query my admiring tone and flow of questions.

A lounge waiter does not sound grand, and seems indeed menial after the sumptuous flaunting in the restaurant among the carvers and spirit-lamps. Mr. Black had a permanent staff of about ten, men knowing nothing about food, service, or folding napkins, but all quicker and brighter than restaurant waiters and making, I soon found, three times the money. And all quite cunning enough not to go buying Jaguars and attracting the attention of the Inland Revenue. These plain, humble men, running about with little trays and glasses of sherry, were richer than almost all the customers.

The last restaurant headwaiter left around eleven at night, after the bars shut. One could then drink in a private room—if one was a resident. One could eat in the lounge. The oddities of the English licensing laws were meat and drink to Mr. Black, one person with a proper gratitude to the battle of Neuve Chapelle.

The lounge was really a suite of semi-private rooms, full of steps and archways, angles and palm trees, a good place for skullduggery, and for solid drinking too. Remember that this was nineteen fifty; difficult still to get butter, whisky, or good woollen clothes: the atmosphere of black market, knowing a man who knew a man and fiddling round restrictions, was strong and omnipresent. The lounge was full of imaginary room numbers, illegible signatures on fictitious checks, a pocketing of five-pound notes, and everyone going away happy. For businessmen with secretaries there were smooth arrangements; to be sure the hotel was always full, but one would see what could be done—the reservations clerk was a dear friend and—yes, there had been a lucky cancellation.

Mr. Black had sophisticated these techniques; he knew how to suggest a nice bottle of champagne. 'Freshen you up and between us this is a good one—not on the list. . . .' His call girls were classier than the hall porter's, who were the usual elderly ladies in fox furs enjoying the fresh vitalizing sea air of Curzon Street, whereas Black's were Roman contessas—that lounge was simply a goldmine.

Snags there were to be sure; cheeky little boys from advertising agencies, car salesmen and other riffraff. Naughty men, drunker than they seemed, inclined to clutch waiters and vomit—this, said Black judicially, could be quite profitable, costing five pounds a throw at least—no sixpenny sick in his territory! Other naughty men, less drunk than they seemed, who asked persistently where their six and threepence change had got to—and plainclothes policemen who were detected instantly and charged fearful prices for a Coca-cola.

For a party Mr. Black would supplement his staff. Anybody applying for this extra work followed a well-charted course. He needed a white jacket and a tray, and for the hire of this valuable equipment he paid Mr. Black five pounds a day. His tips were his own. How much might they be, I asked, and was told at least ten pounds and better for a good worker. Blackie himself had a gay stockbroker's house in Stanmore.

He had never been abroad, having been, naturally, exempted from military service. He now rather fancied a holiday in Tangier, perhaps, or did I recommend Casablanca? I had never been in either of these places, but it was easy to fool Black. What ought he to write on his passport? Executive, I told him—he was greatly pleased.

By the time I left the California Black had been promoted to Banqueting Manager, had acquired a graver, portly air, and wore a dinner jacket. I asked him whether the promotion was worth it, since prestige could not, surely, balance the diminished income. Black frowned a little—he no longer cared to be seen talking to cooks—and poohpoohed at me: the Stock Exchange, he hinted, made for richer pickings. He will never, perhaps, be on Boards in the City, because of his accent, but Sunningdale should not be beyond him.

13 MOTORBOAT GOING

Scruffy came out of the plonge—the plonge is the scullery next
to the kitchen where the pots and the big copper casseroles are
washed. He felt in the deep kangaroo pocket of his apron to see
if there was a biscuit there, or perhaps a nice piece of cheese. He
was disappointed at finding nothing, but seeing me he brightened,
closing the nutcracker of his face—Scruffy did have teeth sometimes but had a way of mislaying them. The tiny eyes gleamed,
all the face munched, just like the sailor's wife with chestnuts
in her lap. The nutcracker opened and closed in silence, several
times; he burrowed both hands deep into the kangaroo pocket
and spoke, in a casual, conversational way.

'Motorboat going.' I was startled.

'Where to?'

He looked disgusted, then cheered at dredging up a piece of

biscuit, which he popped into the nutcracker before lurching back into his scullery. I followed, looking for a pot. His back was to me, but he knew I was there. A rhythmic howl, like that of a rag and bone man, began and developed.

'Motorboat goo-ing. A-ny more for a lovely ride out?—'s lo-ovely on the water.' He turned, munched at me, and added 'Bring yer own 'ores.'

This time I got the point; it was a lovely May day. All the leaves in the square were in tiny pale green leaf.

Directly he saw me again it began afresh.

'Down to Brighton—motorboat going—all along t'th'end of the pier.' Allegro vivace, clutching his stomach, vast boots well apart, the whole person a crooked pile of antique jocular crevasses in the dirt.

'I calls him Scruffy,' said George, the other potman, 'because he *is* scruffy.'

The idea refreshed the gloom of a steamy basement. Down to Brighton, down to Atlantic City. Out to the Valley of the Marne, the Wiener Wald. Slaves revolt—break your bonds. Fine notion.

Scruffy disliked work. If genius is an infinite capacity for not taking pains then he was a genius—why not? By self-report he was a relic of the Old Army—Private Mulvaney's Army— 'wounded by 'orrible machine-gun at Arras' and with a limp to prove it, a limp always bad at busy times and at Christmas terrible to watch. The kangaroo pocket was full of chicken bones, hollowed crusts of Parmesan, blackened bananas—he had a devotion to swillbins. He was like Rat the Marine Cellarman, in John Masefield's books for children.

Apart from eating he loved dressing up. Behind the scullery were cellars, mouldy and cobwebby, where rusty trays were stacked, pots needing to be re-tinned, kitchen junk. Here he had an old waiter's tailcoat, a strange corset with tapes, a sort of Salvation Army bonnet, and other costumes. Arrayed, he would sing.

' 'Ungry, 'Ungry, 'Ungry.' More a Gregorian chant—Lamentations of Jeremiah; Aleph and Beth.

We had also lyrics, jaunty, in march time.
'China—
Carolina—
'Ong-Kong—
Anna-Mae-Wong
My ol' man said follow the van—
'N' don' dilly-dally onna way—
Dilly-dally ally-pally on the cheminy de Parry—
Arras Cambry grab yerself some ankypanky—
Get inside of Sally in our lovely alley' rubbing the stomach in happy lechery. Crash went the pots in the big zinc-lined sink.

If one took any notice of Scruffy he turned instantly pitiable. ' 'Ungry 'ungry.' He would sidle up and use his tapping voice, a sinister mendicant's whine.

'Give us a fag, then, give us a butt, ain't had a butt in munce.' Given a fag he would go away to smoke it in his cellar.

'Motorboat going,' he chanted behind the door.

I went down, too, to Brighton, on the first free day I had. Lovely it was—I had no trouble at all falling in love with Brighton—smell of Guinness and rotting seaweed, of ice-cream and celluloid, of urine and sunshine on creosoted wood. Sound of pebbles rolling hollowly as the southwesterly pushed the spring tide higher, soft twanging whine of the trolley-bus going up the Race Hill. Suck and boom of the wave striking the sea-wall in Hove, scattering a bucket of sand and gravel across the drenched promenade. Smells of wild fuchsias in the hedgerows of Roedean, of cherries and hot asphalt in Western Avenue, of gasworks in Southwick, and the pie-shop in Kemp Town. Brighton—policemen with blancoed helmets and hairy reddened forearms, minuscule pubs selling Tamplins Ales and cold lamb sandwiches, where June sat drinking a pint of bitter, June with her unwashed hair and her trumpet-playing husband and rice at every meal.

Oh how right Scruffy was.

Back in the kitchen old George was leaning on his broom, saddened at the thought of having to push it. His big body had shrunk into a cocoon of patchwork pullovers, he walked in a stumbling lurch that threatened any moment to land him on his nose; the pitch of his voice was a man's but the words were those of a good, uncomplaining child. He enjoyed little errands, bringing beer or coffee. His humility was complete and touching: he was always ready to help anyone he thought had fallen upon

hard times and lacked the food, the warmth, the security he himself enjoyed. It was to the credit of the Hotel California that it never sacked people like George: there were dozens of these decrepit old men in the basement, the twilight of their lives contented by half-eaten steaks, half-emptied glasses, half-smoked cigars that were flung out of the restaurant and appreciated in plate-room or silver-pantry.

George was a real soldier, who had fought—with hardly any imagination—at Minden. If one bawled at him he would heave his shoulders back in a remnant of parade pride, what was left of his shoes at the correct angle, broom parallel to his trousers.

Scruffy was simply Shakespeare's Vice, with uncouth nails and matted hair, roaring threats, tangled mumbled tales of his heroism at Arras, how he would show them and how dare they talk so to one that had deserved better of his country. He had been a soldier, I suppose, the kind that always knows the King's Regulations by heart, and complains at being put upon.

I could not find the pot I wanted.

'George, where's Scruffy?'

'Sat in the back, doing football pools. Dustbin ain't bin emptied neither—lef' to me, see—not fair, that ain't.' George spat in the offending bin with indignation. 'Dirty ol' bastard, don't clean the pots right neither—lazy, 'ats why.' He threw his broom on the floor and staggered out. I found my culprit polishing the pot; he had certainly been listening. He held it out pathetically.

'Done it special for you, I 'ave.' Behind me came the voice of the fish-cook, acid, carrying, sharp French accent heightened.

'I want that big pot.'

'Got no big pot.'

'Yes—in tank.'

' 'At one's all burned, gotto soak.'

'Don't care. Want that big pot in two minutes, or put you in tank, scrub you too, yes, with sand and lemon.' Out he marched. I was expecting the usual aggrieved mumble when the tiny eyes sidled towards mine and gleamed, the nutcracker munched at chestnuts and suddenly opened in a grin of wickedness and complicity. He winked.

'Motorboat going,' he said softly.

Only Scruffy and I understood.

In the kitchen, our main pipeline to the world of upstairs was the printer, a kindhearted, gossipy old soul with badly fitting teeth and a talent for eavesdropping; he was always standing just outside doors with bits of paper that needed signing. His main job was translating menus, which were in French with English underneath—a difficult business since the technical terms of the System had no English equivalent; nor indeed has most hotel jargon. How, wailed the printer, to translate Timbales, or Cromesquis? He had evolved a glossy journalese. 'Chopped steak in Rich sauce.' He read American magazines, and one day turned Fritto Misto into 'Tender Titbits, Crisply French-Fried' and asked proudly what I thought. 'What's inside, bits of tit?' Much shocked he put his blue pencil through it. No mention was ever made of breadcrumb or cornflour, nor of Monsieur Bonvalet's favourite phrase 'No much meat, but you put cauliflower, stretch him a bit.' Those dubious mixtures of turkey-scraps, well stretched, were the printer's nightmare.

When there was a party, Mr. Hawkes made it a duty to appear in the kitchen and see that all was as it should be. Mr. Hawkes was the general manager of the Hotel California. He wore a midnight-blue dinner jacket and a sulphur-yellow carnation, both exquisite. He would stand at a safe distance from activity, sucking a peppermint to disguise the flavour of gin, rattling change in his trouser pocket and balancing preciously upon his heels. Then he would turn to the sous-chef.

'Aha—the British Medical Association—everything all right?'

'Certainly Sir.' ('Think if anything *wasn't* all right—then you wouldn't see old Hawkeye for dust.')

The banqueting manager—before Black; a dim sycophant—laughed heartily at the idea of anything not being all right, settled the lapels of *his* jacket and smelt at *his* (common, crimson) carnation in careful imitation. Hawkes looked at him with distaste—counter-jumper!

'You're all organized?'

'Oh certainly Sir.' Inspection was over, there were no defaulters, and Hawkes could float tranquilly back towards the gin.

He was very handsome, brushed and narrow, with a borzoi look. In the mornings he had a Newmarket flavour, horse-chestnut shoes, long droopy jackets with dog-tooths and flaps and cunning little pockets for one's gold watch-chain and one's shooting-stick. He was a local figure, indispensable sitter on tourist boards and watch-committees, rather like those lords who are on the Court of the Bank of England and chairmen of practically everything. No club, reunion, dinner was complete without Hawkes: he was one of the boys. Never did a stroke of work, but worth ten thousand a year to the hotel. He was the armour against embarrassments and awkwardnesses. An old boy,

a king of ers and mms, he could and did fix police, ministry-of-labour, sanitary-inspector, wages-council, licensing-justices, London-county-council, and the Lord's Day Observance Society. Never would the California be threatened by slum clearance, road widening, compulsory purchase, or any damned socialist claptrap. Alas, I fear that in the end Mr. Hawkes fell victim to

Jack Cotton, and even the League of Empire Loyalists was powerless to save him.

Of course, the general manager of a hotel never does do anything—Ludwig Bemelmans says that he is there to frighten the pageboys into good behaviour and be in charge in case of fire. He has assistants. Mr. Hawkes had three. Mr. O'Toole was given to signing notices. He had a saddle-soaped face and wavy blue hair: his trousers were always new, his linen steel-starched. He fiddled with his cuffs, like Mr. Toots. He was very patriotic.

'No French fiddle-faddle here,' he was fond of saying.

The restaurant manager, poor old Perkins, was a good heart, gone in the nerves, with no control over his chattering clique of Greek waiters, a face like a broken clothes-horse, and a tendency to mutter. Customers liked him; he was so reassuring after the perfumed menace of a waiter speaking such broken English that you could never be quite sure if you were being offered toast melba or somebody's sister. Perkins was there to smooth out such misunderstandings. He knew nothing about food, which did no harm: he had once offered hollandaise sauce with a grilled sole to royalty. Royalty, quiet and kind, with a face much like Perkins, had not wished to hurt anyone's feelings. He also had sang froid. He had to cut up a duck one day when everyone was busy: having no idea how he pushed the dagger in at the wrong place, too hard, and the duck leapt across the room. He did not turn a hair.

'Campbell, get another duck, will you,' nonchalant, and his chef de rang carried it into the kitchen where the sous-chef dusted it, made a knife-mark in the right place, and sent it back.

(The last undermanager, Mr. Waters, was a sort of clerk, who did all the work. The chef called him Vatère; everybody else said Poor Old Closet, or Silly Old, or Bloody Tiresome old— but always with a certain affection. The combination of age, poverty, tiresomeness, and imbecility aroused somehow universal forgiveness.)

Of all the powers in the Hotel California Campbell was the only one to have a definitely sinister aura: it was this indeed that made him a power, since he was only a chef de rang, a 'station' waiter in the restaurant. He was small, thin, very upright; his attitude was always that of a person on most important business, and quite determined to brave overwhelming odds on the way. To tell the truth, the odds were rather on his side, since he was a flourishing moneylender (like the Pastryswiss in Paris: there are a few twenty-per-cent men in every large hotel).

To look at he was not very pleasing, for both his body and his hair were so thin that he looked like a skeleton splashed with black paint. Around this time—March or April, I think—I was suddenly given ten days' holiday (it takes several years before one has enough seniority to get a summer holiday, in a hotel) and with happy ideas of a week in Paris I went to Campbell to borrow an extra twenty quid. He said importantly that he would let me know, and later that day he beckoned me aside.

'My enquiries about you are satisfactory,' he said, and asked me to sign a paper across a twopenny stamp, agreeing to repay twenty-five pounds within six weeks. He had a pen ready; I signed with pleasure: after all, every tuppenny stamp in London could not make Campbell's paper any more legal than an ancien franc in a gasmeter.

The twenty single pound notes were screwed into the smallest possible compass; I wondered where the Campbellite Bank was.

I came back from holiday, and in four weekly pay-days stumped up the twenty quid.

Campbell did nothing for a couple of months, when he sidled up and said, 'Five pounds.'

'Not a ha'penny.'

'But I have your signature.'

'Your left trouser leg.'

Campbell went off like Silas Wegg, saying that I was the minion of fortune and the worm of the hour, and kept his big punch for a week after, when he approached me with a sombre mien.

'I shouldn't joke if I were you. Five pounds.'

I said a rude word in Italian, learned from waiters. His sick-coloured eye turned red.

'Ever heard of black magic?'

My mouth, I suppose, opened.

'You've heard nothing yet. I'm not telling where, but if you knew what went on—behind Marks and Spencers.'

I could not stop laughing—black magic behind Marks and Spencers!

'What are you laughing at you fool?' in fierce, intense rage, 'if you knew anything about the devil you wouldn't laugh. I'll put a curse on you—you'll carry it for years.'

I had never hit anybody before. I haven't hit anyone since, though it did not hurt my hand, and gave me much satisfaction. I left Campbell disentangling himself from a dustbin. The parallel with Silas Wegg stayed good to the end.

Next day I gave the Hotel California notice. My head was full of summer sunshine, and the smells of Brighton. Scruffy's motorboat had worked a subtler spell than any demon Campbell could conjure. Nor have I ever been alarmed at the thought of shopping in Marks and Spencer. . . .

The odd thing—when I think about it—is that for many years I was to have no luck. I could not keep a job, I had many catastrophes, and even quite horrid things happened to me oddly often. Should I have taken Campbell seriously? I do not think so; I had an unstable area in my character, a fault or flaw, crack across the cosmos that was earthquake country.

I stepped out to the rhythm of the different drummer.

Motorboat going!

14 'FEELING RATHER ILL, PETER WENT TO LOOK FOR SOME PARSLEY'

He had eaten too many carrots. Was I Peter Rabbit—or perhaps a donkey? Scruffy's motorboat led me from carrot to carrot, quite often tempting ones, ending invariably in disillusion.

The most enormous, outrageous, absurd of the carrots met me one spring a good few years after I got on the motorboat for a lovely ride out all around the sceptred sea. Restless in my skin, I was looking at a trade paper when an advertisement caught my eye. A manager was wanted, 'with first-class Continental or American experience', which was me. It would be for an 'exclusive restaurant shortly to open in the centre of the city'— one of those large Midlands towns which look like cities till you know them a bit, where, it just happened, I was sitting.

Said manager must have a comprehensive knowledge of

modern catering techniques, and be accustomed to highest standards. This had not been me lately, but could be made to fit. Salary would be generous, which was kind.

I wrote, and got an answer. Would I come for an interview? Yes, but I would like to know a bit more first. The letter was headed 'Wintergarden Entertainments Co.' I knew about the Wintergarden without having been in it; huge flashy building in a little park, belonging I supposed to the municipality, all floodlights and neon signs, like a pier. There was a cinema, a skating rink, an amusement arcade with slot machines, a dance hall, several bars and cafeterias. At the back was a suite of conference rooms for trade delegations, municipal receptions, banquets and such junketings. It did seem an unlikely place to have an 'exclusive restaurant' under its wing.

I went to see a waitress I knew, a prudent woman who now managed a teashop. She knew all that needed knowing.

The Wintergarden had indeed belonged to the Corporation, and had been a great traditional goldmine.

'But it's a bit out of date—you know—television and all. People don't go dancing or to the cinema like they used to; it doesn't do the business now, and it must cost a lot to keep up. And it isn't modern.' The ventilation was a bit antique, the paint peeling, the carpets a bit grubby, the place was full of things like cinema organs that changed colour which had been a riot back in 1936.

In short, gone downhill. Then there had been some great local scandal—the Civic Entertainments Manager had embezzled vast sums. Town Council had been red around the ears.

'Some of them may have been involved—a lot had to resign.' But the exclusive restaurant? Aha; the council, in a fit of petulance had shuffled the whole thing off, leased to some businessman who reckoned he knew how to make it pay. It was he who stuck up all the signs, made the skating rink, put in the jukeboxes and slotmachines. Place was now a stamping ground for Youth from suburban housing estates.

'Doesn't sound very exclusive.'

'Well, people are richer—there's supposed to be money in places for them to eat out.' It was time for my interview; perhaps I should learn more. I could understand the business man, thinking that municipal authorities never knew how to administer anything; he'd show them.... The first-class Continental whatnots sounded a bit misplaced though.

The letter bade me ask for the catering director. The request got puzzled looks; it was decided I must mean Mr. Sleet. I sat, and waited at a café table, and got tired; Mr. Sleet was a very busy man, and took a time to arrive. I was assured that he had said Oh yes, he knew, and would not be a sec.

Twenty minutes later there was a strong draught; important executive in a hurry. I was to get to know this perpetual bustle, with pauses in flight for muttered conferences behind urgently flapped pieces of paper. He was a man in a grey suit, its pockets so stuffed with papers and pencils that he must have been quite a lot narrower than he looked. He was not fat, nor bald, nor middle-aged, but on the way towards all three. He had a bagman's face, with pale grey pebbly eyes behind heavy hornrims and a foxy look of knowing, of always having the answers ready. He had much self-importance. But he did not seem disagreeable, nor was he, even when one knew him.

'Very very sorry,' he said with much warmth. I didn't think he looked that sorry, but we shook each a cordial paw.

'I know I've kept you—have a cup of coffee—but the rush, my god, I really won't be a minute—very very busy this morning.' He was gone again with large strides and I lit a cigarette with resignation, and sipped the usual café Nes, but to do him justice he was back before I finished either.

'Very very busy today—party of three hundred and fifty, soap conference and I've got it all—all falls on me. But wonderful organization I've got here, I direct it all through loudspeakers, you'd be amazed.' I would be amazed, but not impressed, having often enough seen larger parties without so much running and without loudspeakers: it sounded like the train now standing at number five platform.

'Well now—' paper and pencil; sorry wrong pencil, try again—
'you're here about this job. Wonderful job, outstanding opportunity.'

'Is it here?' cautiously.

'Oh no, down town, right in the shopping centre, best situation
on the street. Going to be a wonderful place, designed it myself.'
His enthusiasm was warming: he now slipped into caterers'
jargon.

'Did the whole layout—revolving brush washup, dirty plates
on a moving continuous belt, battery of thermostatic cold-zone
fryers, silver grill, infra-red rapid grill—all visible service—
infra-red canopy over hot plate, refrigerated cold plate, the
lot.'

I opened my eyes, dazzled with this gadgetry, which pleased
him.

'Spring loaded pop-up plate feed, anodized aluminium gold
front to the service counter, choose your steak from this special
display unit and watch it cooked.' I was quite carried away and
Sleet beamed: even a practised bagman is comforted when his
patter palms a new sucker.

'Now yourself—got your letter here somewhere—can't find it
but never mind; was impressed with your qualifications—just
run over your history again for me.' I did, with my own patter,
adding a lot of nonsense about costing and percentages, and was
in turn gratified at palming Sleet: salesmen have a touching
vulnerability to other salesmen.

'That's good, very good; in my opinion you're the man we
want, and I'll say so. Now I tell you what I'm going to do,'
dramatically.

'I'm going to take you in to see the managing director, that's
Mr. Kutchik, and we'll see what he thinks.'

I was taken affectionately by the arm, and hustled up stairs
to a large marbly hall, through a door into an office with files, a
PBX switchboard, and a very cool secretary. The picture of
relaxation; when we bustled in she was poised in an elegant
attitude, like the swans that cooks in expensive restaurants carve

out of ice and fill with caviare, smoking a cigarette and cradling one of her phone sets on a neat black jersey shoulder.

'I got into touch with him this morning and he promised to go into the whole question of the licence right away. Yes, certainly, yes Mr. Kutchik, I'll tread on his tail.' She put the phone down and gave us an innocent sunny look.

'We're just lighting a fire under the Corporation Legal Adviser, but you can both go in.'

The inside office was small, nine-tenths filled by a large man at a large desk, a huge baby, with the cross face of a baby that wants to belch, and can't quite make it. His meaty shoulders were further widened by a shaggy tweed jacket; his shirt was open, with a lot of horsehair stuffing which came crowding out, threatening to burst the next button. When one saw him walk, the small legs in sky-blue trousers, and a fondness for sandals greatly increased the resemblance to Toad of Toad Hall. His friends called him Ben. His motto was: 'Ben, Ben, and White Men.'

He told us crossly to sit down. There wasn't room so Sleet stood, his head bowed in an attitude of reverence, like Keitel in Hitler's presence.

Ben launched into noisy grievances, against the Legal Adviser, the City Engineer, the City Architect (I was fascinated to hear all these dignitaries getting busted back to the ranks) and against a man, very naughty man indeed, who as far as I could follow had been encouraging homosexual manners in the Ranch Tavern, whatever that and these might be. Ben banged on the desk with swelling veins; his stuffing inched further out of his shirt and tickled his inflammatory neck. Sleet made chucking, cooing, tutting noises, and my presence was utterly ignored.

The Ice Swan—she was wasted here; should have been in Miami—interrupted twice on the phone, once to say that the man with the jukeboxes.... 'Don't let him in,' roared Ben, 'I won't see him—ridiculous—much too dear.' The second time was to say gently that the police were complaining; Mr. Kutchik's car was causing an obstruction. This created an outburst.

'Damn it, those silly bastards are more of an obstruction than fifty cars. What do I pay them for? Send them about their business.' I concluded that the Ice Swan would have spare keys, that the police would patiently move the executive Bentley themselves and that godalmighty would never even notice. Her function was plainly to cool not caviare, but his hot little mind. She probably had a cool swan-like name, Diana or Irene. These daydreams were interrupted by Ben turning on me like Rataxes the hasty Rhinoceros (that awful Arthur, Babar the Elephant's naughty little cousin, has just tied a firework to his tail).

'Now I've got these new premises, magnificent, best in the town, best in the whole damn country for that matter, and I want a name, fancy French name, something eye-catching, Toynbee and my wife wanted all sorts of rubbish, Epicure, Aperitif, stuff like that, I didn't like any of it. I want something that's already well known, some famous place, perhaps known for entertainment—I want you to make suggestions.'

I clutched at my wits; nearly said Diana or Irene.

'You mean like the Tour d'Argent or something similar?'

'Yes, I've heard of that—go on.'

'Well there's Maxim. . . .'

'No no, not that kind—have to pay copyright.'

I stuttered out the names of half a dozen gilded French places.

'Never heard of any of'm,' ominously.

'The Lido. . . .'

'Casino' said Sleet helpfully: I nearly said Reeperbahn and something came to my rescue, probably the Evil Genius of the House of Kutchik.

'Fontainebleau? . . .' It seemed feeble but Ben was pricked.

'Yes I quite like that—yes that's definitely better—what is it, anyway?'

'Well, it's a palace.' A palace . . . he was much pleased.

'Yes, that sounds quite good—what you think, Sleet, eh?'

'Not bad not bad.'

'Know what I like?—have a big neon, blue one, fountain playing, fountain in gold see—that's the thing.' Ben sat rapt gazing at a blue fountain playing gold drops and then started drawing it on his blotting paper, which didn't come out very nice so he seized the telephone instead.

'Miss Sims—Miss Sims, what's the name of those people who make neon signs?—well, tell him I want him up here today, got it?' He pointed the phone at me. 'And the name in blue script—get it, get it?' I got it at least far enough to keep my mouth shut, and Ben looked approving.

'I like people who are constructive, not just a lot of comment and criticism. You seem quite smart, I daresay you'll do all right. Now get out the lot of you; I've a hell of a lot of work.'

Outside Sleet drew me to him in a pally way; I was in favour.

'I think we can definitely say the job's yours—but I'll get his endorsement definite, first. Come back this afternoon.'

I went off and built happy castles, a bit like Ben, for a few hours. Something about Sleet's last words were familiar, vaguely. Presently I got it, gottit—the newspaper magnate in the Evelyn Waugh story, whose aide used to say 'Definitely, Lord Copper' when the great man was more or less accurate and 'Up to a point, Lord Copper' whenever he talked nonsense. This discovery convinced me that I could handle both Ben and Sleet. In the afternoon I did indeed get it, gettit, and I went off sanguine as a blood orange to buy a notebook and fill it full of useful memoranda to self on how to run a restaurant.

These were a bit vague, as I noticed presently after the euphoria died down. I had to see the structural design before having any proper idea how much staff I should need, and what one should have to pay. What exactly had been planned? Sleet, next day, offered blueprints.

'I have to see physically—I mean the actual place.'

'Builders still altering the structure, old boy; nothing really to see yet.'

I persisted; we climbed into Sleet's nasty little stationwagon.

Indeed it was a nice position, with furs on one side and flowers on the other; like both a shopfront which was fairly narrow but went back deep to a kind of alley behind. Back door: good news for staff and deliveries. We had the ground and first floors, and also the basement, though I groaned to hear that Ben proposed to have a discothèque in the basement. Sleet explained further that the first floor would be my exclusive restaurant: street level would be self-service, he said. That was not very clever: I stared at Sleet—surely he knew this to be a bad idea.

'Are there separate entrances?'

'No no—up the stairs.'

'Your exclusive customers have to go through a cafeteria?' This was a dirty word; Sleet was shocked.

'Not a bit like that. Don't start flapping; this has all been worked out. Everything's laid on.'

It was his great word. When I asked technical questions about drains or ventilation or fire-escapes it was always all laid on.

'I see no bar in the blueprint.'

'No bar—not yet. Provision made for later, of course. The licence was just a bit tricky. Later, when we can show need.'

'Can't Ben swing it?' thinking of Mr. Hawkes, who had been to school with everybody and especially licensing authorities.

'Well, Ben's a bit in the doghouse at present—bit of difficulty, nothing much—fool of a barman served some boys under age.'

Mentally, I crossed out the exclusive restaurant. No bar—no apéritif. No table licence—no wine. Neither—no profit. I thought of a fantasy involving steak—choose your own and have it cooked. That would give point to the visible service, and it would matter less about the cafeteria. Lyons did this a year later, with no help from me.

'What about entremets—sweets and cakes and stuff?'

Sleet was exultant; I had asked the right question at last. In addition to the 'restaurant' first floor we also had the one next door, on top of the flowers. A hole in the wall was all it took. Complete self-contained patisserie and bakers' unit, would make all that the heart could desire.

'Got first-class London artist, straight from Claridges, costs a fortune—like you. Coming tomorrow, and I want the two of you to dovetail into a really smooth unit.'

I went off with elements of my steak idea, which seemed to me pretty good, taking shape: I went to take counsel of my teashop woman, where I rather exaggerated the joys to be had of modern equipment. She wondered where all the money was coming from.

'Kutchik was bankrupt not that long ago, but I did hear that some new man saved him from being chopped, someone with simply pots, Bates he's called. Financed this new notion I dare say—you know the slogan: Diversify, boys. Fellow's got garages, dozens of them. The Wintergarden can't make real money any longer—too much overhead.'

'Do you know Sleet?'

'Very slightly.' There was a faint nuance of not particularly wishing to improve the acquaintance.

A certain pessimism had succeeded to the euphoria, but hell, I was getting paid, and more than I had ever had. Finance was shaky, but guaranteed by a dozen garages apparently. Now that one thought of it, Ben's finances would always be shaky.

A little restaurant specializing in steak—mm. No licence, and precious little space. But it could be done. Steak didn't need that much—except for a refrigerated chamber, which was essential. In jargon, a cold-room.

Memo: get on to Sleet about cold-room.

15 HOW TO CUT A RESTAURANT
OUT OF PAPER

I was now committed as a loyal and enthusiastic member of the team: constructive, as Ben said. I began to haunt the Wintergarden, with bits of paper and preoccupied expressions.

This afternoon I found a great heap of tables and chairs being unloaded from a lorry and shovelled into one of the many dungeons. I followed and found Sleet directing, not over a mike, but pretty loud.

'For the Fountain,' he said, beaming.

'What, all that?'

'Nono, half is for the Island.' Oh—didn't I know about the Island site—? It was going to be terrific, as exciting as the Fountain—I showed jealousy hereabouts, so he set about converting me. Fact was, place was called the Wintergarden but there wasn't any garden, so we were going to build one. I knew the flat concrete roof, huh, on top of the cinema? Here, high above the town, would be built a house of glass, filled with bamboos, palms, tropical orchids—nono, we'd see that they *didn't* get pinched. There would be a circular mosaic dance floor, cabaret, a restaurant with a licence: they'd got this one, I noticed spitefully. Would be perfect heaven; air-conditioned in summer, underfloor heating in winter—absolutely the last word in super and was to be called the Seven Seas Café, only that was rather long so we all called it the Island.

The Café of the Seven Sinners: memory threw up an ancient Marlene Dietrich film in which all the furniture got broken at the climax; I hoped it would happen here.

Sleet was going on with his fantasies but my mind was drifting back to my narrow fountain, where there was no licence and no Dietrich, but where there was a great shortage of space. All that fancy equipment and you couldn't swing a cat. . . . Hey!

'Up in the Fountain,' I shouted, 'where are the stores?'

The layout genius stopped in midflight: his recovery was rapid, up to a point.

'Easy—make an indent on the stores here; wagon brings it up each morning.'

'No. One packet of spaghetti forgotten and it all breaks down. No control over stock, too many possible errors—system's bad; you know that.'

'I'll see to getting it laid on,' a bit shaken. I was learning, I thought: have to be independent—rely too much on Sleet and sink without trace. I would have to go and have a thorough session with the architect.

Worries were shelved just then by the arrival of the gilt-aureoled pastry-cook; we liked each other at once. We were both cooks, and he was not Swiss—a Jewish boy, rapid and gay, with a Cockney accent. In no time we were drinking coffee together, loaded with pencils like Sleet, brief-cases full of diagrams and catalogues. Heavy machinery was already on order, and here Sleet seemed to have done a reasonable job: we had to buy tools, plebeian things like wooden spoons and staff, and wholesalers.

Hard facts began to emerge. The staff had to have a changing-room, there had to be a linen cupboard, a vegetable store, a space for spare furniture, an office for our paperwork. Several other mundane affairs—like dustbins—had been plain forgotten. Ben's Disc-jockey in the basement had to go: this was the most salient fact. Les the pastry-cook, the architect, and myself would encompass Ben in a united front. As for Sleet, we agreed, he could go and.

During this interlude we became aware of other characters who would affect our lives. Who was the tall pale gangster, always smiling and silent, who drifted in and out of the Fountain taking notes of our plans? He seemed to be called Kay, had a Baltic look, said that he was the publicity manager, but it was born in upon us that he was the designate to manage the Island. Since he knew nothing about the business this ruffled us: he seemed to have Ben's ear too, which was more than we did. Ben ignored our existence, there was no virtue to be had in Sleet, time was getting on, problems piled up and we got no answers from the policymakers.

The workmen were the biggest of the problems. They would not be ready in time—this astonished no one, but why did they behave so whimsically? Concrete was being laid at the Island, and steel girders going purposefully up, but my first floor, my Fountain Floor, was alarmingly untouched. Les and I had planned to keep our stores in his annexe over the flowershop: Ben, we learned, had vetoed this. Save for the bakery unit at the back, this was all to be restaurant space, with the intervening wall removed altogether. All very well; we would have to keep everything in the basement, with in between a self-service place functioning busily. I disliked this gap, with a vision of scruffy cooks ambling up and down for steak and sugar.

I was trying to visualize; behind me came a bumping on the stairs, shuffle grunt shuffle, Easy-does-it-George. A large shiny machine was dumped, of which its porters disclaimed any knowledge. I called Sleet on the phone.

'Who sent the silver grill up here, where the builders haven't

even begun yet? Get destroyed, valuable thing like that—should
have been stored down at the Wintergarden.'

I was told not to be an alarmist fusspot, and banged crossly
down to the basement. The plumbers had made it their own:
lavatories, washbasins, piping and spanners, solder and blow-
lamps lay about in a greasy and oriental profusion, but there was
no plumber to be seen. Crossly, I went in search of the architect.

He was a young man with a nervous pipe, whose matches
always went out before reaching the tobacco, and he knew
nothing of the technicalities of restaurants, but he was quick to
take my points.

'Potatoes—say here—' blowing ash off a blueprint. 'Lockup
for dry foodstuffs hereabouts; linen and so on—yes I quite see—
must be pilferproof, all this. Swillbins—uh—here—' rattle-
rattle with the matchbox— '—here at the doorway into the alley,
and dustbins, yes there's space there behind the lavatories. Your
cold-room huh, yes, at this end here. Concrete draining area,
let's see what the slope is, yuh, draining into here—urhh, yes,
health inspector'll pass that, yes yes, of course; I'll put it up to
Kutchik. He'll be tiresome, of course, he always is.'

At the Wintergarden, where we went to work because we had
no table, a new cloud was gathering. A woman with a loud
penetrating voice was running about arranging flowers; bits of
stalk and leaf were littered everywhere and she was commanding
everyone with loud cries: these antics were distracting.

'My dear would you just move this chair so I can climb on it?
Oops, there goes the water—get a rag, somebody. Deardear, I'm
so sorry, didn't realize you'd just swept round there.' It was
clearly impossible to work, so I gazed.

Careless blonde curls, limegreen sweater and very impudent
bosom, rusty tweed skirt over expensively-corseted behind;
very sunburnt. Freckled hands brightly painted and covered
with diamonds. All of this waved a lot in sweeping artistic
movements that knocked things over. I studied hands and
throat; hm, nearer fifty than forty. She came suddenly sailing
over.

'My dear, I'm very happy to know you—I'm sure we'll get on fearfully well. I can see you have an artist's eye; we must have a long talk soon. Lots and lots of things I want your opinion on,

all my plans for this wonderful place you're going to manage for us.' I did not know quite what to say, having no idea who the preposterous woman was, and badly alarmed besides at the lots and lots of plans. I could have said please-do-sit-down, but she already had, with a graceful flexion of the expensive girdle.

'Please forgive my appearing rude; to be honest I thought you were the florist.'

'Oh my dear, what a lovely compliment, I do so wish I were, flowers are the Great love of my life. You must come up to Larchgrove—some of mine are the only specimens in the country outside Kew.' I breathed shallowly with my mouth open; plainly she was not the only specimen outside Kew. I said I would be charmed. Mercifully she did not stop.

Sleet popped a pebbly eye out of the service entrance before advancing with caution.

'That poisonous bitch gone yet?'

'Yes—at least, I hope so. Who is it?'

'You mean you didn't know? Philippa—Ben's wife. Look, come back a bit early after lunch; we've got to put you wise— we'll all be in the Ranch Tavern.'

Sure enough a conclave was in session; whispers, smelling of conspiracy. I knew these people by sight: Toynbee, a pocketsize Groucho with a dry, level voice, was the general manager. A dark man with glasses, heavy and hairy, was Mason, the accountant. Sleet. Carmody, the cinema and ballroom manager, got up after shaking hands.

'Got to run. Count me in, anyway.'

'Glad you've joined us,' said Toynbee with his thin smile through a small cigar. 'It is most important that we should resist all encroachments. I gather that you have met Philippa; she made herself agreeable no doubt, since she certainly plans to ensnare you. The woman does nothing but interfere; she insists that she is a director, which she emphatically is not. She does have a certain financial interest, making it difficult to ignore her entirely: I do ignore her entirely—haven't spoken to her in a year. The point to grasp is that we must be united. Don't let her inside the Fountain; she'll turn it into a brothel full of flowers. Don't gossip—be chilly, be distant. Ben's all right, once you know his funny little ways.'

He was of course right; I should have agreed. Then I would have been informed about many troubling little things; I might have got help. Toynbee would be a useful ally about the cold-room. But I disliked the categorical imperatives.

'I don't want to get involved in squabbles,' I said foolishly. Toynbee raised eyebrows, and was about, perhaps, to answer. Sleet, who had been nodding portentously, now leaned forward with a leer. 'Seen Kay today? Was at Larchgrove all yesterday—sunbathing. . .' The loudspeaker clicked and hummed; the Ice Swan's tanned voice asked Mr. Toynbee to be good enough to come to the office.

'Ben with his pants on fire.' A look at me. 'Bear in mind what I've said.' I was irritated, stupidly.

'I'll use my judgement.' He shrugged and went away. Mason, who had not spoken, stretched and yawned; I rather liked him. I was not worried about Philippa, who could be distracted. I saw no need to climb in to the Toynbee clique. This was my worst mistake.

At the Fountain was a most disagreeable surprise; a vast espresso coffee-machine, and a man demanding gas, water, and electricity, none of which were in the building yet. Ignoring Sleet, I phoned Ben direct, in a rage. Ben said he was coming up anyway that afternoon.

He arrived soon, rumbustious. He had a way of making a lot of noise with a hand on his head, palm across his ear. Then he would shout— 'What, what?'

He made a beeline for the coffee-machine.

'Very nice. Everybody's got one.'

'Everybody's getting rid of one. This is a self-service, no? Thing's too slow, too complicated, too dear. Send it back.'

'Can't; I've bought it,' almost humbly.

'Down to Wintergarden.'

'Got one for there too.' A voice of classical tragedy. 'But I know—upstairs in the restaurant.'

'No,' I screamed. Ben looked at me with a new respect.

'Well I've an idea—see that shop window? I've a display unit for there, wonderful thing, and we sell cakes. Now why don't we mount the machine here, and the shop girl can tend it. Two selling units, see—cake and coffee.'

'That would be all right.'

'Engage a girl, pay her a decent wage—she can have her own cash-register.' Ben had played me the trick I wished to play Philippa: giving in on something of no importance would silence me for some time. This was about to be demonstrated.

In the middle of the floor the joiners were assembling the self-service counter, to be fitted on chalk lines drawn from the architect's measurements. Ben stood gazing with the cross baby look, hand on ear.

'What you *doing*?' Jack the foreman rattled off technicalities.

'Yes yes, but I don't want it there. I want it *there*.' Squashed back against the wall. I opened my mouth—mistake.

'You shut up; I gave in to you about the coffee—now kindly allow me to be the judge. How far is that from the wall?' Jack scratched with a folded footrule; less said the better. Ben moved the counter back two foot six and happily fitted in three more tables.

'Turnover, my boy. All that space wasted where we could be making money.'

'Can't make it in that tiny space. Thirty per cent available area for service, that's a classical rule. Without equipment.'

'Plenty of space for the equipment.'

'But none for the goddam staff,' I howled, 'the architect . . .'

'Don't talk to me about that fellow—wasting my money. Thought up a heap of damn things, mucked up the whole basement—*that's* where the coffee-machine should have gone. Look at all the space I'm losing there. Told the fellow I didn't want his stupid drawings; I can do better myself. Now Bill, this radiator. What?'

The counter was knocked to pieces and reassembled several times. An ice-cream freezer was pushed in, and eighteen inches sawn off the end to fit in the cashier, whose little cage was abolished in favour of another table-for-four. I hoped she was thin, for her sake.

Memo: thin cashier.

Ben changed everything, having decided that this needed doing once and for all before he concentrated on his Island. I tried to tell him that he had hired me for advice on the technical side.

'Yes yes yes; now don't get on a high horse. This isn't technical, man—all you need here is common sense; allow me to say I've more of that than you. Goddam, don't *argue*.'

I should have persisted: I was frightened, and kept silence.

I excused myself by saying that this was the cafeteria, for which Sleet was supposed to produce a hitherto unseen manager. I would be busy with my restaurant, and devoutly hoped that Ben would be too busy with his island to muck me about. I went to see Les, feeling nightmarish. So was he; his quart had been stuffed into a pint pot too, and he had flour and sugar all over the restaurant floor. The plumbers had flitted one after the other to the Island, leaving everything half-finished: Ben had been dissatisfied with the rate of progress.

'Production starts tomorrow,' said Les, morose, 'with nowhere to wash our hands.'

Oddities pursued us, creatures of Philippa's fantasy. A Hungarian guitarist who would entertain with song. A poor old soul who could make Viennese strudel thinner than a cigarette paper. A stout glittering personage that jangled, covered in bracelets, bangles, and all manner of sweet harmony, who had been engaged as cashier by Mr. Kutchik personally. Ben disclaimed all knowledge of this, and I got rid of her at last by demonstrating that the cashier had to get off her stool every time the telephone rang.

Philippa was active, pursuing workmen with pots containing exotic treelets: she mourned like Niobe over each casualty. Would not Les sell clotted cream? She knew a little man who made wonderful quince jelly. Would Les please have little brown scones for tea, fresh daily. 'Quince jelly inside my bleedin' head is what I've got,' said Les.

I connived treacherously at making the shop depend on the pastry.

'Only natural, Les—shop only sells your stuff, plus chocolate and cigarettes and there's no costing there. There's only coffee, and that'll help your profits.'

'If there are any.'

Sleet arrived, car full of cigarettes and chocolate—it had been fresh that day in Ben's mind. Since there was no cupboard anywhere but the fuse cupboard he put the chocolate in there and hid the cigarettes inside the silver grill upstairs, under a dustsheet. The workmen would henceforward run short of neither, but Sleet told me not to be obstructive. I asked about the self-service manager. Yes yes, he was around, but had been temporarily diverted to the Wintergarden, where they were very very busy as I would realize if I had any loyalty. If I did not propose to be a saboteur I would now occupy myself with the impending opening of the cafeteria, since I had nothing as yet to do in the restaurant, all the workmen being now very very very busy with the Island. I had engaged staff, hadn't I?

I had; some even seemed reasonable, apart from having asthma, or only one leg, or only speaking Spanish. I had concealed all connection with the Wintergarden, well known to catering staff as a hell ship. I had never worked in a cafeteria myself, but this was no problem compared to finding an early-morning char-woman, and midnight washers-up. I read too the lengthy texts of the Shops Act—a desolate experience, because there was a great deal about the exploitation of staff, but nothing about exploitation of managers. I was, I learned, going to work a sixteen-hour day. Underpitching the language a bit, I seemed to be in kind of a false position.

16 'PADGHAM BY NAME, AND PATCH'EM BY GODDAM NATURE'

It had become an obsession as well as a matter of professional pride to try and make the building into a workable machine. Heavy equipment, for Les, for the self-service, for my all-but-forgotten restaurant, was being delivered; daily some new expensive object got lugged in and dumped among the ends of flex and the sawdust. At first I tried to have them taken to the Wintergarden until we were ready. I gave this up after realizing that in Ben's mind we were ready, or would have been but for Mr. Padgham.

He was the builder, and had succeeded the architect as Number One Enemy in Ben's mind. He had contracted to have the work ready by a specified date—a date which had been meaningless for months, ever since Ben had had a vision of bamboo and orchids on the cinema roof. If Ben took all the plumbers, having decided first to open his cafeteria, then go up a ladder to the Island, then to go back down a snake for the restaurant, Padgham's mind was tranquil: his deadline no longer existed. He was not going to trouble himself for lesser idiocies, and when the shopfitters were told to install the glass and marble display unit while the cement round the front door was still wet—the whole job had to be done twice—nobody bothered less than Padgham. I bothered, having an anxious and meticulous mind that goes psychotic quite easily, and until the Carpet I worried all day.

It was the restaurant carpet, naturally; the special linoleum for the self-service would not be seen for a long time yet. Since the restaurant did not even have a floor the carpet was a horrider calamity than most—eighty feet of it in a monstrous torpedo.

Nobody even knew it had come. Through the front it might perhaps have been got up the stairs, but with a perverse humility the lorry men brought it to the back, carted it past the damp cement-stinking skeletons of the lavatories, and left it in the basement between tea-chests full of china, where the builders found it pleasant to sit on. Like Scarlett O'Hara I said that I would certainly think about this tomorrow.

Ben discovered it, on one of his tours changing things. He now wanted to have the basement area laid with plastic tiles. It didn't matter at all about the plumbers, who could make themselves useful at the Island. He slapped me on the back, bonhomous.

'Goddam staff can keep the service area clean then, huh?'

Bonhomie vanished at sight of the carpet.

'Cost hundreds and the plumbers are all sitting there on their greasy oily backsides. What? I don't care, get it out of there. What? Well carry it up the stairs. Where's Jack? Where are all these tea-drinking four-letter bastards got to? What?'

Everybody had disappeared. The plumbers had had to go home; forgotten their male and female joints again. The gasfitter lay down flat on the floor behind the cafeteria counter and stayed quiet as a mouse. The joiners were at their sacred tea-break round the corner. The electricians had a different technique—dialectical materialism. Honest, they would love to help but the union would not let them: sorry, but demarcation and all that.

'Union won't know,' tried Ben. Ah yes, but suppose one of them hurt himself in this dangerous operation—why then, he'd have to put in a claim, wouldn't he, and then the union would know and the hullaballoo then. . . .

The plasterers were up in the restaurant annexe, where Les was their daily and unwilling host, but both turned out to have bad backs. Ben danced on the sand heap like the great god Nquong. When the joiners rolled in wiping their mouths he got all silky and placatory. Beer: bonus. They only held out a while to get a better bargain; the idea appealed to them really. It was a novelty, and pastime. But the carpet, they said, would never go up the stairs.

Ben thought otherwise, and said so. Willing hands, backbone: all right, come on Bill, you get that side Ted, onetwothree Urghh; once more, boys!

The carpet was not bendy, though Ted did get a bit of a kink in half way along. The stairs made two turns, of a hundred and eighty degrees. Halfway up, when the carpet would go neither forward nor back, the hypnotized electricians forgot all about demarcation and helped. . . . The carpet reared up like Cleopatra's Needle and prepared to put down roots: Ben looked at it, both hands to his ears.

'I'm feeling very ill. You'll have to drive me home, my boy.'

I did, and went straight home myself.

The builders brought a crane, and rigged a tackle: Padgham, like Mr. Baldwin, smoked his pipe and said nothing. The carpet was wrenched out backwards, breaking all the banisters, and hoisted up outside to the first floor level. Here, swung like a battering-ram, it arrived through the window of the future kitchen, dynamically knocking over the silver grill and breaking all the firebricks. It took everyone all day, we enjoyed ourselves immensely and my anxiety neurosis, weakened by laughter, dissolved once and for all: nobody saw Ben for three days.

I lay on the floor alongside Harry the Gasfitter: we were good friends. He lit my cigarette and his pipe from the blowlamp and became philosophical.

'Ben?—pinko. All these businessmen have slipped their trolley—know about figures 'n' such, so they reckon they know everyone's job better'n he does. Reckon a building's something you can cut out of paper. Take me, now. I'm told a gas stove's got to go here. Show me where, I says, exact, no people after- wards telling me I done it wrong. Yes, there: all right, I says, that can be done, 'n' I'll do it. I makes exact measurements, drills holes, cuts the woodwork, gets the piping, bends it the right angle, makes the joints, seals it all. I got it all connected up 'n' tested when along comes his lordship and moves the whole thing three feet the other way because he's forgot about the ice-cream.

'Why it's nearly July now. Could have been all ready a month ago but no. He has the men and he has the stuff, but all arse- ways first. Carpet but no floor. Paint, but the walls isn't plastered. Men hanging about, can't get on—all right, he says, get'm all down this other daft place, this Island. I'm not saying it isn't nice, it looks fine, but mark my word it'll never work. Whole kitchen's a bare ten foot square. Panic here then, bring'm all back, 'n' go back three times for stuff what's been forgot. Look out, here he comes.'

The gasfitter fell flat; Ben had his worst face on and all the milk in the world had gone sour. Jack the foreman joiner, waving his hammer to drive home unpleasant truths, climbed over piles of rubbish.

'Sanitary inspector's been here: kicked up stink he did.'

'Goddam we've got a sink.'

'Wants two more.'

I had said a month ago that one could not wash food and plates in the same sink; it had done me no good.

'Quite easy really,' went on Jack, 'by the window; we build a

partition in front with frosted glass. Only lose four tables an'
we can get another in by that radiator. Oh no, I'd forgot; there's
a plant coming there.'

'What plant? I won't have it.'

'Well Mrs. Kutchik, she said. . . .'

'I won't have her interfering and you have my authority to
tell her so.'

'Thank you sir,' sounding really grateful.

In the restaurant I found a horrible heap of rusty iron. I went
in search of the gasfitter and found him next door, where Les
was conducting a tirade.

'Can't get hold of a joiner to do my shelves in here; the fridge
is on the blink and so's the bleeding phone; that sanitary geezer
says the stores must be transferred immediate to hygienic
conditions Ha ha ha, and I want an extractor fan in here before I
bleeding well melt.'

'Harry,' I said, 'what's that junk in the restaurant?' Pious eyes
were raised to heaven.

'Condemned open-top household stoves, pre-war pattern.'

'Come from where?'

'Couldn't say but I seen stuff similar down in the Wintergarden. Mr. Sleet might know. . . .' I went to see the Gas Board.

In the middle of chaos stood Ben, bellowing.

'Where's this bloody builder? Where's Padgham? Why isn't this lino being installed according to my instructions? Nothing's ever done here unless I do it—Padgham by name, and patch'em by goddam nature. . . . You, where have you been?'

'Gas Board.'

'Well, get Sleet on the phone and tell him to get up here—he's supposed to have designed this layout and my god look at it.'

'Did Sleet get those stoves?'

'Don't waste time.'

'They won't work. And neither will I. You've disregarded every word I say and I'm better out. I don't care: I'm supposed to have been hired for my skill and you go listening to Sleet.'

'We're spending too much money.'

'You can't economize on a thing like a stove—that rubbish. . . . Gas Board won't let you install them anyway; they're condemned. But it will make you an allowance against something of some use. Thirty per cent off list price,' I howled.

Ben was looking at me with his benign face.

'You're a good fellow, a likeable chap, but you mustn't cost me so much money.'

'I'll do a good job if only you let me.'

'Very well—go ahead,' suddenly. 'And don't bother me any more; I'm going to chase this bastard Padgham.'

All the builders were standing still, with mutinous sulky looks: won't do it without the governor's sayso. I went back to the Gas Board, where I spent rather less of Ben's money than it had cost to get the carpet upstairs. On the way back I met Padgham, walking slowly. We entered together; he stood with his pipe in his mouth, unflappable.

Ben was upstairs; it was now Les' turn for the high soprano wail. 'We can't do nothink, winder won't open, there i'n't no water, there i'n't no ventilation, it'll get so 'ot in 'ere no staff'll

stay, 'n' the work won't be no good neither. Got to 'ave it cool
for pastry, I'm ony askin' for what's reasonable, Mr. Ketchup.'
It was reasonable; it was even forcible, and something might
have been done if a stupid plasterer had not just then put his
head in. 'Guvnor's-'ere-now.' Ben forgot everything but his
desire to chase that bastard Padgham.

'Now look Padgham, you're a nice fellow and all that.' It
seemed to be his phrase of a sudden. 'But what's this nonsense,
dammit, everybody dragging their feet, nothing's been done,
dammit. I've put an advertisement in the paper saying this place
is open for business tomorrow.'

Padgham remained quiet, but suddenly became personal,
detailed and unanswerable.

'You'll have to put in another one then and cancel it, won't
you. You can't faze me, Mr. Kutchik: I know good or bad
plasterwork when I see it. Nor can you paper over wet plaster;
the archbishop couldn't do it. . . . So it could, so it could, but
just so happens the men were taken off without my agreement
and put premature down at the Island. . . . Yes, I sympathize;
you're in a hurry—never had a customer yet as wasn't.'

Certainly it was true, all true; the basement wasn't ready
either, but those plastic tiles hadn't been in the plan, had they
now? Place had been a disc jockey when he saw it last. And if
Mr. Kutchik was going to talk about dates, if he'd never set foot
in the place it would have been ready six weeks ago and it was
him, Padgham, who ought to be doing the shouting round here
because he had plenty of other contracts, he was the one getting
held up, and he was the one losing money.

Having spoken with wooden calm Padgham went away,
leaving Ben so squashed that we would perhaps have a week's
peace. But upstairs Les was turning over piles of paper; seeing
me he made a sound like Awk.

'Forms . . . gotto fillem in . . . we think we got trouble now!'
I looked, appalled: material used, production sheet, work costed
out, weekly stocktaking.

'Mason's not this dense surely?'

'Comes from Bates—this garage geezer—Mason says it only adds to his work. . . .'

There were other jobs after all. They might not pay so much but. . . . Still, if we got the basement straight, if the cold-room was installed, if . . . it might still be made to work. In a final effort to 'be loyal' I went to see Sleet and fired it all at him. He heard me out quite reasonably, and read me a long lecture of calm and reassurance. Everything was laid on, everything would be done ahead of time, he'd only that day had a long talk with Mr. Kutchik. I need have no fear. As for the paperwork it didn't affect me anyway.

'Les is running a production unit—stuff for the Island, for you, for downstairs, for us here. Accounts must be kept distinct.'

I allowed myself to be hypnotized and to be bought a beer in the Ranch Tavern, where Toynbee joined us, in relaxed mood; Philippa's philanderings kept Kay, whom he detested, out of his way.

'I've hardly met him; tell me more.'

'Name's not Kay of course. Latvian or something. Cool type.'

'Does he really know nothing at all about the business?'

'Heavens no. Vacuum-cleaner salesman. Ben took to him, the way he does. . . .' Shrug: the day was warm, the beer cold.

'How's the Island getting along?' lazily.

'Very nice, come and have a look.' It was nice, I was bound to admit. From below a free-arch staircase and a kind of catwalk led to the roof. Here was the mosaic floor in a huge smooth circle; the glass walls were up and venetian blinds were being fitted: it was easy to imagine the bamboo facings and the profusion of foliage.

'When's it supposed to open?'

'After you was the original plan but it all took too long. So Ben decided first downstairs, then here, then your place last.' My mellow frame of mind was daunted by the thought of Ben standing round my restaurant helping.

'I'd like to meet the cafeteria manager.'

'All laid on,' said Sleet, 'ready to take over the moment it opens.'

Next day was Saturday; I looked forward to a weekend of peace. Wallpaper was drying streakily; joiners were hammering away like Pepito: there were no sinks because there was no plumber. I talked to Jack, who promised to start on the basement (dry stores, linen-cupboard, vegetable-store) on Monday; I had made careful drawings of all this. The fridge engineer reckoned he could install the cold-room in three days. Another week should do it, I thought, cheered.

Meanwhile the joiners were doing the shop window, over which there had been acrid controversy: display of eatables (Ben) or decorative plants and some really tempting goodies (Philippa) —Ben had won. A great gallows-like contraption of stainless steel was being tugged about, nobody could tell top from bottom, there had already been a lot of cursing and hacksawing, and two glass shelves and a rubber-plant had been sacrificed to research. Ben hove in sight, followed by Sleet. I paid no heed, preoccupied by reminding Jack to order the wood and the hardboard for Monday morning.

Man and superman halted to look at the view, hardly an encouraging one. Two joiners were tinkering with the gallows. 'Must be wrong way up, Ted, she don't *go* this way.' Two more were covering the counter in heatproof plastic. The floor was deep in filth, which did not conceal bubbles where the new lino had been laid too hastily. From lamps hung long tentacles of flex; two electricians were on a ladder. A painter lay on his back on the stairs, busy with the banisters. Ben advanced, hand on ear, stomach out, forceful as hell.

'All right—the lot of you—out by lunchtime. That window's the very last thing; I want the entire gang down at the Island first thing Monday morning. The entire town's been notified that this floor is open for business Monday—nine in the morning till midnight.'

I did not take this seriously: we had after all heard the same song before. Sleet turned on me with an executive face.

'Where's the staff you've engaged—why aren't they here?'

'Nothing for them to do—don't be daft. Be here when it's necessary.'

'Necessary now—place has to be cleaned up.'

'Well,' crossly, 'I can't just wave a wand. They've got to be notified. What the point anyhow?—the sinks aren't in, neither's the cold-room—the basement's not even begun yet.'

'That's all right,' said Sleet sunnily, 'we'll manage without.'

17 IN WHICH THE FOUNTAIN PLAYS

And in which Congress would dance: if anyone happened to feel like jumping off the bridge he was invited to waste no further time. I suppose that incredulity and stupor, a grating sort of cynicism and a hearty grin as though induced by a stomach-pump were all written large across my face, but nobody took a photograph. Sleet noticed something for he held his hand up importantly: rookie policeman his first day on traffic.

'You worry too much—I'll be here. I'll take charge.'

'Welcome.' All would now move upon a flowery slope, and the incompetence of such lazy stupid bastards as myself would become manifest.

'Grocer's arriving today with the order.'

'Where do you propose to stuff that?' Sleet, anxious to

demonstrate his flexibility and swift reflexes, tumbled down into the basement.

'Plenty of room, once it's cleaned up a bit.'

'Openly? On the floor? Just like that?'

He had stopped by the door of a peculiar cell known to Philippa as the Ladies' Powder Room. No plumber, plasterer or paperer had ever desecrated this sanctuary. Far back in time a bricklayer had built it, a joiner had hung a door; that was all. Ventilation depended on the ignoble cells next door, the bare cement was sweating like a stoker in the Persian Gulf, and the smell was not nice.

'Do grand for stores.' I did not utter, and he moved on to the lavatories, a handbasin in each.

'There you are, till you get the sinks—won't be more than a day or two. Don't need these anyway; hang a notice on the door saying Out of Order—don't let anybody in the basement at all.'

'The Sanitary Inspector. . . .' I groaned feebly.

'I've never known anybody make as many difficulties as you over the simplest things.'

'Where's the new manager?—things to get acquainted with.'

'Be here when I've someone to take his place. Nine different catering points down at the Wintergarden—you think you're the only pebble on the beach.' Not before it was time, I lost my temper.

'And what about swill—or laundry—or potatoes? You've no fridge bar that matchbox upstairs. Where's the staff to change? Where's the manager—god help him—to work? Everything you do is against all sense and judgement, and goodbye!' I tottered up to Les to tell him I'd had enough. His materials lay in ghastly profusion on the floor, deep in dust, radiators, paintpots and loose plaster. Two cooks, sweating in filthy singlets, were working; a new dustbin was three quarters full already.

'Carry that down two flights of stairs . . .' muttered Les. 'You know what Sleet said!—use that flaming Meccano thing.' This was the tackle used to haul the carpet up; it was still in place outside the window. 'Reckons to leave it up permanent now it's there—bring stores up 'n' everything.' It was imaginative and I could not help admiring Sleet.

'He's made a total fool of me—I'm going.'

'I envy you,' groaned Les, mopping his forehead on a rag with which a painter had wiped his brushes. I felt cowardly. A heavy tread behind me announced Ben, who looked at me the way Caesar looked at Brutus.

'You wouldn't do a thing like that,' he said with certainty.

'Oh no?' stung.

'Five pounds a week extra till you're relieved.'

'Uh. . . .' Ben tapped me on the shoulder and made me a knight. I sat on the carpet and smoked a cigarette. Then I went downstairs, borrowed Sleet's car, and began to round the staff up.

By ten o'clock on Sunday night the lights were all working, the wallpaper gleamed, plants were massed everywhere, the floor had been polished, and the fridge was so full the door would not shut. An ancient icebox smelling of rust had been unearthed in the Wintergarden dungeons and now stood in the basement.

'Not to worry,' said Sleet, contriving to sound sanguine and saccharine in the same breath, 'we'll turn it over so fast nothing will have time to go sour. Thing is, order everything fresh each day, just like bread.' The lavatories were full of lettuce and two new dustbins stood full of peeled potatoes. Everyone was brimful of confidence and co-operation. By the restaurant stairs stood a large notice saying 'No Admittance': by the basement stairs another said 'Toilets temporarily Out of Order'.

Monday: customers, impelled by curiosity, arrived in droves. Sleet gabbled with glee at seeing real people, who actually paid, and announced that all troubles were now at an end. He spent a lot of time on the telephone ordering things that had been forgotten; all these were put in the basement where the staff, pleased, helped itself. He was a bit daunted by the length of the day and so was I; we locked up at one in the morning after seventeen hours. It had been foreseen, and I had counted on sharing the day with the self-service manager. Since he was apparently a figment of the imagination, and since Sleet, bless him, did not appear on the second day, I had a staff problem.

I had several; I sat in the basement on a spare chair, wrestling. Quite a lot of the staff, exhausted by their labours, had not reappeared either. The sixteen-hour day meant employing two shifts of cooks, of washers-up, of counter hands—and since we were open on Sundays, which meant that everyone had to have a day off somewhere there was what Sleet called a Challenge.

I had tried to persuade Ben that the idea of staying open late was uneconomic, but had been beaten by the great god Turnover. At the Wintergarden, where cinema and ballroom emptied late, and a number of brightly lit nooks invited people for coffee and hamburgers and having their fortune told, there was something to be said for his argument: what he could not see was that the Fountain Blue stood in the shopping quarter, silent and deserted —since this was England—after six in the evening.

Staff is always the biggest problem in the catering business. These jobs are made for people of low intelligence and small skill, who have no union, and are protected by no proper agreement. By definition the pay is bad and the hours long and irregular. People who will accept such work are unstable. One must assume that half of one's army at least is incompetent, unreliable, quite possibly dishonest and certainly eccentric. To fill the gaps caused by absentees, and to spare the few steady workers who are treasures, one falls back on casuals, the staff's aunties or sisters-in-law, people who do not officially 'work' but help-out-in-a-pinch. We had not been afloat long enough to collect this indispensable 'shadow staff', and I had to fill the gaps in my army by ringing the Labour Exchange, who cheerfully sent me a flock of undesirables, those hordes of sad people to be found in every large town, who seem capable of wiping a table, washing plates or mopping a passage, and whose loose wheels are not at first sight a great handicap.

The counter staff appeared in a body, unable, they said, to tolerate Mrs. Biggs' foul language any further. I was startled:

she had seemed inoffensive, and commendably brisk on the washup. I asked her why, in her view, anybody should feel a grievance, and she replied with some heat that the wrath of God would descend upon fornicators. Doubtless that was so, I said soothingly, but perhaps the counter staff were upset at being called fornicators. She told me sternly that she was not to be muzzled, and that the *Daily Mirror* should hear of this. I sighed, sacked her, put the lumpiest of the table-hands in the washup, and filled the gap with Rosemary.

One does not ever really want to employ Rosemary, even for the work to which she has obviously been called—she was a bit too tacky; a thin pretty girl of eighteen or so, looking tubercular as well as. . . . But she had a nice smile, told me she enjoyed working at night—yes, quite—and set to, I had to admit, neatly and with energy. She broke no cups, solicited no customers, and in her overall her scarlet blouse and mauve skirt passed un-remarked. Even on the second day she arrived punctually, gave me a luminous smile, and set to. Mother Johnson, a fat and fussy soul, came sidling up.

'Really—that girl—her feet. . . . I hardly like to say it, but she doesn't wash.'

'I have noticed, Mrs. Johnson—I'll try to get her to wash. Meanwhile we're not really settled down yet. She works hard, and it doesn't show so in electric light.' Mother Johnson bridled off and I retired to the basement: the daily battle to assemble material, list it, try to stop it being stolen. I was in the Ladies' Powder Room looking at the condensation that ran down the walls when there came a faint scratch at the door and Rosemary's timid voice.

'Mister—I've such a pain.' I did not bother to turn.

'Sit down for a moment, have a cup of tea, ask Dolly for an aspirin.'

'Such a pain Mister—I know you could fix it.'

Belated, I raised a leaden eyelid. Oh Rosemary!—what would Mother Johnson say? Her quite pretty face had a half-cunning, half-simple expression.

'Rosemary you mustn't worry me—I've a lot of work.'

Sleet appeared next day all right, in a gale of wind; induced probably by his extreme terror of what he might find.

'Can't stop, fearfully rushed, big party.... I won't be coming any more—Mr. Kutchik says he has complete confidence in you; so have I of course. You've done wonders—keep it up.' I was too tired to argue; my numb bloodshot eyes bothered him more than yelling would. Kay was upstairs, he said—he would help out till the Island was ready, when the new manager would certainly bring his crystal mind and powerful muscles to bear upon the fermenting potatoes and the reeking meat—to choose just one manifestation of psychopath minds. Why did I not seize Sleet?—plunge him headfirst into an over-ripe swillbin as Sloppy does Silas Wegg—fit reward for servility and treachery.

'Oh, one other thing—the shop chargehand's got to be sacked, right now, one minute's notice—express instructions from Mr Kutchik.'

'I'll do no such thing—why?'

'Confidential.'

'Your sister.'

'Well between you and me she has convictions for shoplifting.'

'Then we can sack the whole staff, unanimously, right now—and close the bloody door at one minute's notice. There isn't a single one hasn't helped himself to all this stuff lying about.'

I might have saved my breath: before I got upstairs Sleet had sacked the woman and vanished, happy. Kay volunteered to look after the shop—he didn't mind, he said.

I found a new girl, coy and shapely—when Penelope went upstairs to give her cake order and have her till checked there was a lot of giggling and shaking out of the sultanas that got put down her neck—Les casting about for distraction. He had solved the worst of his worries—space—by taking over the whole first floor. We had found too a solution to the staff problem: to put a permanent advertisement in the local paper, charged to the Wintergarden. It was not a very good solution—nobody of any experience was taken in by our smiling mendacity. Using the first day's takings—which were never equalled—as a basis we could see at once that the ceiling for wages this gave was far too low: put the other way round this meant that we had far too much staff. We got a nucleus together of more-or-less possible people, nearly all on overtime, and filled the gaps with the Girls.

The Girls were paid by the hour from Petty Cash: they did not mind what they did, and were always happy: a great comfort. They earned little—they came for sociability as much as anything: this was before the invention of Bingo.

They were middle-aged women, often with grown children; three or four members of the family bringing money in. They lived in the new housing estates, with cars and motorbikes, washing machines and television sets, expensive furniture and all-electric kitchens; bought on time the lot of it, so that their pretext for working was that they never had a penny and were constantly being seized or repossessed, living in the shadow of the bailiff. Since what they earned could make no difference to these catastrophes the real explanation was that in the Fountain they found life, animation, jokes. At home the days were dreary—what was there to do but have a quick dust and go for a cup of tea with Iris? At weekends they were lavish—huge joints of roast meat and drinks: they got through the week on baked beans and cornflakes.

They would come in beaming, take their coats off and produce bags of sweets, which they offered generously to everyone. Talkative and open, they told me all about their private lives, gleefully and with loud collective laughter.

'Margie's ol'man only has her on Wednesday night and she has to put on a clean nightie, that's right innit, Marge?' Shrieks from Marge.

When they could not come they sent their friends, wonderfully adaptable; frying eggs or scrubbing the steps was all the same to them. Often they found friends who had dropped in for a cup of tea, and exchanged broad jokes in public. They drank a great deal of tea themselves and smoked all day, recklessly borrowing half-crowns from me. Without listening, while trying to check invoices, or find out where all the dirty teacloths had got to, I heard what Stan and Ernie said in the pub—the Girls went every Saturday night, religiously to drink gin and bitter lemon—what our Ivy and our Carol did in the stocking factory, what our Johnnie said to that policeman who gave him cheek, and all about that nosy probation officer—I felt sorry for him; his job sounded like mine: hopeless. They were all good-hearted and all cheerful; I could tell none of them apart, except Janice who had missing front teeth and violent lipstick.

I tried, I suppose, to keep the System going; costing, stock-taking, efforts at bulk buying. When I added up debits it was obvious that there were no profits—how could there be? Sausages going home in staff shopping-bags, cigarettes moistly brown at the edges, sloshy chocolate in the fuse-cupboard, the incredible waste of everything. . . . I sent all the papers, with long memoranda added, down to Mason, but nobody paid any attention, blind and deaf to everything but their Island. I had been trained to see a minus percentage as black disgrace, the utter collapse of the System, and took a packet of figures down to Toynbee, who seemed to have some detachment, but he was unconcerned.

'Nobody could make a profit with that set-up, and I certainly wouldn't expect you to be the miraculous exception,' with a disagreeable smile. 'Just try to rationalize gradually, step by step—you're getting paid, aren't you?' I got back to the Fountain and found two customers who had disregarded the Out-of-Order notices and were standing aghast in the basement, which looked like a Delacroix drawing: the Sack of Constantinople, possibly.

Sleet never showed his face; no more did Ben save once late at night: he asked for some supper and did not shout at all, seeming in a mellow mood. He promised me a fridge and swore that the second the Island was ready I could have joiners for the basement: it could not be more than a day or two.

'If it's that nearly ready Kay will be going. I must have this other manager; I haven't had a free day in four weeks.'

'Tomorrow,' said Ben '—you'll have him tomorrow.'

'He really exists?'

'Certainly,' startled. 'Wonderful chap, always cool, never flustered.' A palpable hit at me. I said nothing about Kay, who refused to touch any paperwork, and had hired all the reject staff—a gaudy collection of maladjustments—for the Island. I was no longer jealous of the Seven Seas Café, where even without Dietrich the furniture would get broken up for sure. Ben was now describing it in glowing terms—everyone was bored with me and with the Fountain; their Island, that glittering mirage, was going to arrange everything. Alone, I thought about the crafty cooks and the vanishing food, about Mother Johnson who made the espresso machine shriek with steam like a wounded horse, about the Girls, still with us on peoples' days off, for everyone got days off, except me of course. About Penelope, with whom Les was beginning to exaggerate, and Rosemary, who had been exaggerating for some time and whom I had had finally to sack, together with a cook of numerous other vices.

Next day was the first of August, and it looked like being beautiful weather.

And next day—it had indeed been lovely and a splendid blue twilight was coming down over the town—I was grubbing in the basement as usual, holding inquests, when Mrs. Jenkins appeared upon her unusually heavy feet, like two Russian soldiers together in step, and said that the new manager had arrived.

18 'SAVE OUR SONS AND SAVE OUR DAUGHTERS'

'Excuse me Mister Manager Sir,' Mrs. Jenkins drew me secretly aside, as was her habit when there were matters of heavy moment afoot, 'for interrupting when I know you're very busy.' Her usual preamble, which I had learned to bear patiently. I had stolen her from Lyons Teashops; with us it was 'more human-like' which I could well believe: too human by half.

Would she, in deep confidence, tell the new manager that I was coming? I could say so for myself—but she had already rushed ahead. I found a stocky man with amused eyes, in a maroon shirt and a dark-blue bow tie, who shook hands and said his name was Chris. I had been prepared to loathe anyone Ben had taken such a hearty shine to, but I liked him at once. I sat down, forgetting happily about the corpses below, and sent the hovering Jenkins for coffee.

'Splendid woman that.'

'We've certainly plenty worse.'

'No doubt of that. She threw me in the chair here, shouted "Now smarten up, girls," and said first she'd get me a nice cup of tea and then she'd see where Mister Manager could be.' He looked at me poker-faced; I had found another human being at last: high time.

'Mister Manager Sir,' I corrected: we assisted gravely at the spectacle of the coffee coming wobbling in and Jenkins, breathing heavily, wiping the saucer with a dirty dishcloth (surely I had bought two dozen new ones when the laundry did not come back, day before yesterday?) Jenkins lurched off down to the lavatory to be first with the hot news among the girls.

'She has queenly airs,' said Chris. 'I re-christen her Marie-Antoinette.' He glanced round peacefully. 'Modern you are here—if what one might call a bit cramped.'

'Cramped, as you will discover, is an understatement.'

'But anything is better than Welsh Rarebit in the Ranch Tavern, and Sleet's moralities about being Part of the Team.' He stirred his coffee while I enlightened him about the fuse-cupboard and the powder room, the facts of life as illustrated by Rosemary or Penelope, this and that: he shook with laughter. The phone rang and the cashier, blessed woman, got obediently off her stool with an interrogative glance.

'I've gone to the bank for change,' I shouted.

'Too late at night.... I think he's checking the laundry—yes sir, I'll mention it.... Mr. Kutchik has just driven past and noticed the sign wasn't on.'

'Oh god, forgotten the bloody nylons again,' Chris raised an eyebrow. 'Your new girl friend, Marie-Antoinette—she calls the neon sign the nylons. She shepherds customers across the floor, flapping with that dishrag like an overweight bullfighter, shouting "This way, lady, here you are lady, Eggs and Chips this way"....'

'There don't seem to be many customers.'

'There never are much—word got around. None today—too hot.'

I described our start; Sleet washing lettuce in the lavatories. The day no washers-up appeared at all, so that Kay and I did it till we got some Girls. Ben moving the counter to get more Turnover; Sleet's ideas on fridge-space: Chris laughed consumedly.

'Our present crisis concerns the mews at the back. We finally got a large extractor fan, which makes a din, pours out stink, creates television interference, and the neighbours complain all day. They also complain about the garbage bins, the deliveries—wait till you see our Meccano set—and a very large pile of straw which came out of the china'—the Girls had unpacked all the tea chests—'and which the bin men refuse to take away.'

Chris took up the fight for the cold-room and the lockup space and for the lavatories to revert at last to their proper function. He got the same answer as me: we would have to wait a teeny while, just till the Island was ready. Chris was much more competent than me, and we might have managed somehow if there had not been an August heatwave. There was a wholesale desertion of staff at once, nor could one blame them. The tiny insanitary washup nook faced south, as did the bakery upstairs, where Les in his singlet battered on alone, paperwork piling unheeded, till he hired a new cook, a very shady man but we were all shady by then.

All the food went bad. We stowed things on the floor, covered in dustsheets soaked in cold water, which was not of the slightest use.

We lived in expectation of typhoid or polio. The pigman, who in theory took our food debris, no longer appeared, unsurprisingly, and the dustbins filled with bad food, which the garbage men said rightly was insanitary: they refused to touch it. Complaints from the back increased hourly. Chris took Happy Pills: I fell asleep and dreamed of the Pest; the town became Camus' Oran in my mind and I was ready to see the rats appear at any moment to die in heaps in the gutters. Chris and I loaded the filthy bins into the van at three in the morning, left them at the Wintergarden where we stole empty bins, and hoped fervently that Sleet would be the first plague victim.

We abolished all meat, fish and vegetables: we bought things in tins. We did think of ringing the health authorities and having the place closed, but in August where would we find another job? We rang Ben instead, who said that in a day or so he would come himself, with an army of plumbers, joiners and fridge engineers, and do everything to our entire satisfaction. I met a joiner in the town; he bought me a beer, being rich, and said that the Island, delayed again and again by whims and fantasies, really was almost ready. The weather had clouded over, heavy and abominable with thunder; a movement brought one out in sweat: there were, thank heaven, no customers at all.

On one of these quiet, sultry Oran days Chris was asleep in the café, while Les and I drank mint tea and tried to make sense of out-of-date paperwork. We went upstairs to take his stock, and were aware of strange scufflings and thumpings, and muffled squeaks: the shady man was busy raping Penelope. We bellowed, the girl flew off, trying to straighten herself and shriek at the same time, Les gave the shady man one minute to vanish, and Chris was enchanted.

'Got rid of that bloody shop at last—now if only someone would rape Mother Johnson, I'd be almost content.'

That evening came rain: torrential, superb. It would pause half an hour, and come blinding down again. It continued all night, and was still falling next morning: one could not see out of the window, for busy little men with buckets threw solid masses of water at them.

It was midday, and not a customer in sight, when all the joiners came rushing in, soaked but hilarious: we understood that there had been a catastrophe but had to wait for the uproar to subside. After the sweltering days on that concrete roof, banging away in the dust and shavings while Ben changed his mind about things, they were revenged and so were we. The monsoon had come to the Seven Seas Café.

They were confused but dramatic—electricity fused, plants drowned, floor awash, Sleet running very fast with squawks, Philippa jumping up and down—'My flowers, my precious flowers' (joiner: soprano)—'a thousand pounds gone. . . .' The roof, it seemed, had been open all night; had been for days to get what fresh air one could, for the air-conditioning installation had been the source of endless trouble.

When this was discovered in the morning it had been a good while before anything was done, because nobody could find a ladder to climb up to the glass skylights whose cords, mysteriously, had never been attached. The rains went on tumbling in while the floor, sunk in its concrete surrounds, brimmed because there was no drainage. We sat contemplating this picture with enjoyment: Chris was first to find his voice.

'Save our Sons and Save our Daughters,' he intoned mournfully, 'Der Sieben Sees Kaffee ist Unter Die Waters.'

We had been disconcerted by an apparition—it was during the Oran time, after our superlative complaint, when he walked in and said that Ben had asked him to help us out a bit. Distantly, for he was rather fine, while Chris and I smelt a bit of the basement. We did not know quite what to do: we needed a cold-room, not a new manager. He was tall, with red hair and an Australian accent. He had a black jacket, and freshly pressed stripy trousers; he was called Mr. Watson. One could not put this fashion-plate to work in our pest-ridden hole.

This was a big mistake; we should have stuck him straight in the washup, trousers and all. We asked him to relieve the cashier during her lunch break, and had a hurried conference. After thought, and anxious assessment of the political angle and possible consequences, we sent him down to Sleet, where he was no more seen.

Sleet himself had been no more seen for such a time that we were taken aback when he bustled in a day or so after the monsoon, full of goodwill, which was well received. He then allowed himself some criticisms of the food and the linoleum, which was not well received. We reminded him acidly of the fuse-cupboard and its insanitary puddle of chocolate, of the cigarettes now so autumnal round the edges that our affluent staff no longer cared to steal them. If we had succeeded in tidying a scrap, it was no goddam thanks to some of those present.

'No need to get upset,' said Sleet hastily. 'In fact one of the reasons I came up was to say that we're all naturally very very grateful and very very appreciative of the immensely hard work you've both put in. While I was here, by the way, I did just want to ask you if you'd help out with our opening tomorrow night. Gala reception for the Seven Seas.'

'No.'

'Oh come—fair is fair isn't it now—Kay helped you out.'

'I helped *you* out—this wasn't my department either, remember?'

'Well anyway we all felt,'—who were the we that Sleet kept talking about?— 'that you'd do the same by him. Chris is pretty well fixed up, here.'

'You think so?' said Chris nastily. 'Do you now?'

'Well of course, yes, we're all very overworked.'

'I'm not going near the place. Broken my heart here with one ghastly fiasco; not having that again.'

'What d'you mean, fiasco? Everything's laid on; the place is superb. Now I tell you what—you can see this surely, you're reasonable—I know of course you're both tired—will you come for the opening? First-class party menu, invitations gone out to the mayor and everyone, the whole town in fact, we want it to be absolutely excellent and everybody knows you're a top flight cook and all that. When we wanted something special naturally we thought of you.'

'Hasn't Kay a cook, then?'

'Of course—naturally—that's all arranged—just the opening night?'

'Very well—if Chris agrees. The opening—as long as that's clear and properly understood.'

'Good fellow,' said Sleet enthusiastically. 'Knew I could count on you.'

'All right; I'll talk to Kay.' For Kay had taken to dropping in again at night, looking he said for staff. I had given him my notebook, full of people I had never seen, or never wanted to see again. That night I brought a cup of coffee over to where he was sucking his pencil.

Hors-d'oeuvres he wanted, and fish—nice fish—and a main course, something to look pretty you know, and a party dessert of course: what did I think of Siberian omelette? Since it appeared that I would be doing the work I abolished all this.

'These people only come for the free drinks; they're not interested in eating. You'd spend too much money and it's all too complicated. Anyway, it's only the goddam mayor.' I suggested a cold meal, with a minimum of serving; I was suspicious of Kay's waitresses. Cold consommé now; lobster—no, salmon, couldn't go wrong with salmon and sauce verte—and a cold lemon soufflé. All standing ready; no last minute fluster. And a lot less work for me, I added privately. Kay, pleased with all this, in a burst of Latvian enthusiasm suggested cold Bortsch. 'And I'll make it myself.' Which was all right by me.

Ben arranged himself at a small table in the middle of the mosaic floor and announced that he wasn't going to budge till the place was ready. There was no need for these dramatics: the place was ready bar the shavings that still had to be swept up underneath Ben. I had arrived with my salmon, full of curiosity.

It did look nice. Pale-green cords had been attached to all the skylights; the fans worked; it was hot and dusty everywhere but here, where all was fresh, cool, attractive. Say what one liked, the project had been imaginative and the realization was bold. It wasn't perhaps perfect; waitresses were hanging about in a strange get-up—sarongs with a hint of Watch-Committee decency, and artificial camellias in their hair. Sleet hurried in; he had been sent to buy tablemats and proudly unwrapped large green plastic leaves.

'Where's Kay?'

'Downstairs—main kitchen.'

'Isn't there a kitchen here?'

'Certainly.' A grinning joiner, waiting to see my face, guided me towards the stage, a small platform towards one side, covered with a striped marquee and looking like a Punch and Judy show. At the back of this was a shack, or sentrybox, which I studied: it was most ingenious.

One side was for cold things; a chilled display counter, with a wooden flap to dodge in at which became a serving hatch when down: I dodged in. The other side was for serving hot things, with a warmed plate-cupboard and an espresso machine. The back, which faced a semicircle of tables and the glass wall of the Island, was blank but for a letterbox where dirty plates could be passed through: inside were two little sinks, an electric fryer, and a little household cooker. As for the fourth wall, which formed the back of the stage, it was all shelving and stood full of plates, glasses, and various household gadgets, a toaster, a mixer, an infra-red grill. This might perhaps be a bit hot and noisy for the musicians in front, but they would be amply revenged: one high note on a trumpet and all the china would fall off the shelf. I had suddenly remembered the words of Harry the gasfitter. 'Whole kitchen's ten foot square, washup and all.' He had not exaggerated in the slightest.

It was like a little caravan where you fold the table out of the way before going to bed, and like the little caravan it was isolated. Here would stand a cook, a counterhand, a washer-up, back to back in happy promiscuity except that there was no room to fornicate. I looked upward—above my head was a sheet of cardboard: there was no ventilation or even a fan. Sleet had based his design on a mobile van. No cook had been in here, nor been asked for an opinion. This was the kitchen we had seen advertised for meals à la carte. There was room at the tables for sixty persons.

On the cooled shelf was a dozen of Rhine wine, and in the little fridge below were bottles of lager beer and Coca-cola. There was no food, nor storage for any. Sleet would have said that it could be brought from the main kitchen and the stores, along the catwalk, down the steps and two more flights of stairs, down in the antique bowels of the Wintergarden.

Here I found Kay, in Sleet's office, changing into a dinner jacket. There was a smell of boiling beetroot.

'What's that?'

'The bortsch.'

'Will it be cool in time?'

'If it isn't I'll serve it hot.' I kept silence and unpacked my salmon, which was already cooked. Chris had helped me make Russian and potato salad, little boats of cucumber filled with shrimps, and plenty of greenery—stretch him a little bit. I had only to arrange this and sprinkle chopped parsley. I had been told thirty people and proposed to assemble four times eight on the biggest silver dishes—but perhaps I had better think again.

'What's your final figure for the guests?'

'Thirty-seven—Sleet hadn't counted some friends of Ben's.' Kay was perfectly calm; his notions of bortsch were a bit odd but on the whole I felt sorry for him, and prepared to be flexible as I changed into whites and began breaking salmon steaks in halves.

'How many waitresses have you got?'

'Two—we only kept the pretty ones. To look better in the costume, you see.'

I did see. Let's think, the soufflés—four times eight was thirty-two and four times nine thirty-six. Mm. . . .

19 AN ENTIRELY NEW POLICY

The evening went very well, filled with disgraceful events not quite credible but perfectly laughable, and made enjoyable by everybody getting drunk. There were fifty guests; I shuffled bits of salmon on to plates, splashed salad all around to make it look bigger, added ridiculous things like pickled onions (a large jar I discovered in Sleet's kitchen and instantly stole) and stacked it all on the shelves of the sweatbox. There was nowhere near enough soufflé but Kay produced a large piece of pale-grey cheese: I abstracted a bottle of the Rhine wine and observed the antics. Nobody ate the soup, which was water with carmine colouring and saccharine, with a flavour of Oxo (this is what happens when one boils beetroot)—but there were pickled onions for all. Ben made a speech, to which the mayor replied; the usual on both sides. Philippa made a speech, which was embarrassing and full of superlatives, during which Kay hastily opened a lot more vino. Everyone then moved closer together for the serious drinking to begin, and the cabaret started.

There were no musicians, though I recognized Philippa's
zigeuner guitarist. The evening began to swing when the French
students appeared; twenty or so on holiday and quite uninhibited, playing all sorts of musical instruments with verve, and
singing: nobody understood the singing, which was as well.
They were prepared to enjoy themselves as long as the vino
lasted, and Sleet ran about sweating with bottles while Kay made
coffee. Nobody did any washing-up: I stole two more bottles
and slipped off to tell Chris.

'It would make a good beer garden, though—there isn't a
cook in this world would stay there five minutes. I'll make you a
drawing—if you took out all that fryingpan nonsense, and put
refrigerated shelves on both sides—yes, and the third side too,
why not. . . .'

'No food at all?'

'Salted peanuts. . . . Perhaps one could load a trolley up with
stuff from downstairs, club sandwiches or something, and push
it about; lot of salty smoky things to make them drink more.'

'Sounds like the Ranch Tavern all over again. So there's no
cook?'

'Of course not—but I see it now; I bet they're counting on
me—ha ha ha.'

Toynbee, coming down to collect money (a figure of speech)
after midnight confirmed the diagnosis.

'Fool's paradise,' he said acidly. 'Wait until tomorrow.' At
one in the morning we went down to see.

Revelry had reached a peak; the French boys had found jazz
records and a player somewhere. Ben sat in a nest of creditors
and empty bottles; the tough executives beginning to look a bit
glassy. The workmen had all reappeared in Sunday suits, and a
joiner was doing a tango with Philippa: the others sat at tables,
supplied with bottles while Kay washed glasses. The waitresses,
the mayor, and all the respectable guests had long ago disappeared. Sleet greeted us, vinous and sweaty.

'Great success,' he kept saying.

Next day the workmen arrived back in the Fountain, subdued

but glad to have seen the last of the Seven Seas Café; they looked around the familiar scenery with pleasure, as though glad to be home. Chris and I had coffee with the foreman joiner, digging out my plans which had been untouched for six weeks. I made new drawings for the restaurant annexe—little larders for Les and myself, a corner left as an office for the three of us. We were determined to yield no further about working space but thought we should have no trouble, for even Ben, surely, would now see that the sweatbox mentality paid no dividend.

News of the Island was not long in coming. Kay had no staff. The French boys had volunteered to cook, serve, anything: Toynbee, who knew something of labour permits, had put a stop to this. The Seven Seas Café had reopened for afternoon teas and closed again, for the little electric stove could not boil water fast enough, so that customers waited half an hour and then left.

That night, we heard, there were musicians. There was also Kay as cook but neither of these temptations aroused enthusiasm, and some people made scenes. The evening paper carried an advertisement offering colossal wages for a cook, and we pictured them turning up, talking to Sleet, and then focussing their dazzled eyes upon the sweatbox.

Sleet came to see me next morning. The floor of the restaurant was being sanded preparatory to laying the Carpet, the gasfitter had brought new firebricks for the silver grill, electricians dragged flex about: it was as though they had never been away.

Had I any spare staff? asked Sleet. No. Well, had I engaged staff for the restaurant? Yes, and taken great pains over them. Good; in that case it was all very simple—they could all go and work in the Island until the restaurant was ready.

No they couldn't.

'One look and they'd all give notice. I'd never get them back here, then. They were dubious already, seeing the washup downstairs, but I swore it wouldn't be like that here.'

'Well if you're that well organized why can't you come and lend a hand?'

'Now look—the six square inches theory has ruined everything. I'm staying here, to see that this place at the least isn't buggered up: the basement's got to be done and this annexe too converted for working space, and some sort of policy arrived at and stuck to—let Kay play about in that bamboo brothel; can't you see that no cook'll ever work in it?'

'All right all right—you won't co-operate. Heard all this before.'

He went off abruptly, furious. I went down to Jack the foreman.

'How long will the basement take?' If Ben found out they were down there instead of upstairs. . . . Chris met me with the news that the fridge engineer refused to work any further till he was paid.

'And I can't somehow see Ben giving us a cold-room when he finds his precious annexe gone too. . . . But there's a drain there; at the worst they could build a shack with slatted shelves, put block ice there, and a powerful fan—be better than nothing; at least we could keep meat.' Had we got to go on improvising? I wailed. Were we never to get anything done properly? The phone rang, the cashier gesticulated; I went crossly over.

'Mason here. Can you come down?—something I have to talk over with you.'

'Oh, all right—after lunch—what's the matter; butcher's bill wrong again?' He sounded a bit fussed, which was unusual. He was always unexcited—needed to be, since half his work was persuading people not to cut his credit off.

He had a little funkhole in the basement, where two slaves pored over accounts by permanent artificial light. He gave me a wry sort of grin, fiddled with papers, and seemed at a loss. I realized with unusual lucidity that my problems were about to be solved for me.

'I have an idea I've guessed.'

'Well, no use beating about the bush then—yes, I've been instructed to pay you off—sorry. . . .' He offered a cigarette, something in the style of the prison governor who's had bad news from the Home Secretary about the reprieve. I did not feel this way at all. I felt humiliated, to be sure. I felt fury at never having been given a chance to do any real work. I was angry and disgusted, but above all I felt joy. I was free. Mason, relieved, gave me a friendly wink.

'I gather you spoke your mind a bit freely to Sleet. You haven't made too many friends here. The vultures gathered round, and said you'd let the side down, disloyalty and all that, spreading alarm and despondency—well, forgive me, I know nothing about the technical side. Anyway, Ben took a look at the Island this morning, and he's looking for a sacrifice as you can understand, and you were it. I wouldn't worry is all I can say—you won't be the only one. I fixed it to give you a month's money—no notice I mean, and all that.'

We went upstairs: he had no money, he said, but there might be some in the safe in Toynbee's office. I waited in the hallway. No sign of Sleet, obviously, but Ben came out of his cubbyhole suddenly, and did not try to avoid my eye. He had his own brand of honesty, and I liked him at that moment. He looked tired too, and genuinely harassed; so many of his own dreams were collapsing.

'Hallo my boy—waiting to see me?'

'Not really—waiting for money.'

'You've a right to an explanation, I know.'

'No, you don't have to explain.'

'You're a likeable fellow—I've always said so. But you're not very competent, you know.' For the first time, I realized that this was quite true. I had made so many jokes, had been superior and sarcastic so often—was this not to conceal from myself my own shortcomings?

To be sure, none of them were competent either, but what had that to do with it? I had got and kept this job under false pretences: I knew nothing about administration, and had no talent for it. I had pretended to be a manager, when I was just a cook. My self-satisfaction fell off: for three months I had been walking around thinking no one knew anything but me. I had been rightly served, no?

'You're quite right really,' I mumbled. Ben was looking puzzled.

'There it is, I'm afraid. Economy—unavoidable—we've spent too much money.'

'Good luck with all the projects, Mr. Kutchik.' I held my hand out in a stupid way; he was disconcerted but grabbed it.

'And the best of luck to you, my dear chap.' He stumped off, not sure what was going on. Everybody had let him down, and nobody was sorry but me—but I was the one he'd just sacked, wasn't I? Mason came back with the money.

'So long old boy.'

'So long—spit on Sleet from me.' Mason wrinkled his nose and glanced both ways, lowering his voice.

'No need, I'm thinking. Smudger's days, between us, are numbered. Bates is due back day after tomorrow.' Bates . . . who was Bates? Of course, the garage man, the millionaire, the source of all the money. 'I think, when he sees my figures. . . .'

I got a job in a little Italian restaurant, where they listened to my stories and laughed, not believing them. . . .

A fortnight afterwards I met Chris in the street. A lovely summer evening; he was walking very slowly, his hands in his pockets, not a care in the world. I had always admired his refusal to ruffle, his way of being at peace with himself—so unlike me. We had supper together.

'Two days after you went—that was all it took. Bates came in suddenly, with Ben in tow behind squeaking out complaints, just like a little dog being dragged along the pavement.'

'What's this Bates like?'

'Big fat thing in a brown suit—affable, but decidedly not to inferiors—iron hand stuff. Looked, I may say, in the very devil of a rage.'

'Mason tipped me off.'

'I think he was the only one who knew, but Toynbee guessed—cunning little bugger. He resigned, you know: said his doctor had warned him not to overdo it—not bad, that. I had a word with Mason after; he wouldn't tell me anything precise but he did let fall that Bates has dropped over thirty thousand, and I don't suppose even Padgham has much to show for it.'

'Is that all?'

'Not counting the value in the properties. Just on work done, or if you prefer not done.'

'Go on.'

'Tore all around the building, Ben panting behind yapping out remarks like Now just look at this, what did I tell you. . . . Bates never said a word—the tight grim jaw, no good morning, no nothing.' His eyes crinkled at the corners: the recollection was enjoyable.

'Marie-Antoinette in a dickens of a flap—I didn't have the nylons switched on, either—you can just imagine it.'

'The basement. . . .'

'Just as usual and upstairs Les tearing his hair according to routine—you know; sacks of sticky goo lying about.'

'What happened to the restaurant, finally?'

'Well, you know, Ben wanted little lamps with rose-coloured shades on all the tables, but it hadn't of course occurred that they'd have to be wired up. So the electricians cut neat little circular holes for plugs, all over the carpet—looked as though the moth had got in. Bates really went wild; I heard him lighting into them—fornicating nincompoops was one. They walked straight out of course, said they wouldn't stay where capitalists used insulting and obscene language. Well, I reckoned we'd better get packed before any of the obscene personal expressions came floating our way. Word took about an hour—phone call from Mason who'd been appointed chief executioner pending the arrival of the receiver, presumably.'

'And?'

'Oh, me sacked, naturally, Les sacked, Kay sacked—you'll be pleased to hear Sleet sacked. Crows came home to roost there; bad planning, incompetent execution, lack of directive, should never have hired us all in the first place, fiasco directly traceable and that's all she wrote. Toynbee's nervous exhaustion was a master stroke. It shows us up, my boy. The difference between an amateur and a professional. Why did we stay in that dump getting hit on the head and liking it?'

'We needed the money. And we had that queer idea about loyalty—you know, like Sleet.'

'Not like Sleet. By the way—know who the new general manager is?—Watson.'

'Who's he?'

'You don't recall?—red hair and striped trousers. Come to see us one day and we rather foolishly laughed at him. Back to the sausage rolls and the Ranch Tavern, you clown. We were wrong, you know.'

'I do know.'

A day or so later my path took me past the Wintergarden. Large notices were everywhere much in evidence. Eggs and

Chips. Plaice and Chips. . . . Visit our Island site, went another. Hamburgers, Hot Dogs—the Homeliest Holiday Atmosphere in Town. And the largest of all announced the Entirely New Policy—the Sieben Sees Kaffee was unter die waters this time for good. As for the Fountain, it had had a jukebox installed and the window was full of cheap cake from a multiple bakery; Ben by now convinced no doubt that this had been his wish the whole time.

The ludicrous episode, trivial as it was, had a lot of weight in my life. I believe that it marked for me the difference between being a boy and becoming a man, what Joseph Conrad called the Shadow Line. But his experience off Bangkok, in equally nightmarish and often equally comic circumstances, was for him a resounding success, while for me it was an ignominious failure. Two lessons were to be learned from this: the first a simple lesson in material facts: that I had no talent for figures and never would, that one didn't make a cook into a chef, or a manager, by calling him a different name, that a job—any job—was more than offering up incense to Loyalty, Application, Perseverance.

The second—a little more complex—was that it is too easy to see people as laughable or pathetic, absurd or contemptible. This was a convenient way of masking the painful impact they could have upon my life—but they were right; I was wrong. Sleet had been more imaginative, more active than me: I had stood around being superior. He had known, instinctively, how to handle Ben without there being a grave crisis: more clever than me. It could be said that if Sleet got the sack it was my fault. He had been very well where he was, doing no harm to anyone, before I arrived full of arrogance.

Realizing one's own clumsiness and ignorance, I suppose that the reaction is always to adopt these airs of cynicism—viewing Sleet as I have seen him in these pages. For years I practised the little slogans of egoism; playing it cool, keeping the head down, keeping the nose clean—though luckily for myself I was never any good at following such sage, sad advice.

A year or so after Mr. Sleet, I found myself working in Germany, in the dismal town of Düsseldorf: I was lonely and miserable. I bought a paperback copy of *From Here to Eternity* and read it twice: it took me a surprisingly long time to realize that I had not Prewitt's courage. His talent for putting himself in the wrong was, by itself, not enough. The book would be nearly faultless but for the overblown romanticism of the imagery, but then perhaps it would not have appealed so much to people, and would have sold a lot fewer copies.

THE COOK BOOK

THE FLEISCHKLOBBER

Unless a writer be more than somewhat vain and bursting with inflated self-confidence, or be indifferent to the charge of defrauding the public (and then who of us shall scape hanging?) the idea of writing a cook-book ought to fill him with dread.

So (tone hereabouts majestic and rhetorical) am I filled with dread? Yes I am, but not really more so than at the start of a novel, another ungrateful, self-defeating and probably fraudulent occupation. Anyway, being hardened in cynicism by too many years spent in hotel and restaurant kitchens, I have before now maintained stoutly that writing a cook-book, as opposed to a kitchen-book, was impossible, and very likely I was right. The craftsmanship of a blacksmith, a potter, or a carpenter—or of a novelist—cannot be explained on paper, however lucid, brilliant, numerous and expensive the accompanying photographs.

My publisher, aware that the pen is mightier than the sword but with a healthy respect for all the weapons both blunt and trenchant wielded by cooks, spoke his mind to me.

'Having' he said—his logic was inescapable—'taken pains to shoot down every cookery book in sight in your last effort—' (*unspoken*—with which it had been his misfortune to be associated) '—well, I greatly fear, dear boy, that if you now have the damned audacity to pretend to write one yourself, I fear that they will all reach for the Fleischklobber, that's all.'

I was enchanted at his erudition. How the devil did he know about the Fleischklobber?

We would call it a steak bat; it is a heavy piece of forged steel polished smooth, oblong in shape but prolonged at one end into a handle. One side is flat, the size of a man's open hand but shorter and broader. The other side thickens to a central ridge whose solid metal lends a punishing weight, and bevels at both sides to straight edges which without being purposely sharpened can inflict a frightful wound; I have a hand which bears witness. Of all people I have cause to respect such a weapon.

A steak bat when not thrown at me is used to slap and flatten meat: steaks, cutlets and escalopes are hit with it to make them even, to present a larger surface to a source of heat, and to break down and weaken the sinews and fibres knitted into meat. It can also be used with cheap meat, to flatten out the nubbly bits, crush tough muscular contractions, pound and repress all individualism into humble and horizontal conformity. Quite a hitlerite sort of weapon; admirable choice to use on me.

In fact in German—hats off to my publisher—it sounds nastier still. I have an immediate vision of Goths in the pictures by Hansi ('The History of Alsace Told to Our Children' around 1890; it drove the unhappy occupiers absolutely wild). They are crouched in their savage forests along the Rhine, bloodshot eyes peeping out of uncouth mats of hair at the glimmer of the Roman watchtowers. One and all have 'Wotan Mit Uns' inscribed in barbarous gothic lettering upon their belt-buckles, and one and all are clutching Gothic Fleischklobbers in hairy knotted fists. How is it that I am not afraid?

I lit a cigar and told my publisher that living in Alsace (I learned to read from Hansi) I was not afraid. Nor of the steak bat. I did not mean only that I was used to cooks grasping knives—throwing them too, quite frequently—but that I knew most of the tricks phony cooks get up to. I told him about Joe.

Joe was a warrant officer in the Royal Air Force, a lumbering but soft-footed bear with a bland ham face and tiny eyes, chief of the kitchens in a large camp where I used to scrub floors. He was a great man, and could produce bananas where there were no bananas (it was a period in history when pregnant women were entitled to One Banana, other ranks not for the use of). Many a catering officer, commanding officer or even grander personages had tried to topple, undermine or otherwise infiltrate Joe, who went his placid way and grew rich. He was a good cook, too.

Finally a terrible sort of F.B.I. man appeared, technically the new Station Warrant Officer, a figure who was and probably still is the most important person on an R.A.F. station. But this was a little man, and nasty. Since Joe was nice, and good to work for, all the cooks were solidly pro-Joe, down to me. I was humble, a Roger-the-Dodger who had feigned migraine to get away from Radio Telephones—the war now being over, there was no further use for these contrivances, which flourished rankly none the less. I had been reduced in disgrace ('scrubbed down') to Aircrafthand General Duties, which is very low, and means you scrub the floor. I scrubbed the Officers' Mess Kitchen, and since I got it clean Joe used to walk past and push a banana down the front of my battledress.

'Ere's yer rations, chap.' He called everyone chap.

The horrible man now came bursting in, a suspicious sniff upon his face which was crafty, mean and hideous.

'Where's Joe, eh? Not ere, eh? Thought not. Well I'm going to look around, see? Joe's on the fiddle I ear, all right I says I'll ave im, I bin a cook too. I knows all the fiddles, I bin ospital cook in 'alton twenty year.'

I am glad to say that this boasting was as naught. Joe when told of this naked threat said nothing. He expressed no contempt of hospital cooks from Halton; he had had ten pre-war years at Uxbridge, but did not boast of having beaten T. E. Lawrence. He neither poisoned the horrid man nor starved him to death; he said nothing, and did nothing. He was not afraid of the Fleischklobber.

While meditating on my dictum that writing a cook-book of any use to the zealous but untrained aspirant would be futile and ridiculous, I slowly developed a theory that perhaps one could do something after all. Not, to be sure, with the classic, and generally tedious dishes of the Almanac de Gotha repertory in which I had been trained. Nor with the snobberies of experts, who have been everywhere, seen everything, and tap you out in their weekly column a Saddle of Camel Bulgarian Style which will get your husband promoted to sales-manager just by inviting the managing director to dinner. One such dish, I read recently, had become the Rage of the freshly-ground-black-pepper belt, and the expert the toast of these ambitious folk: I am not in the least surprised.

I thought of a very simple affair, which might even help someone. I would write about perhaps thirty simple dishes. Remarkably few people cook more than that habitually: as a French friend of mine says gloomily about his wife, who has small taste for the kitchen, 'Every time it's liver I can be sure it's rice and raisins.' Thirty everyday dishes of simple materials available to all. I would cook each one for my family at my own stove, and eat it too. While working I would observe myself carefully, especially things I do automatically, from trained experience or instinct. How did I start? What next? Why?

I would ask myself, too, the basic questions which a schoolboy, if he is properly trained, keeps in mind as he listens to his professors.

How does he know?

How can I be sure?

I would try to think how best the details could be described briefly and lucidly. I would write each recipe down, with its mechanics. I would give it to friends to try. If told it was confused, unintelligible or idiotic I would throw it out, and begin afresh.

This was quite a large field already and would easily exceed the limits of readability. Such is the risk of accumulating detail. My limits as a cook would be seen too, at once, many and various like my limits as a writer. Oh well, I decided, I would bear that. Why should I not be criticized? Should I not try at least to be humble about it? For that is what I really object to and complain of in cookery-experts. They tend to speak ex-cathedra, to aim at dazzling with their mastery and erudition. They taste, and say 'Quite good, but not as good as the last time I ate it in Andorra, which is of course really where you have to go'. They have kitchens stuffed with objects of decorative folklore in which they are sometimes photographed, as in a Royal Enclosure, wearing hats.

The public, it seems to me, has the right to say 'Stand out of the light, you frog-footman you; what we're interested in is what happens in that pot there in the stove'.

WHAT OUGHT TO BE THERE, BUT GENERALLY ISN'T

Kitchens are always full of rubbish, mine as much as anyone's. Tin-openers which don't, ladles whose handles come off, knives nobody can sharpen, gadgets for grinding, whirling or shredding which cannot be washed, so that one takes them to pieces and can't put them back.

There are rules, about which I do not hesitate to be dogmatic, because I have now twenty-five years of experience, and there are others about which I refuse to be dogmatic, because I still get caught.

Most of my equipment is French, because I live there. Some of it is very good. One can get very bad things here, and very good things elsewhere, but most French kitchen equipment is good. Some of the things I describe, or think essential, may have been originally French, but all as far as I know are made everywhere, and are everywhere available.

Stoves: they get their heat from all sorts of sources and it is a truism to say that it is difficult to get gas stoves to go really low enough, to get solid-fuel ranges really hot enough quickly and flexibly, and electric stoves that will regulate themselves with precision. I am not going to say anybody *must* do anything, but a stove should have, besides sources of fierce flame or heat, an area of solid metal where things will cook very gently. If this cannot be found on top it can generally be found in the oven. My gas stove has a horrid oven, with too much bottom heat and not enough at the top.

It has three burners, a big bear, middle bear and tiny bear, and an area two feet by one of solid metal with a small burner underneath. This when turned low will simmer a stew, and keep things warm at the back: when turned high it will boil two pots together, or three smaller ones. This is adequate for seven people. I have also a range burning any solid fuel, which I use in winter because it heats the whole kitchen. Because its metal is much thicker it cooks better. But it is sensitive to changes of wind, goes too fast or sulks, and is difficult to regulate.

Pots and saucepans are thick and heavy, cast iron or stainless steel, enamelled both inside and out. Frying-pans are the same. They discolour inside and are difficult to clean, because one may not use abrasives at the risk of dulling and scratching the interior, but they are the only ones which I have found any good. I have some cheap old-fashioned French ones and some very expensive Swedish ones.

Casseroles and cocottes, or pots without handles, possessing two ears and a fitting cover, exist in every size and type of flame-proof porcelain or glass. I find them indispensible and so does everyone else.

Cutting or chopping boards should be of real hardwood and made in one piece.

Everything, from a stove down, should be very simply shaped and easy to scrub. It is extraordinary how many things are sold which are neither.

Knives are a problem. A professional cook collects dozens, of which a few favourites emerge. It is best to buy professional knives; they cost more but are shaped by centuries of experience, easy to hold, handle and sharpen, and last a lifetime. Household knives are never any good. When buying a knife look at the blade; put it flat on the shop counter, hold the handle and press on the blade with the other hand. It should give springily like a golfclub, neither stiff nor over-flexible. Look along the blade; it should taper in thickness from base to tip. It should have a good depth of metal bevelling gradually to the edge, so that it will sharpen easily. The forged metal of the blade should be in one piece going right back to the tip of the handle, which is attached by large solid rivets. The handle should be wood and not plastic, and should have a large comfortable grip which will not slip.

I think that the amateur cook with any ambition needs three knives. But before describing them one has to settle the awful problem of weights and measures, since I have to describe knives, and a lot of other things, in these terms.

I use metric measures and have done so all my life. When in England my wife and I always had to do sums in our head, which we found tiresome, so that I sympathize with anybody English who now has to do the same sum backwards and finds me tiresome. But it looks as though the United Kingdom, despite prejudices I find sympathetic, will adopt the metric system, for my stern and learned English daily paper has just told me, rather sharply too, that in future technical handbooks—and it mentions cookery specifically—should give all detail in metric terms. So I am afraid that this is what I will do. But since all pedantry is abominable, one can approximate without breaking any bones. Except in a few delicate pastry recipes, a slight variation in measuring does no harm at all. I always say 'about' anyway, since one is never quite sure how much flour will thicken a sauce, and where possible I have given no measure at all except that used by cavemen: thus a walnut of butter. Americans talk of cups, but how big is a cup? Everyone knows how big a tablespoon is; it will just go into your mouth, though not if you have nice manners.

For our purposes—and this worked perfectly well in England for us—250 grammes is half a pound, 500 is one pound, 750 a pound-and-a-half, and a kilo is two pounds.

A litre is two pints, roughly. (Actually a shade less, but this makes no real difference.) Pedantic civil servants and phony cooks to the contrary, I have never in my life, anywhere in Europe, heard anyone ever speak of centilitres. A pint is half a litre, a half-pint a bit over two decilitres, a quarter pint just over one deci.

A foot is thirty centimetres. Fifteen centimetres is six inches. A metre is a bit over a yard.

My wife bought everything including children's clothes, on this principle for five years and never got anything wrong with the food either.

To get back to knives. . . .

One is simply a little vegetable knife, with a blade of eight centimetres or about three inches—you see that the measures are no real trouble? When mine gets mislaid, as it very frequently does, I use my penknife. The whole point is to have a knife of good enough quality to keep sharp, because few things are more frustrating than peeling tough onions with the little household knives the ironmonger sells.

The second is a most important knife. It bones meat, splits vegetables, fillets fish, chops onions and peels them too when *both* the little knives are missing. . . . Mine is a French butcher's knife, thirty centimetres long, with a blade just over half that in length and four centimetres deep at the base. The cutting edge is nearly straight.

The last is a big knife. Mine is Swiss, with a blade 25 cm long and nearly seven deep at the base. The cutting edge is nearly straight for three-quarters of its length and then curves abruptly up to the tip. It cuts steaks, splits chickens, chops cutlets, beheads fish.

These knives are kept sharp on a butcher's steel or a fine-grained carborundum stone used in the same way. About every six months the metal gets too thick to hold a fine edge and you give them to your butcher and ask to have them ground along with his.

Only a few years ago the steel people learned to make knives in stainless steel; the same applied to razorblades. This was a big technical advance, for a stainless knife which really cuts (the trouble before had always been that they didn't cut) does not rust and is easy to keep clean.

Remaining kitchen equipment is a matter of taste. The only potato peeler I have known of any real use is the French type called 'économe' which peels clean and fine, right or left-handed, and does not clog itself. And to strain a sauce or soup, an every-day occurrence, the handiest is the French conical wire strainer called a 'chinois'.

Now we can start cooking. One thing altogether missing from this book is descriptions of cake or pudding. This is my first, and most glaring, deficiency. I never had any training as a pastrycook, nor ever tried: it was a corner of the kitchen for which I had no taste or interest. I have regretted this since, and often. I love pud, and my English blood comes out strong at the mention of Bakewell Tart—still the heart is Highland and I in dreams behold the Hebrides. . . .

My wife, who loved England, makes nice pud. But I can't and however I try my shortcrust comes out tough and nasty. So that despite hankerings for suet pudding I have avoided the subject in this book, because I promised to describe nothing I couldn't guarantee.

I

SERVE IT RIGHT FOR
BEING SO DEAR

Mr. Squeers, we recall, asked for two'pennorth of milk and said 'Just fill that up with water, will you?'

'But the milk will be drownded,' protested the waiter.

Mr. Squeers' retort, tart, brief and unanswerable, should be taken to heart by all cooks. It is so easy to make a flashy menu up with expensive things, but people want to cook something cheap most of the time. Not just at the end of the month, either. The first meal that comes into my mind is not only cheap but one of my own favourites: *Shepherd's Pie.*

To me this means something made with mutton left-overs. Perhaps the name has become vague—some people speak of cottage pie. But in general people think of beef, I believe, and not left-overs but fresh meat: what the butcher calls mince. This is very vague—the butcher intends it to be so. He shoves all kinds of gristly scraps through his mincer, and what is more he uses the coarsest mesh, so that it comes out with nubbly bits, and lots of fat, which isn't at all nice.

In France this became such a scandal that everyone refused to eat it, and the law now says that the butcher must do the mincing in front of you and show you the meat he uses, as well as how much fat he is putting in. For a classic 'hamburger' mixture, such as is good for meat-balls, meat-loaf, or shepherd's pie, there should be 25% of clean suet and he should use the medium mesh. This sized mince, and this amount of fat, is needed to keep the mixture juicy and tender.

For four people I would take a pound, which is 500 grammes, and I base the other quantities I give on this amount.

Take a round heavy pot. Mine is enamelled cast-iron. This type can be heated very hot without burning, and that is what is needed. Put it on the fast flame, and in it a tablespoon of fat.

What fat? Oil, lard, butter, dripping, all have their uses. I never use marge, which is only vegetable oil emulsified, with custard-powder colour added, a butter-substitute for the poverty-time of the depression which now—thank heaven—has outlived its use. I would use beef dripping if I had any. Not butter, which burns when fiercely heated. The French would use vegetable oil, which heats well and does not smell nasty, and the Germans take schmaltz, which is rendered pork fat. Either is acceptable. Bacon fat would give a nice flavour, but it sputters rather and burns easily.

When it is really hot and beginning to smoke, put in the mince, a bit at a time, distributing to make it brown. Bad butchers have wet meat which spits. If such is your bad fortune hold the lid of the pot in your hand as a shield for your face, your apron, and the floor.

When the meat is really sizzling stir it a little with a wooden spoon, to brown it evenly. You have time to cut a large onion coarsely, the size of small lumps of sugar, and to dice two washed leeks (or one big one) the same size. Add these to the meat and stir: the meat should now be browning nicely and the vegetables should fry a little with it.

If the mixture seems wet and reluctant to brown, stir in a good teaspoonful of tomato purée from a tube; it will help the mixture to colour and give flavour.

When everything seems about to burn, lower the flame as far as possible—or pull the pot back. Stir in a good (slightly heaped) tablespoon of flour and let the mixture cook well through. Add enough water to make a slack sauce; it is not nice if thick and clawky. While it is coming up to the boil, season this sauce with salt, pepper, and a small branch of thyme.

Instead of plain water one can use wine and water: an ordinary wine glass of plain dry red plonk from Spain or Algeria. It gives extra flavour and colour. The essential point about using any wine in cooking is that it must cook for at least thirty minutes to evaporate and get rid of a vinegary flavour which would be nasty.

Once the sauce is seasoned and the right consistency, cover the pot and put it on a very slow fire, where it will just barely tick over.

Cut peeled potatoes to an even size, cover them in a saucepan with cold water, bring them rapidly to the boil, let them boil for a minute, and then put them back in the sink with a thread of cold water from the tap running on them. This gets rid of dirt and scum, whitens them, and makes them easier to cut. When they are cool drain them and cut them in slices one cm. thick, a bit less than half an inch.

Most people use mashed potatoes for shepherd's pie. It is nice, but I think that with mince it is a mistake. It gives the dish a bland pappy texture, over-soft and suitable for very small children. The sliced potatoes I describe are I think better.

By now the meat has had twenty minutes or so to simmer, enough to cook the sauce well out. Take it off the fire and let it settle. Some fat has been absorbed by the flour but if there was too much it will have melted and come to the surface; skim it off carefully and keep it in a cup. Now take the dish in which you serve the pie, ovenproof and oval or oblong. Grease the rim slightly. Pour in meat and the sauce; ideally the dish will now be about two-thirds full. Remember to use a wooden spoon; metal scratches enamel. The sauce will have reduced slightly, and is no longer sloppy. Taste it with your finger to see if the seasoning is right, remembering that the potatoes are unsalted, and absorb a good deal. The sliced potatoes will be arranged on top of the meat, overlapping like roof tiles. When they are all in take the cup in which you had kept the skimmed fat and brush the potatoes over with it, using a small paintbrush or pastry-brush.

The dish is put in a medium-fast oven, about halfway up so that it will get some top heat and brown prettily on the top. In thirty or forty minutes the potatoes will be tender and will have absorbed nice juices from the meat. Some cookery books insist on giving cooking times for meat: I find this absurd and misleading. Mince will be tender in a total of an hour or less, depending on how fresh the meat was. Ten minutes extra will not spoil this dish. If you allow a total of an hour and a quarter, you should be able to take the pie out of the oven and sit directly down to table.

There is no risk of failure with this dish, except that if the oven was too hot, or the dish itself filled too full, the sauce may boil over, making a nasty stain and a burning smell.

Since there are onions and leeks in the sauce an extra vegetable seems unnecessary, and since it is a solid filling dish one would not want to eat much to start with. Would it not be a good idea, and a compromise with the absent vegetables, to start this meal with a raw salad? Everything in shepherd's pie is cooked soft: it would make a good balance of texture and colour to have a salad of raw carrots or winter cabbage, or celery. It gives an extra vegetable too, is good for the teeth and does not make one fat. It only takes five minutes' work.

Grate a carrot, quarter a small white winter cabbage, or pick the flowers of a fresh cauli and blanch them five minutes in salted water—they must stay crisp. When you have cut away the cabbage-stalk it can be held flat and finely sliced into shreds with your big knife. These salads are flavoured with thin cream, or top-milk which is seasoned with salt and pepper and a few drops of lemon-juice. For cabbage add a pinch of fine sugar and a pinch of dry mustard.

A pinch is a saltspoonful, a very tiny quantity. A coffeespoon is double this. And a teaspoonful is double that.

After a meal of this sort one might like to eat milk pudding, or fruit, but I think cake or pastry or anything with butter would be too heavy. And with it a glass of red wine, because of the sauce and the onions.

Another cheap dish, but this time a French one instead, and like shepherd's pie a dish one can eat all the year round, is *Boiled Ham with different Purées*. Ham is dear, it will be remarked, but salt pork isn't, and salt pork is just as good as ham.

It is wet-salted, which is to say that the butcher throws it in a barrel with brine, and leaves it to pickle for a few days according to size. It comes out a beautiful clear pink, and the skin or fat is white. You choose a piece according to your liking. I find it most tender and juicy when the fat and the lean are marbled together, so I choose the breast, which when smoked becomes streaky bacon and when salt was known to my father bluntly as sow-belly.

One can have shoulder, rib, loin, or hindquarter—it is all ham, but the hindquarter, or gammon, takes too long in the brine barrel and is generally 'injected'. The brine-barrel pieces, generally cheap corners, are called in France 'petit-salé'.

It is cooked in a saucepan which is just large enough for the piece to swim in. Fill this two-thirds full with plain cold water, early in the morning, for this dish takes plenty of time, although there is little work involved. Season it with half a bayleaf, four peppercorns, two juniper berries and no salt. Do not put in wine or cider or anything else; this dish is very plain, tasting of nothing but itself. When the water boils slide the meat in and arrange the pot that the surface just quivers. Fit the lid on and forget it for an hour, which is about what a piece of sow-belly weighing 700 grammes or just under a pound and a half takes: this is enough for four to five people. Whatever the piece you take maybe you have time to make the beds, drink tea, and read the morning paper.

It is ready when you stab it with an ordinary fork and you notice that the fork slides effortlessly in and out. Any bones there are will detach readily from the meat. Put it on a plate to cool.

My father ate this dish with a very simple and delicious country vegetable he called pease-pudding, which is no more than a purée of dried split peas. It tastes lovely but is a bit clawky, which is why in France it is always varied with another kind of vegetable. Suppose you have mashed potatoes too—good, that makes two purées. The French add a third, and have a party dish, fit to serve to the Shah in Shah should he happen to turn up in time for lunch.

All these vegetables are cooked in the salted-pork stock, which is strained and divided among four small saucepans.

I would not dream of dictating to anyone what their choice should be nor how they should blend the flavours. This is strictly a matter of personal taste. I will offer a few possibilities.

Dried split peas. They take about an hour and a half before they become a true purée, and need frequent stirring on a very slow fire, or they burn.

Dried white, brown, pink or freckled beans. About the same time, but must be soaked the night before. Have often tough skins, difficult to get rid of.

Green flageolet or Lima beans. Much the same applies. Resist the temptation to use canned or deep-frozen substitutes. Quicker, but tasteless.

Potatoes. Cooked in the stock till very tender, drained, dried, mashed with walnut of butter.

Carrots, swede or kohlrabi turnips, yellow or white turnips (the white have a violet-tinged skin and the true bitter 'turnip' flavour). Thirty, forty or sixty minutes, depending on how old and how wintry they may be. Mash with a little stock for moisture.

Parsnips. These, also carrots and swedes, are slightly sugary. They combine very well with peas and dried beans.

Jerusalem artichokes. Have no sugar. Delicious, and good for diabetes. Very delicate, so be careful what you combine them with.

Apples. Ordinary cooking apples, cooked fluffy with a little butter in their own juice (no stock needed). Add perhaps a tiny pinch of powdered cinnamon.

Celery. The root variety called 'celeriac' like a round parsnip is best. Stalk celery is inclined to be stringy.

Onions. Large 'Spanish' onions, cut in quarters, braised slowly with a little stock till very tender.

'Soubise'. The same, with rice added and mashed together. Makes a firm purée with a very good flavour. A little tarragon can be added. When this is used, no potato is wanted.

'Dubarry'. Cauliflower instead of onion, otherwise like soubise.

Beetroot. Take pre-cooked peeled beetroot cut in quarters and simmered with a few drops of red-wine vinegar.

Salsifis. As Jerusalem artichokes.

Spinach. Braised in a buttered saucepan with no liquid at all. Has to be mashed mechanically, with a mincer or liquidizer.

All these vegetables have different cooking times and some are more difficult to reduce to purée than others. One could put them all on together, in four dear little pots, an hour before serving time, or one could cook them at any handy moment during the morning: a purée is not a difficult thing to keep warm or even reheat. A few drops of the cooking stock will moisten it if it seems unpleasantly dry. The more floury kinds, like potatoes or dried vegetables, can do with a hazelnut of butter added. When they are all ready, say a quarter of an hour before sitting down, they can be arranged in a shallow fire-proof dish, the salt pork is trimmed and sliced and arranged on top, moistened with a few drops of salt, and the dish with its lid on can then be heated well up before serving. Sprinkle the whole thing well with chopped parsley at the last moment, and serve it with a little stock in a sauceboat separately, horseradish, and Dijon mustard. Cider or beer would be good to drink with it. To start off, perhaps a good beef consommé, and perhaps for dessert a fruit tart.

Fanaticism about food is as disagreeable as it is anywhere else. People easily develop fads, begin to imagine that such-and-such does not agree with them, and launch into ardent proselytizing which quickly becomes boring. For normally constituted persons there are very few things which are at all indigestible, let alone harmful in any sense. Much of the success of a meal lies in choosing a nice balance. This dish is a good example: it would be foolish to have more than one floury vegetable. Carrots with dried peas make a pretty colour scheme; they also make the peas more digestible. Most diets are no more than the art of combining aliments to avoid an accumulation or exaggeration of one type, and it takes only a very small knowledge of chemistry and physiology to become skilful at this. To avoid the colour scheme—and chemical scheme—of what my father used to call 'Rhubarb, tomato and rhubarb' does not really require a great effort of the imagination. Yet there are people who will complain of the acidity in the tomato.

2

FRANÇOISE

How to Roast—Boulangère Potatoes—Gratin Dauphinois

A professional cook is formed by training. The discipline in old-fashioned kitchens was severe, and a young boy with no feeling whatever for food could in four or five years be turned out with a skill not perhaps ingrained but worked so thoroughly into his skin that he might never be a good cook but would always be a competent one. But the amateur cooks for love, because she enjoys it and has feeling for it. When we say that Mrs. Chose is a good cook we very rarely mean that she has been to one of these little *cordon-bleu* schools: we mean that she has a good instinct.

The style being catching, here is a sentence a paragraph long.

When, after setting out on that solitary swim across the entire ocean which is the first reading of Proust, we reach the first and most famous seamark, the episode in which he eats the *petite madeleine*, then we know at once that whatever else Proust may be —at the least he is the most acute and penetrating of prose fiction writers—he is going to tell us more about food than we ever dreamed exists, and sure enough within another thirty pages, or no more than a blink of his eye, we have reached a tropical island which is the richest tribute ever paid to the French countryside's genius for giving one an appetite, a character-sketch of genius which is Proust's own, and the best description I know in literature of a cook. The portrait of Françoise would do credit to Rembrandt, but that is irrelevant and anyway banal; my concern is with this one page of text (pp. 97-8 of the Gallimard edition) which is of high literary interest, being a good example of the poetic, evocative transparence and lucidity in these huge, sea-sounding sentences. These monolithic blocks of prose would be so extremely turgid in less nimble fingers, and the Literary Man is open-mouthed before this limp and languid person (so easy to confuse with Rimbauds and Beardsleys) showing himself an unequalled marathon athlete. But to a cook the page is much more: it is holy writ, a Song of

Solomon of food ... in which prosaic objects of nourishment reflect the unchanging beauty of the French countryside, and resound with the sonorities of those huge horizons. Illiers (it is called Illiers-Combray now) is not far from Chartres and the landscapes share the flat immensity of la Beauce with the livelier air of the uplands. Fruit, flowers, herbs and vegetables have the scent and savour of the country markets a hundred years ago, which still lingers in rural France and promises us the best and simplest food there is. The very weeds around Combray are fragrant, so that we bless this most olfactorily sensitive of writers.

In the dual quality of cook and Mister Gigadibs the literary man I set to with relish to translate this page, a gargantuan task which left me ready to eat the whole of that turbot, that turkey, that leg of lamb, for the fresh air of Proust hollows one out so, and gives such an appetite! The effort left me with respect for Mr. Scott-Moncrieff's magisterial labour.

Unfortunately, as my publisher was to tell me, sharp quillets of copyright made it impossible to print my effort, of which I was somewhat vain, so that I was vexed. I could, he said, by the kindness of the English publishers quote the page in Mr. S-M's translation but I did not feel much like this; it seemed like cheating. I invite anyone who feels like it to read pp. 93-4 of the English edition and I think they will agree: these no longer smell of the hawthorn blossoms Proust so loved, but of bibliophiles become a little dusty, a trifle musty, an ossuary of Combray. Neither the leg-of-mutton to be eaten after one of those tremendous country walks, the Swann way or if the weather were really settled the Guermantes way; nor Françoise who cooked it with her incomparable feeling for the countryside and its produce, reflect here more than a prim and somewhat desiccated pedantry: they do not give us the same appetite. The 'raspberries Monsieur Swann brought specially' have come by dusty ways; Gower Street as it were. . . .

My favourite of all the examples from Françoise's repertoire is the *gigot-parce-que-le-grand-air-creuse*. Perhaps this is because I live in the Vosges, splendid land for fruit but not really sheep country: our *gigot* (the Scotch call it a jiggot) comes from the Alps, and that ought to awaken a Southdown echo in an English heart. It is very expensive, so that we keep it for feasts as a rule; this rarity and expense, vague feeling about that dam' gigot being worth its weight in gold, make of it a thing to be approached with deep respect and as it were a beating heart. But Françoise was such a good cook because she approached everything with respect, and dignity, and simplicity. There were more like her; Osbert Sitwell had such a cook, called Mrs. Powell, and speaks of her in his memoirs. Nowadays we have lost our respect for food, the moment's recall of the work and the love which a piece of bread has cost, and we view food with awe only when it is dear, which shows our snobbery and base materialism. It is true that neither Françoise nor Mrs. Powell would have had a great opinion of the sodden and insipid fishfinger world in which we find ourselves.

When I am in the kitchen with a leg of lamb the truth of an old cliché hits me—cooks are trained but a *rôtisseur* is born. Anyone can cook a simple thing like a chicken but to roast a joint . . . it is the one thing above all for which one cannot give rules. All that stuff about twenty minutes to the pound is the crudest of guides by thumb: how large is the oven, how thick the metal, what is the distribution of heat like? You can be a born roaster but nothing will replace experience of your own range. And this is why I began with Proust, and why the *gigot* is dedicated to Françoise. When roasting, the cook needs training and experience, but above all sensitivity. Physical to be sure; the ear alert to the crackle and mutter of the oven, the eye to any sign of precocious shrinkage or hardening, the nose to any acridity of flavour. And an inner sensitivity: the good roast cook is the person who can look at and see that lovely chrysanthemum, that startling cloudscape, and, like Mrs. Powell, 'a really beautiful turbot; I wish you could have seen it.'

I have some of this—a writer without a share would be very poorly equipped—but even as a cook in constant practice, and constant practice is another essential, I was never more than a fair roaster. Is it affection that is missing, such as Mrs. Powell felt for the turbot? This seems contradicted, if not by Françoise's cruelty to the kitchen-maid, by her ferocity in killing a chicken. Perhaps some country blood is needed, an ancestor who has spent a lifetime among beasts and has the 'feeling for meat' so very few butchers have.

One must remember, too, that in Proust's day, and indeed much later, up to 1939, cooks whether professional or not had single-mindedness and concentration. Nowadays a ballet dancer will whip you up a soufflé while the cook is displaying his talent for social climbing on television and we are all hindered in the practice of any craft by haste, restlessness, discontent, gadgetry, and envy. We forget that not long ago the working-class housewife with no servant was in her own kitchen very often an excellent cook. Narrow perhaps she was in ambition and achievement, but she could roast a joint! Whereas now, even given a cooker with a thermostat, remote time control, an infra-red grill, an automatic turnspit and a self-cleaning oven—gallimaufry of modern tech-notautology—she 'has no time for all that messing about'. It is not her fault; she is divorced from her kitchen.

In winter we roast on our big wood-burning range. One has to know its little ways. The gas stove is easier but the result in no way better. I have tried electric '*rôtissoires*' from time to time but never been seriously tempted. The skilful publicity—visions of beefy medieval barons eating barons of medieval beef, of a little electronic man in a glitter of chrome, doing all the work in a cockpit full of dials—is seductive, but I have not been able to convince myself that one really gains anything. Roasting in the oven is sneered at by the precious, but like digging one's own garden or sharpening one's own pencil it is a satisfying, rewarding task.

The first enemy of a good roast is the butcher, who does not know how to bone or cut meat, and increases his profits by leaving on the sinews. He tried to impress you with a great deal of elegantly entwined string and—shall I tell you?—a proper joint needs no string. A lot of string means a lot of sinew, when it does not mean a detestable rolled roast, like a boned loin, a thing suitable for a cheap hotel. A proper roast has bones on it, which protect the meat and give flavour.

But even a bad butcher cannot do much to spoil a leg of lamb, beyond, of course, giving it to you much too fresh. He cuts it off and cannot mess it about. There are only three bones and he leaves them alone from laziness, thank heaven. The shank, or shin-bone, joins on to the thick thigh-bone in a nice round joint; they run through the centre of the meat, hold it in shape, and are no trouble to anybody. The propellor or rotary pelvic bone at the thick end joins at the middle to the thigh-bone in a simple ball-and-socket joint, and is easy to cut out neatly after the cooking, when it goes in the gravy with the sawed-off shank. This shank is joined to the meat by a thick ligament which runs alongside the bone; it is easily cut through, and there is virtually no other thick sinew in a leg of lamb. At the corner of the thick end there is rather too much heavy fat (except, of course, in real spring lamb) and this is cut out, together with the small gland the size of a hazelnut which it encloses. The layer of fat surrounding the meat is left alone; the tough transparent membrane at the outside is peeled away, and the fat itself scored across diagonally, four or five times each way making a diamond pattern on the fat, and that is all.

The seasoning comes next. Lamb—one uses the word now in a general sense because real full-grown mutton is now hardly seen—is a strongly flavoured meat. It can be coarse, and even rank when of poor quality. This robust flavour can support strongly-perfumed spices, and co-exist with them happily. For example, it is very good in curry. Nor have we forgotten Kipling's excited exclamation about the cinnamon stew. But leaving aside these oriental delights, nearer home anyone who likes garlic can have an orgy hereabouts. Garlic in the *gigot* is so classic as to be banal, but it is unfailingly delicious. Very simply done; a goodsized clove of peeled garlic is cut lengthwise into six or eight 'nails'. At intervals across the meat and especially the thick end, make narrow deep incisions with the tip of a vegetable knife and push the nails well in. The roasting will close these tiny gaps, leaving the garlic embedded in the meat, which it will flavour admirably. Garlic cannot be left outside; it burns very easily. The often-recommended rubbing of the surface with a cut clove is a waste of time with a thick piece like a *gigot*: one does this with little chops before grilling them.

One of the nice things too about garlic is that a strong-smelling herb can be used with it, and without any clash. But One herb. My love for Nero Wolfe, most characterful—and delightful—of all private detectives, is surpassed by no one, but he is an awful cook! There is a notable moment in the canon when Nero, plus a whole gang of gastrologers, is busy tasting a most nauseating con-coction of—I quote textually—celery, cayenne, pepper, chervil, tarragon, thyme, parsley, chives and shallots—and the author of this amalgam gets, one is mightily relieved to note, a knife stuck in him. This medieval abracadabra is of course just Nero being upstage, an art in which he has no peer. It is based on the theory of secret recipes, magic formulae, love-philtres and the philoso-pher's stone. There are no secret recipes, except for Coca-Cola. There is, to be sure, the art of the blender, of coffee, tea, cognac, non-vintage champagne and the like, which is a skilful balance of his standard ingredients with regard to their seasonal variables to achieve a 'house flavour'. Similarly, commercial *apéritifs*, vermouth and the like, use a blend of herbs varying with the type of wine they use.

But the art of the cook is different. He tastes too many different things, with disparate and often violent flavours, to be bothered with such subtle alchemies. He uses two or three local ingredients at a time, and the local water, and this is quite enough to give the subtle regional flavour. Why are there so many different kinds of cheese in France, when a cow, a sheep, a goat are much the same anywhere? The answer is in a local micro-climate and the local soil-chemistry. Such recipes cannot travel, either to Nero's house or anywhere else, and the cook makes no secret of the ingredients.

There is as well a simple reason why one does not use herbs and spices in great numbers together; it is the same reason why the painter does not mix several colours on his palette. The result in both cases would be mud. Mix several ingredients of any sort together, anywhere: they will cancel each other out. The cook, like the painter, knows the elementary rules of contrasting and complementary flavours—or colours; the science of adding white for a tint and black for a tone; and both types of craftsmen tend to simplify rather than to complicate as they grow in skill.

I do not know what Françoise put with her leg of lamb. It should be easy to find out, since Combray is a real town and there will still be old women alive who cook in the same style; the local products, even if vitiated by chemical fertilizers, will not have changed since Proust's day. She would certainly have used one or other of the *aromates*—thyme, rosemary or marjoram—which grow easily in a garden, for we may be sure she would have had little use for the commercially dried and powdered herbs we are too often forced to use. She would certainly sometimes have used a *persillade*, a thickly-sprinkled mixture of parsley chopped with chives or chervil, which is added at the last minute.

There are a hundred regional variants, many so successful that they have become classic, but these can be found in other cookery books. To me there is nothing better than a simple roast. There are very few rules to it, and those exceedingly simple: a roasting fire should be really hot at the start and allowed to die down progressively. Spring lamb like veal must be well cooked; older lamb should be pink, not *saignant* like beef, but all the meat should have a rosy tint. A leg weighing two kilos, or between four and five pounds, will take an hour and a half in the oven. It should be well basted at the start, and every half-hour. It should be started round-side downward, not touching the metal but resting on the bones and a few pieces of carrot and onion coarsely sliced. Half-way through it is turned on to its flat side. The first half-hour's cooking should be quite fierce, to seal the meat well in, but the last hour should be gentle, so that the heat goes through to the bone but without drying or darkening. And that is quite enough of the word 'should'.

Boulangère potatoes are splendid with roast lamb. They are very easy if one possesses an oven with an electric turnspit. Have ready potatoes which have been sliced fairly fine—one centimetre thickness—and well mixed with raw onions sliced thinner, the whole seasoned with salt and pepper.

When you open your oven to baste the meat for the first time, after half an hour, the drip tray below the spit will have become 'lined' with roasting fat. Fill it with the potato mixture and leave it under the meat where it will receive any drips of juice. Whenever you would have turned the meat if you had no spit, turn the tray round, so that it cooks and browns evenly. When the meat is ready the potatoes will probably be ready too, but if they are not quite done they can be left another ten to fifteen minutes, for a roast needs that amount of time anyway to rest, before it is carved.

If you have no spit, or if you dislike the greasy effect of potatoes done in the drip tray, then do the meat in a pot or on a tray, and make a *dauphinois gratin* instead. The potatoes are sliced as for *boulangère*, but without onion. They are put in a buttered fireproof dish, quite wide and shallow, and just enough milk to cover them, mixed with an egg well beaten up, is poured over. This is cooked in the oven with the meat as described.

Almost any green vegetable goes well with this, or of course salad. Instead of salad I think I should like an artichoke with vinaigrette to begin with, and fresh runner beans, or French beans, with the roast. Or a tomato soup and then a lettuce salad after the roast. And then fruit, fresh or stewed. It is not a heavy meal, and one could well have a splendid pud, but the oven is in use, so it would need to be cake or something made beforehand.

I should want to drink Beaujolais out of a jug, or any light red wine from the Côte d'Or district.

I haven't mentioned mint sauce. I love mint sauce, but not when it is made with English chemical vinegar. It tends to be overwhelming, but is of course famous for being delicious with fresh summer peas, if one were lucky enough to have any.

3

A DAM' ROTTEN TEA, MY DEAR

Jessie Conrad was an admirable woman, with no great gifts of brain or beauty but stable, patient, sensitive, and with a highly developed sense of the ludicrous. Perfect wife for a man with an exaggeratedly nervous temperament as well as high literary talent. She was also an excellent cook. Sometimes when there had been a large dinner, and there would shortly be a lavish supper, Jessie's common sense would decide that there was no need of tea —that delicious meal which is so much the nicest of English meals (nobody minds a bad lunch, and perhaps a worse supper, when tea comes in between).

Being Polish as well as living in Kent, Joseph Conrad particularly enjoyed tea, and when his greedy appetite was put on a leash by naughty Jessie's deciding that today bread-and-butter would do nicely he used to mutter venomously at her, and always in the phrase quoted at the head of this chapter: Jessie herself tells the story gleefully.

It has become a classic in my house, rapped out with great severity when my wife has an economy drive, or perhaps could not be bothered; it is hard to tell. Joseph of course was utterly convinced that nothing but Jessie's dam' idleness was responsible for the rotten tea. Inevitably too my wife says it to inflated head waiters in bad French restaurants: they retire perplexed behind pillars, in a dudgeon. '*Qu'est-ce-qu'elle a, cette bonne femme-là qui rouspète en chinois?*' And inevitably it is used for meals in Holland, that extraordinary country where they give you deep-freeze chicken, roast with lots and lots of marge and served with tinned fruit-salad. Being Dutch, my wife is sarcastic about Dutch kitchens.

So of course was Arlette van der Valk, who suffered from Dutch kitchens but to do her justice was alive to the many virtues of Holland as well as obstinately loyal to her tiresome Dutch husband, who complained about Holland all day but was perfectly happy. Being French Arlette never did learn how to make tea; she thought it was tisane and used those awful paper bags, and this was a secret grievance of his, but there, she did make proper coffee. And coming as she did from the south she took with enthusiasm to hearty wintry northern dishes, like Belgian stewed steak with beer ('*carbonades au lambic*') and above all to pea soup, which used to be the Dutch national dish till that became chips with tinned apple sauce. Arlette dated the decadence of Holland from that moment.

The recipe, then, is not truly Dutch. My wife says that there are several details wrong and that she, for instance, uses no onions. Arlette does have a tendency to exaggerate onions; she also puts in a carrot, which is completely wrong. This is partly a vague French notion that carrots always should go with dried peas, partly because the colour is attractive, and partly, too, to annoy the greengrocer, a young man with an inflated notion of his importance. He had trouble too with the letter 'r', which sometimes awoused dewision. This was not his fault, but he would lay down the law so. Arlette, shopping for her pea soup, had said 'and throw in a few carrots': he remarked pompously that one didn't put cawwots in pea soup.

'Well, I do,' she said crossly 'and if you weren't a wotten gweengwocer you'd be glad of it.' There were sniggers, and thereafter he hid in the back pretending to be busy when she came in. His father, an elderly gentleman with the good old Dutch habit of always having a huge pale cigar in his mouth, was a much better business man and seduced her with cunning phrases like 'Real biological potatoes, Mevrouw'.

The carrot then is not essential, nor is the onion. Two large leeks are, though, and a big celery root of over a pound. A pound of dried split peas. This is all for four persons, and will be generous. A piece of smoked streaky bacon, about a pound. Half a pound of smoked but not dried sausages. Beef bones for stock. A packet of pumpernickel, the coarse black rye bread which comes ready-sliced in cellophane.

To be at its best this dish takes a long time. It is no great trouble but does properly belong to the 'three-days-ahead' category. At this rhythm, there is only an hour's work in all and one has plenty of time for other kitchen chores.

On the first day: put the bones in a large heavy pot with plenty of cold water. Bring to the boil and skim well to get a clean stock. Add six peppercorns, three cloves, a bayleaf, a small branch of thyme and any parsley stalks you may have, for a nicely flavoured beef stock, exactly as though next day you were going to make consommé. Simmer gently for three to four hours, take off the stove and allow to cool.

Second day: strain the stock, throw out the bones and herbs, put the cold stock back in the pot with the peas. Bring to the boil and skim again thoroughly. Add the bacon. Arrange the pot on a very gentle fire so that it just barely ticks over, and leave for two hours or till the bacon is very tender when pricked with a fork, and the peas have become quite liquid.

During the last hour, the soup must be thoroughly stirred three or four times with a wooden spoon, because the peas have a tendency to settle at the bottom and stick. Lift the bacon out on to a plate and let it go cold. Take the pot off the stove and allow the soup to cool in it.

One could eat the soup this day, but dried peas, while they need no soaking before they are cooked, do improve very much by being left overnight after they are cooked. But fresh vegetables cannot be left in this way, so are left till the last day.

Third day: the soup is set to jelly, with an opaque layer of *purée* below. Put it to warm up on a gentle fire, stirring it from time to time. Meanwhile the vegetables can be prepared. If after climbing back to boiling point the soup seems unpleasantly inclined to stick, or overthick and heavy, add enough boiling water to correct it. There is a legend that this soup should be thick enough for the spoon to stand up: on the contrary, it should be fairly light.

As the vegetables are cleaned and prepared they can be added. The celery root goes in whole, and the other vegetables fairly coarse—half an inch long, one or two centimetres according to taste. The reason is that this soup is a meal in itself, containing meat, vegetables, and carbohydrate roughage, and is treated as such. The Germans call such a dish *Eintopf* or Single-Pot.

Arlette hereabouts added four cloves of unpeeled garlic and a large pinch of chervil or marjoram. This again is a matter of taste, and I would not like to be dogmatic about such things. Some people like cold consommé set to a jelly as solid as aspic: others think Buckingham Palace a handsome building. One must beware of becoming like the gweengwocer.

Allow a final cooking time of around an hour and a half. When the celery feels tender (but not soft) when tested with a fork lift it out and put it on a board to cool. Twenty minutes before serving time the sausages are put in to poach gently. During this time peel the cold cooked bacon carefully, trimming the rinds, the surplus of fat, and the small round bones. Slice it thinly lengthways. Then cut the celery in half and slice that too, rather thicker. Now spread each slice of pumpernickel generously with mild mustard, add a slice of ham, and celery on top. These sandwiches are arranged on a plate to be served with the soup.

It happens sometimes in England that root celery is unobtainable and this is a pity; it is more delicate than the stalk variety which also tends to be stringy. If I had only stalks I would slice and cook them with the leeks, but I would regret the celery sandwich deeply, for it is superb.

The sausages are taken out after ten or fifteen minutes, according to their size, sliced and put back into the soup so that they can be eaten with a spoon. It happens that smoked sausages have a tough skin, which has to be peeled when they are cooked. Very irritating of them; it applies mostly to the big ones five centimetres across in thickness. Since there are innumerable kinds, from Poland, Hungary or where you like, it depends on what the pork-butcher or delicatessen has to offer.

The soup is served just as it comes, from its own kitchen pot, for this is a peasant dish. If a tureen is used it must be a type that can be kept hot: this is a meal, people want second helpings, and third ones too. The soup is better in a large shallow soup-plate than in a bowl. The sandwiches are handed round to go with it. In France one makes 'soldiers' of fried diced bread to go with pea soup. The 'celery sandwich' is a variation specifically Dutch, and to my mind it is unbeatable.

When I said that this was a meal in itself I meant that quite literally. These tremendously filling solid peasant dishes need nothing before or after except salad, which ought to be something crisp and crunchy for a change in texture, like iceberg or cos lettuce, or endive, with something pungent in the dressing, like tarragon, or mustard, or Roquefort. For dessert too something tart and crunchy, like an apple turnover.

To drink with this meal there is nothing better than a dry fruity white wine, like a Riesling, and water is all right too. Beer spoils the flavour.

This is above all a winter dish, best of all on a day of iron-hard and biting cold when one's breath is as thick as the soup and nose and feet feel as if they belonged to someone else. Skaters' weather. It is a Dutch dish and skating is a Dutch sport. Think of canals, and of all the Brueghel pictures with names like 'Diversions on the ice at Antwerp'. All the Dutch skate, and they can best be studied wearing pointed balaclava helmets, hands clasped behind their back, head down in an attitude of meditation, moving with slow long swings to the harsh metallic rhythm of the skates, a drummer using wire brushes, all the way from Leiden to Haarlem facing into the steely red disk of sun. To watch these hieratic, hypnotic movements is compelling, and, to any Dutch person of whatever age, sex or waistline, the action is as fulfilling as fox-hunting.

Eating pea-soup—it really sticks to the ribs—one is transported in imagination to this scene. When my wife was a little girl in Zandvoort, a seaside village with no canals, and the winter was hard, the fire brigade played their hoses on the football field until a skating-rink formed by itself, and one stood on the edge of the ice without taking off one's skates (fingers too cold anyhow) and slurped pea soup which old women sold in the street. In Friesian villages I feel sure they still do. When there has been a real freeze lasting a fortnight or more, there are icelinks by canal between eleven towns in Friesland and Groningen, and the Elf-Steden-Tocht is run, a race open to all and really amateur: one sees old gentlemen of seventy with crackly layers of newspaper under their sweaters, secret recipes of dynamite in the pea-soup, and five pairs of socks; and it goes on all day, much like the Vasa ski-race in Sweden.

It is nice to imagine all this; it is also nice to sit and read the Sunday papers, with a pleasurable belch at intervals.

There are other good dishes of the sort in Holland and Arlette became attached to a variation on her familiar *boeuf au gros sel* called Leiden Stamp-Pot. The legend is that the Spaniards raised the siege of Leiden in the sixteenth century with mysterious haste, and the puzzled Dutch crept out very cautiously, suspecting a trap, and (being starving) to see whether anything could be picked up in the eatable line—more sensible than modern Dutch tourists who are so frightened of Spanish food that they take tinned applesauce with them all the way to Granada. Myth has it that in the Spanish lines they found carrots, onions and potatoes, and created Leidse Pot straight away. Arlette viewed this tale with scepticism, saying that she'd have eaten the carrots raw if she'd been that hungry. It is a fact that this stew takes all day, but the Spaniards had perhaps left no horse behind.

We will take a piece of boiling beef, ideally 'flat rib' with alternate layers of meat and fat, which keeps the meat juicy. It is the identical cut to pork streaky, coming between the rib and the breast.

In a pot large enough for the meat (750 gr., a generous pound and a half for four people, or more if it has not been boned) to swim in, put cold water, a tablespoon of coarse salt, a few peppercorns and the usual pot herbs, parsley-stalks, a bayleaf, a tiny branch of thyme, and bring to the boil. Put in the meat and a marrow-bone, exactly as for *pot au feu*, turn the heat right down, and poach the meat very gently for two to three hours until perfectly tender. Take the pot off and let the meat cool in the stock. If left overnight this stock will jell.

Two hours before you wish to eat, lift out the meat and remove the pot herbs. Remove the marrow carefully, keeping it on a saucer. In two different saucepans have a pound-and-a-half (750 gr.) of carrots and onions peeled, coarsely cut, and mixed in equal proportion, and a similar quantity of potatoes. Cook these in the stock till quite tender; coarse or old winter carrots take up to an hour. When done, drain them all carefully—keeping whatever stock is still left—and smash them to *purée*, which need not be excessively fine. Using the pot in which the meat was cooked, mix smoothly together with a wooden spoon. If it seems dry add a little stock. It may need a little more salt. Keep this mixture warm on the corner of the stove while you trim and slice the beef.

You need now a shallow fireproof *gratin* dish, big enough to hold all this. Fill it two-thirds full of *purée*, arrange the slices of meat all over the surface, and over that the sliced marrow. Top up the dish with the remaining *purée*. Sprinkle it with brown breadcrumb, and a few dots of butter. Brown the dish until it is crisp on top, in a hot oven or under a grill. Strew it when ready with chopped parsley and eat it like any boiled beef dish with horseradish, and if you keep the salt to a minimum when cooking, with coarse salt served separately.

This is another substantial peasant dish, and to start with the best thing is *antipasto*; perhaps anchovies with a salad of sliced green peppers, or very thin raw ham with salad, or raw mushrooms, and to end with I should think cheese rather than pud. A glass of red Bordeaux would go well with all this.

Afterwards, definitely, the brisk stroll is indicated, and in the country—for these are really country dishes—one would botanize, geologize, or meteorologize.

Coming back from which we will be much dashed to be given 'a dam' rotten tea, my dear, a dam' rotten tea.'

4

WHERE THE FISH IS
TURNED OVER

Bouillabaisse (fish stew)—Rouille

Banquets are ghastly things. Of all the numerous ways society
has invented of eating dinner, the 'banquet' is surely the most
uncivilized. Only the most rustic and unselfconscious of family
feasts are supportable. The wedding feast at Cana sounds enjoyable
enough, but only after a great deal of vino, and there were strained
moments as well as a few snappish remarks. The prototype of the
family feast has been of course described better by Mr. Polly
than by anyone else: they are all so constrained that even Uncle
Penstemon, as uninhibited a figure as one could hope to find, felt
it necessary to explain his little gastric difficulties.

'This sherry rises—grocer's stuff I expect.' If everyone is on
their best behaviour all enjoyment is swamped. It was by climbing
without demur into a carriage ahead of Louis XIV that the Duke of
Portland earned his reputation as the politest man in Europe.
In other words by his unaffected simplicity: few can say as much.
Even now when one is invited out in France it is the magic
phrase 'in all simplicity' that tells us we are expected to enjoy
ourselves.

Large banquets are much worse, if only because people are
more strange to each other, and feel bound to be on their best,
meaning most strained and anxious, behaviour. But the worst of
such occasions is that the food is always so horrible.

'Go to all the dinners, but eat none of the food' is the advice of
an experienced politician. The explanations are easy to find. Even
if the kitchen is good, and it very seldom is in places which accept
'banquets', the food is detestable by definition. The cooks are
bored, the menu is a lowest common denominator chosen to
please everyone, in other words revolting, and the food has been
kept simmering in a steam cupboard while everybody trickles to
his place—oh those limp slips of meat sweating in a warm, wet,
woolly dressing-gown. . . .

The worst of all banquets are formal receptions at the Elysée Palace, where the food is as diplomatic as the guests and even a Château Margaux of a fine year comes out undrinkable. I have never been, of course, because I have no decorations, as those bits of watered-silk ribbon are so unaccountably known, but a Frenchman—Talleyrand, very likely—who had suffered frequently said a lapidary word upon the subject. 'The thing is, to sit where the fish is turned over.'

He meant of course that the placing is dictated by protocol, so that you have very little chance of being near anyone you know or like, and that the food is awful anywhere, but better for those lowly placed. This is because the formal fish dishes which appear at these dinners, *Turbot Amiral* or *Barbue Cambacérès* are cooked whole, and at a certain point in the service the waiter will 'turn the fish over'. Since the juice of the fish drips from the backbone into the fillets below, the helpings served from this point on may look messier and less grand but they will have a lot more flavour. Fish—or meat—cut into fillets and cooked without bones will always be dry and tasteless even when of good quality: lacking the essential juice—what in English is called gravy, odd and meaningless word; etymology dubious, as the dictionary tactfully puts it.

Suppose now that instead of that frightful dinner one wanted to give a party which really would be a party, conspicuous for simplicity, enjoyment, and something nice to eat. Suppose that one grouped six people; impossible to group more than six people without affectation creeping in. And suppose finally that one were to give them fish that didn't need to be turned over but that had a bit of juice in it. The answer to all these conditions would be *bouillabaisse*.

The affected hostess, preoccupied with imitation manners and anxious to show off, is sunk straight away. Mr. Betjeman's celebrated rhyme about 'Send for the fish-knives, Norman' comes instantly to mind: the poor woman, chained and weighted by fingerbowls and dainty napery, hardly had time for one glug-glug. Any guests worried about what-to-do-with-the-bones will suffer the same fate.

Of course this dish presents problems. The chief one, contrary to expectation, is not how to find the fish, (one of the cookery experts whose columns I read with sadistic enjoyment says in despair that one must be rich enough to have it specially flown in from the Mediterranean) but how to find a suitable pot. Mothers with small children are not the only ones to have a pot problem, even if we agree to exclude the narcotics squad.

One can get special pots to cook fish; narrow *saumonières* and diamond-shaped *turbotières*—they are expensive and few people have them. But plenty of people including me have a large pot in which they cook jam, spinach, or other things which take up a lot of space. It must be big, holding ten litres (a litre is about a quart) because everything is cooked together: the soup, the vegetables, and the fish of which there must be plenty, of several sorts, and whole, including heads, fins and all sorts of limbs which take up a great deal of space. There will be lots of bones. . . .

This is indispensable. Without all this rubbish there will be no juice, no soup, and no flavour, and that is what counts in *bouilla-baisse*: the actual fish is of less importance, much of it is poor quality, and as they say on the coast 'only Parisians are stupid enough to eat it'. Without lots of bones one would be reduced to the flat stones, covered in seaweed, of coast myth. . . .

Choosing this fish is not difficult at all, because luckily there are a great many different kinds of fish, but there are three important conditions which limit one considerably. The first is to have types with firm flesh. The handiest translation of *bouillabaisse*, a romantic but awkward nomenclature, is 'fish stew' but a stew is simmered and this dish is boiled at a gallop. Some fish, nice but fragile like haddock or whiting, would simply disintegrate: plaice and lemon sole are flat little things full of bone into the bargain.

Second condition is no fresh-water fish. This dish should taste of the sea. There exists a very good fresh-water fish stew—several in fact—but this is not one of them. As a witty English person remarked 'Ye cannot serve both Cod and Salmon.'

The third condition is to avoid greasy fish with a strong flavour. Tuna or swordfish, mackerel or herring will spoil this meal. So we are going to choose round or thick, firm-fleshed sea fish. They can be as expensive as you please. One can spend a great deal of money: one can also spend surprisingly little. To speak of twelve different kinds is pedantic idiocy. Six is plenty; in fact the simplest way to go about this is to take three broad types and choose two varieties of each. You can always throw in a few decorative whatnots at the end if you please.

First: a large, thick fish of the type one cuts into steaks—hake, brill and turbot are dear, cod and conger-eel cheap. This type gives everyone a good chunk of boneless fish.

Second: a nice medium-sized fish to cook whole. Red mullet and real sea bass are superb but dear. Grey mullet, gurnet, gurnard, a whole shoal of vaguely-named kinds of dogfish, various weird appellations like 'rock-salmon' are cheap, very often delicious, and at the worst make splendid soup.

Third: shellfish—one can use absolutely anything. Lobster and crayfish are dear; crabs, mussels, scallops much less so. You can use prawns, cockles, sea-urchins, even deep-freeze scampi if there is nothing else ... The only exception is oysters, which when cooked shrivel to tough tiny scraps.

Any undersized and therefore cheap fish can be thrown in for fantasy, colour and variety as well as flavour.

The fish must be cleaned (except red mullet and tiny sardine-sized things) and where necessary scaled. The fishmonger will do this, but must be stopped from cutting off heads or tidying fins and tails. Choosing the fish is a most enjoyable chore: go early in the morning. There will be the most choice, fewer people, and everything will be freshest. Do not be afraid of ugly or odd-looking fish; some of the best are perfectly hideous.

Having got your pot (it must have a tight-fitting lid) and borne home your fish your troubles should be at an end, for the cooking of this dish is very simple and takes only half an hour, but there is still one essential ingredient which can cause difficulty. This is saffron. The herb factories sell it ground to a fine powder, in idiotic little plastic capsules. So handled it goes stale immediately and loses all its flavour. It should be bought whole, when it looks like a tuft of rusty wire wool. It can be got from herbalists, rare birds, alas, in England, and perhaps from speciality shops. It is worth taking trouble over saffron. When found it will be exceedingly expensive, but it is very economical indeed in use; a minuscule pinch is enough. Bought like this, put in a tiny plastic bag and kept in a screw-top jar, it will keep a year.

The remaining ingredients are very simple. For each person you want a fair-sized potato, a large ripe tomato—if over-ripe and squashy so much the better—a smallish onion (or half a big one) and a plump clove of garlic, peeled. And about three decilitres or a good halfpint of olive oil. Coarse sea-salt, a pinch of paprika, a pinch of cayenne, half a lemon.

You need no herbs whatever of any description except a little chopped parsley to sprinkle over at the end.

When one has guests one does not want troublesome food. This dish suits these conditions nicely. There is half an hour's work in all; your presence is needed for five minutes at the start, and five minutes at the end. There are two little extra jobs which can be done a long time in advance. One is to peel the vegetables, and the other is to make the mayonnaise. The onions are cut in small dice —say in eight. The tomatoes in four. Potatoes in coarse dice— ten or twelve. Garlic left whole.

The mayonnaise is called *rouille* which means rust, from its colour. You need a sauceboat full: one egg, half your oil (quarter of a pint) the half-lemon, a little salt and dry mustard, a very small pinch of cayenne for the kick, and the same of paprika for colour. The sauce should be stiff.

When these jobs have been done, you need do no cooking until your guests are settled with drinks. Having had a good drink yourself you put your big pot on a fast flame, and throw in all the oil you have left—it must be real olive oil. It may seem a lot, a quarter pint, but will be completely absorbed; your soup will not be greasy. When it is really hot, almost smoking, put in the fish, one after another, to sear. When all is sizzling add the onions, put the lid on, and grasping the pot with both hands give it a good shake, to settle and distribute the contents. Lift the lid, and throw

4

in the potatoes, the tomatoes, the garlic, the saffron, and a table-spoon of sea salt. Replace the lid at once and give the pot another good shake. In about a minute you will hear a fierce bubbling begin; now reduce the flame enough to keep the contents bubbling without burning; if the fire is too hot an unlucky piece of fish might catch, and the liquid might evaporate too much.

In general, no liquid is added; the juice is enough to make a generous soup. After five minutes boiling take a cautious peep inside. If the contents are not yet submerged add a little boiling water, enough to 'swim' any bits and pieces not covered by the rising tide. Unlike most fish dishes this one does not poach; it gallops. This may break more fragile fish but only the rapid boil will really 'pull' the juice from the heads and bones, emulsify the oil, which with the potato-flour will thicken the soup slightly, and disintegrate the tomatoes. The whole thing needs a good fifteen minutes cooking, and will take no harm from twenty, for thick pieces, or a whole lobster.

When you come to serve you need a soup tureen, and a large flat serving dish or platter, round or oval. Call your guests first and serve only when they are all sitting, ideally at a round table, because the dish is put in the middle, and then it's every man for himself. Take the pot in both hands, and with a dishcloth hold the lid open just enough to drain the liquid off, just as it is, for the soup. The fish and vegetables are now arranged roughly and rapidly on the dish, in a pyramid. The colour is reddish from the fish and the tomato, and golden from the saffron: very nice.

It is too hot and fragile to decorate or arrange. Pay no heed at all to horrible faces staring out, dreadful eyes, fins sticking up at weird angles and the generally dishevelled look—this is as it should be, and half the fun. This is not 'polite' fish, and needs no turning over.

The table arrangement is very simple. The soup is served simultaneously with the fish, so everyone gets a soupbowl, a large plate, and a salad-plate for bones and débris, of which there is a great deal. There are of course no fish-knives. Everyone gets a spoon and fork, to help themselves with, and to eat with in any order one pleases. The *rouille* is handed round with bread. Exactly as with pea soup this is an *Eintopf*, a big dish, filling and satisfying, and nothing else is needed, except perhaps a nice piece of Brie and a tart to finish up.

A lobster or langouste is best left to a man to deal with. Break its tail away from the armour, and put it on a chopping board at a side table. The tail, shell and all, can then be cut crossways into five or six medallions with a butcher's knife. The claws are left as perks to the man who does this and doesn't mind getting his hands fishy.

To drink one has plain plonk, white or pink, dry and a bit flinty. Tradition dictates a Côte de Provence or a Côte de Rhône, and the Cassis district is thought of as the best. There are no pretensions about any of these wines, any more than there is about the dish.

It was an Englishman who wrote *The Ballad of Bouillabaisse*:

> A street there is in Paris famous . . .
> Rue Neuve des Petits Champs its name is
> The New Street of the Little Fields.

The dish is like that, simple and happy. The eating of *bouilla-baisse*—sudden violently-impelled removal of bones where no bones were expected, terrifying confrontations with great glaucous boiled eyes, greedy diggings in the potato-field for a prawn that cunningly hid itself, the discovery that conger is tough but delicious, the slurping of mussels out of their shell—all this is the best possible antidote to *protocolaire* false manners, than-whom persons of all sorts, and a certain stiff shyness which overcomes even nice people when they are not quite sure how they are expected to behave. It is a very democratic dish, and pleasantly aphrodisiac, or should one say uxorious. It can be eaten any time, on the hottest day of the year on the terrace, or in the depth of winter in front of the fire.

It can be very grand and expensive with mullet and langous-tines—or a Victorian Bank Holiday with shrimps, winkles, and Hampstead Heath. It is a great promoter of impromptu art: it has made a classical actor recite the wonderful 'Chowder' passage from 'Moby Dick' and a lyric soprano do 'Flow gently sweet Afton among thy green braes' in the manner of Elizabeth Bennet's pedantic sister Mary (the imagination does boggle at Mr. Collins eating *bouillabaisse*).

Lastly—this too is important—it is a dish which is just about as far from frozen fish-fingers as you can get.

5

BOURGUIGNON

It is one of those French enigmas. The word itself is perfectly clear; an adjective meaning from or pertaining to the province of Burgundy, and here we trip up straight away, because the French do not talk about a bourguignon wine but a vin de Bourgogne. They do, though, talk about beef bourguignon, but have done so only in the last few years. It is a classical dish, and when I was a boy in the kitchen it was called 'sauté de boeuf Bourguignonne', the feminine adjective, like all such, meaning, 'in the style of' or 'after the manner of'. Look up the word in a pre-war Larousse and one finds the original meaning, but in the post-war edition the definition has narrowed mysteriously and we read the blunt remark 'beef done with red wine and onions'. Which is reasonable enough, apart from implying that there is no other red wine in France— well, to the people there of course (les Bourguignons) there isn't... But though Larousse doesn't say so, it means stewing beef. Is there then no steak in Burgundy—are they too poor or just too mean to eat steak?—Enigma.

Come to that, the word 'steak' is another pitfall, because it isn't French at all, but as Concise Oxford tells us effortlessly "ON steik"—in other words the French possessed no steak till the Normans got here, and what is more they still don't know how to spell this simple monosyllable. By itself it is generally written 'steack' and then it is applied to veal, horse, wild boar and other oddities. When talking about ordinary steak as we would understand the word they write things like 'beafsteack', perhaps under the impression that they are talking Old Norse, or more frequently 'bifteck' under the impression that this is English (they also talk about, and write 'rosbif'). When I now hear myself telling the butcher to give me three biftecks and a pound and a half of bourguignon, a thing he understands perfectly, my mind reels.

Why stewing beef? Well, those economical Burgundians were

forever stuffing themselves with bacon which was stewed with onions, red wine and white haricot beans, and the beef is done in the same way except that the beans have disappeared and they were the most Burgundian thing of all—look, I'd better stop this, or we shall never get anywhere.

The vagueness of the appellation is a heaven-sent gift to the butcher. A 'bifteck' means something quite definite; an English steak, cut from the hindquarters (in France happily called le rumsteack), for otherwise you would ask for a fillet, an entrecôte, or a point. A bifteck also means a price-fixing racket which has become a French national scandal dignified by antiquity and immovability, like the pharmacie. These two unmentionables dictate the whole of French life, like the Syndicate and the Mafia in America. They are alive but somehow amorphous, a thing no Nobel-Prize-Winning biochemist has yet worked out, and slink about perpetually oppressing the French populace which between the two leads a wretched life. By comparison, bourguignon is easy going.

The butcher stares thoughtfully at you, weighing up how simple you appear. 'A nice sinewy bit?' he offers helpfully—he means shin. Good too, but over-gelatinous; a bit too sticky in the eating. At this point it is best to say firmly 'A nice piece of shoulder'. Once you have got him pinned down he will become quite reasonable, do it carefully, and even enquire politely how large you like it cut. This is important; if cut too small the stew when cooked will be full of dry horrid little scraps. I like goodish chunks the size of a demi-tasse coffee cup. There should be on one side a thin layer of fat; do not trim this off because it keeps the meat juicy. Running through the pieces will always be quite large strips of sinew, which cannot be got out but do not be discouraged; they will cook tender. You have, in fact, one of the best buys there is. Beef stew is nice anywhere, and in Burgundy particularly nice—the name conjures up not only the bacon, the red wine, the onions and the white haricots but large muscular housewives with broad red faces and cunning little eyes, excellent cooks, with placid temperaments and a subtle humour. Most of Renoir's models, including his wife and a long line of famous servants 'whose skin took the light well' and were forever scrubbing the floor with no clothes on when not eating stew, were Burgundian, and the stew is just like them; marvellously tender, honest, beautiful, innocently sensualist.

Forget about the white haricots, staple of every province of France. They can be awfully good but when eaten continually they are just awful. The bacon and the onions are necessary, and so is the red wine. For four to five people you will want 600 gr. of beef (about a pound and a quarter) and one good glassful of plain honest red wine which can be from Hungary, Spain or Algeria as readily as from France, but nothing thin or vinegary. You also need a 'mirepoix' which is a carrot, a large onion, a piece of celery and a piece of cheap smoked bacon. All these are cut roughly to about the size of a hazelnut.

If the meat looks a suspiciously light red it is fresh, and can be marinated or soaked for a few hours in the wine. A lot of people do this anyway, but I think it has little point. Marinated meat is wet, and even if carefully dried will sputter horribly when fried. The meat will soak in the wine anyway during cooking, which is long and slow. Fresh meat makes it a bit slower still. However, the old French 'three day' tradition of soaking it the first day, cooking it the second, and eating it the third day is a good one. If this dish is left overnight after being cooked, and warmed up just before being eaten, it will be more tender, and will have more flavour.

Have you a heavy pot, round or oval, whose sides and bottom join in a smooth curve so that it has no corners? It will be ideal for this dish. Put it on a fast flame with a good walnut of beef dripping, or a tablespoon of oil, and let this get very hot. Brown the chunks of meat on all sides in this, searing them and also charring them slightly. They are best done a few at a time, so that the temperature of the fat is not unduly lowered. When well browned remove them to a plate and keep them handy. Put the bacon and the vegetables in and fry them too, turning them with a wooden spoon. When nicely brown and smelling aromatic lower the flame right down, or pull the pot back, add a good teaspoonful of tomato purée and stir it in, and a large tablespoonful of flour. Stir it all to a reddish-brown homogeneous mass and cook it gently for a minute before moistening it with the wine and a glassful of cold water—g-r-a-dually till you have a smooth sauce. Stir it at intervals till it boils; the pot should now be about half full. This sauce must not be too thick, for it will reduce during the cooking. You may need to add more water; there must be enough to cover the meat comfortably. The sauce can be seasoned at this point with a little salt and pepper, and a 'bouquet' of a small branch of thyme and a few parsley stalks, doubled together and tied with a thread. When it is to your liking slide the meat into it, stir for a moment till it comes back to the boil, cover the pot with a tightly fitting lid, and place it where it will cook so slowly as barely to bubble from time to time, either on the back of a solid-top range or in a very low oven. The stew now needs no further work or interference and can be forgotten about for hours.

Really forgotten; a failed stew is always the result of over-hasty cooking. The absolute minimum with well hung meat of good quality would be three hours, the average is five, and fresh meat can take longer. So have the courage to leave the stew strictly alone for a very long time. No harm will come to it if the heat is really gentle; it will neither stick, burn, nor go dry.

The flavour will be greatly improved by putting in a beef bone, or in the French style a split pig's trotter. A very small bayleaf can be used instead of the thyme.

There is no obligation to use garlic, but in Burgundy they would put in a clove or two, and Arlette would use three, happily. Garlic when cooked for a long time becomes very mild in flavour.

Do not use too much salt—there is already some present in the bacon. Salt toughens meat, and is not put on a steak or a roast till after the cooking. A bit more can always be stirred in at the end.

Whatever herb you use be very sparing, and do not use more than one. If beans are used soak them overnight first, make the sauce more liquid with another half-glass of water, and cook the beans in it with the meat. One would use less flour, since the beans contain some starch.

When the stew is at last brought back into the light of day the sauce and the meat will be a pleasant chocolate brown colour and a nice consistency, and one should be able to cut the meat with a fork. It needs nothing else added to it, except a little chopped parsley when serving. The bouquet can be fished out by its thread and thrown away: the mirepoix is good to eat. The stew can be transferred at the last moment to a serving dish, after checking the seasoning and skimming any surplus fat that may be floating on top of the sauce.

If there are beans with this stew one needs no other vegetable, and in Burgundy they would just have salad after. A more conventional way of serving it would be to have no beans, but plain boiled potatoes, or else pasta, and nicest perhaps would be the big bicycle-tyre kind. In that case one would want a green vegetable with the stew, something with a good hearty flavour. Depending on the season this might be sprouts, or broccoli, or spinach, or either French or runner beans.

Beaujolais would be good to drink with this. It is not drunk chilled, but much cooler than other red wines, at the temperature of a stone cellar. You might not have a stone cellar, but you can always let the cold tap run on the bottle until it is nicely fresh.

Before eating stew one would not want to eat a large complex hors d'oeuvre. In summer one might choose radishes, with butter and a crust of fresh bread. Or melon. In winter perhaps an egg dish, a little cheese tart, or a grilled trout—or a smoked trout. Come to that, something unstodgy and a little tart in flavour would make an agreeable dessert, like a baked apple or stewed apricots, green-gages or other types of plum. If in an extravagant frame of mind one could have oysters to begin with and fresh pineapple after—doesn't that sound nice, on a grey December day? And in summer the trout, and afterwards fresh greengages, lots and lots.

So far, I notice, I have given nothing but massive, solid country food and while this is very good it is nice, too, to have lighter things offered one from time to time. Here is a light stew, and surprisingly enough a light version of dried beans.

Take a roasting chicken which is not deep-freeze. A weight of about 1200 gr., or two and a quarter pounds, is right for four people. Cut it in pieces—two legs, two thighs, two wings, two pieces of breast, with your big knife. Chop the carcass and neck into four or five manageable pieces. In a casserole heat a walnut of butter till it begins to turn brown. Brown the pieces rapidly on both sides. Take out the pieces, keep on a plate, and do the same with the pieces of carcass. Put in another walnut of butter, and fry four shallots, peeled and in quarters, and, when they begin to brown, four large field mushrooms, sliced. Add four tomatoes, blanched, skinned, and cut in quarters. When they have cooked down a little moisten with a glass of good drinkable dry white wine and a glass of water. When this boils add the pieces of chicken and carcass, and the giblets, and season with salt and pepper and a good pinch of chopped tarragon. Let the casserole simmer very gently under its lid for an hour, or until the meat is very tender. Fish out the carcass and the giblets. Thicken the sauce slightly with a teaspoonful of potato-starch dissolved in two of brandy. Sprinkle it generously with chopped parsley. This simple stew is called *chicken chasseur*: it is good with fried potatoes and baby peas.

Chick peas as a hot salad:—soak dried chick peas overnight and simmer them in slightly salted water for two hours or until tender —they never become soft. When they are ready fry very thinly sliced bacon until perfectly crisp. Keep the bacon fat hot in a little bowl. Drain the peas, put them in a warmed fireproof dish, and season them with a vinaigrette made of the hot bacon fat with good red-wine vinegar. Serve them with little separate saucers of finely chopped onion, sliced gherkins, chopped parsley, and the crisp morsels of bacon. This makes a very good winter hors d'oeuvre. One can make hot potato salad the same way, with the yellowish waxy potatoes which stay firm.

6

PARILLADA

Barbecued Chops, Cutlets, Steaks, Sausages, Chicken, Best End and Rib of Pork and Veal

In the paper, not long ago, was an item about an archaeologist in the United States who made an interesting discovery while searching for stones with which to build a barbecue, which sounded like the first time a barbecue had made a contribution to civilization. That is much too spiteful: they make a large contribution to enjoyment.

The fellow was at least collecting stones, not cooking with a pretend-barbecue which has an electric turnspit (otherwise one has to work) and a gas-fired grill (otherwise you get your hands dirty), a thing guaranteed to please anyone, anyone that is with no sense of smell. People with no sense of smell (or who aim at that ideal) are getting frequent, alas. One could be led pretty easily into a little discussion about correlations between the decline of civilization and the sale of deodorants, which goes side by side with the spread of tasteless food. These suburban barbecues, probably another invention of Sinclair Lewis characters, are just great for rugged outdoor types like advertising executives in Westchester County, but aren't of much interest; about as much as the pretend-fondues of European suburban housewives got up in ski-clothes and looking around for Alps in the hinterlands of Holland. Dolls' tea-parties.

But the real barbecue is as American as chile con carne (the word itself characteristic American Spanish-Indian), and a genuine national dish throughout the Americas: it is easy to see why when you think that only here is found the true open-range cattle country. No longer perhaps in the United States, but the guilt felt at the wanton destruction of so much land, the hankering for lost innocence in cowboy movies, does not come into my theme hereabouts, any more than a chat about deodorants in Lewis-Land. The barbecue is still the national dish of nearly all South

America, and the tremendous parilladas of Uruguay and Argentina arguably the most splendid beef dishes there are, although I have been told that on the range itself they only do lambs, since there is no means of keeping meat from spoiling.

It is tempting to say that in Europe, particularly on the Continent, nobody understands beef. The meat itself is as good as, or better than, anything in America. But even in England it is almost impossible to find a butcher who will hang it long enough. Once with some French people we were invited to dine with a whisky millionaire in Scotland. He went on a great deal about Scotch beef and to prove his point drove us (in his Rolls Royce) to get our dinner from his special butcher. The beef was superb but far too fresh and madly tough. In France the Charollais beef is very fine, and they export bulls to America. But it is seldom you get good steak from a butcher (as opposed to good restaurants) and my experience in England has been the same. One is impressed in America by shopwindows holding carcases put there to ripen and in my days in the kitchen we bought carcases over a week ahead. We hung them that much extra so that they would be tender, but the ordinary person cannot, of course, do that.

In Europe, then, our idea of a barbecue will always be a little silly, pretentious and mincing like a fondue-party, but enjoyment we can have, and let's begin by collecting stones: no man needs telling how to build a fireplace of stones. The enjoyment of a barbecue is getting hot, smudged and sweaty, dropping things in the fire, wiping one's hands on the grass, being very unhygienic indeed, and losing one's temper at least twice. Only when 'really in the country' can one manage even this. Nine-tenths of us have to be happy with a little suburban terrace and charcoal.

We can at least use real charcoal. It can be bought, and it gives a hot small fire with no smoke: it is already an enjoyment to light it, and fan it to get it red. It is no substitute for real wood, to grill on, but can be played with; one can remedy the tastelessness by throwing in things, like old herbs of which one always has too much; a good way to get rid of that stale sage or rosemary which has been hanging about. One can play at producing smells, vivid green sparks and tiny explosions, by dropping in cloves, pepper-corns or juniper berries. Orange peel gives rather a nice effect—as well as getting rid of orange-peel.

For small things I have a charcoal fire-pot, identical to that used by all old women in all 'underdeveloped countries', a large cast-iron mushroom with a hollow stem bought for two sous in Portugal, which will grill sixteen sardines in two minutes, or sausages, or filet mignon. The children enjoy playing with it very much. But it is a great deal nicer to be like the archaeological expert and look for stones, to build a fireplace, and a table, and make a parillada, however mean and mini.

You need, evidently, logs, and the world being what it is one must be content with what one can get; I will only say that pine is the worst, because it flames and spits and burns quickly through, being resinous, but at least one has no regret at chopping down a beastly pine-tree. Fruit wood is nicest for a grill because it smells so good, and for clear even heat the best of all is beech-wood, but cutting down a beech tree is one of the worst crimes in the calendar. Elms are supposed to fall, but one sometimes has to wait a long time. . . .

There is only one rule, which is to make a big fire and let it die down before cooking on it. One needs to start well in advance. Even then you will probably have drunk too much, and the children will certainly have eaten too many potato-chips, before any cooking gets done.

Even when you have a good glow with lots of red embers it is not as easy as it looks to cook on it, so start with simple things like sausages and cutlets before trying anything ambitious. It isn't relevant to give way to my hatred for plastic things. Metal plates which can be dropped, dented, cleaned with earth and have one's name scratched on are what I like, but every man to his taste. You need a spider's-web wire grill as big as you can get it. You need a variety of prongs and tongs to grab and turn things; these can be bought, and very dear they are: they can also be fabricated by ingenuity. Anywhere in the country, looking round a little you can find an ash stump with thin straight rods growing from it. Being a green hard-wood it will not burn readily: a few straight sticks to put across above the fire, a few sharpened spears, and some chopsticks, will help the cook considerably. One can spit meat, and unpeeled potatoes too, on these spears. I know that potatoes are done traditionally in the ashes, but they have a way of turning into charcoal before they are cooked through. The other things you need are your butcher's knife, plenty of oil, a few lemons, a couple of large onions, and any herbs or spices you like as well as salt and pepper. Mix a bowl of oil and lemon juice six to one, like ordinary vinaigrette, and dab the meat or fish with it, using a paintbrush. Americans go in a lot for dipping sauces, tending to have lots of pounded chili peppers in them, and I am tempted to think that this is because their food is often tasteless. These are easily made, with sour cream, or creamcheese thinned with milk and a bit of lemon juice, and they make everything more elaborate.

The stones at the sides of the fire must be built tall, so that there is a good distance between the spits, or the grill poised upon sticks, and the heat. The charry bits are the best, but if too close to the heat everything will burn however much care is taken. Only experience, I am afraid, can dictate times, distances, when to turn things round, and when to yell to people that the grub is ready.

Only one person is cook. A man does not mind getting his hair smoky, the fur on his forearms scorched, and a few smears on his trousers where he wipes his hands without thinking, so that the barbecue cook is always a man, and a wonderful time he has too, pretending to be a gaucho—any man who does *not* want to be a gaucho is better not invited. But his work is hard and he must be given extra perks.

'Give me' my father used to say 'the middle piece, which is the best piece, and Help Me First'. He gets hot, cross, hungry and thirsty. He must be supplied with many drinks, very large, very cold and very good, exactly like James Bond. He also needs a selection of pretty women with a portable pharmacy, to bind him up and make a fuss of him when he gets cut or burned, as being a clumsy ass he quite certainly will.

When he gets beyond the cutlet-and-sausage stage he becomes more ambitious every minute, and starts to indulge all manner of fantasies. Quite a simple meal, but already a test of Barbecue-Bill, is a grilled chicken. In old-fashioned English 'spatchcocked'— lovely word, and delicious to eat, too. You take a large, rather fat roasting chicken, 1,500 grammes, or three pounds, for five to six people. Once cleaned, rest it on a board holding it by the tail (in the same language the parson's nose) and with the butcher's knife cut down each side of the backbone, as close to it as you can— this is easier than it sounds. It will then open out flat like a book, and if given a smart bang in its middle, as one does to badly-glued paperbacks, it will stay flat and need no skewering. Paint it lavishly with oil-and-lemon, and place it on the grill, skin side downwards. Leave it like this for twenty minutes. If the skin scorches too much raise the grill another few inches with a couple more stones, or logs. By definition the fire is dying down, so that all cooking begins fast and ends slow, in the same rhythm as roasting of any sort.

Turn it and paint it again; the bones are now downward. After another quarter of an hour prick with a fork or sharp stick into the thickness of the thigh (always the slowest to cook) and watch the little bead of juice. If clear, the chicken is done; if still pink, leave it another five minutes. Even if pink, the wings are done and must not be overdone—the thighs can be put back separately. If the chicken is put on a board and rested for five minutes the thighs peel off easily and are put back with their skin side down after again being painted. The fine rib-bones can now easily be lifted off the inside of the wings, and the soft breast-bone from the centre.

Double cutlets, thick chops, or a T-bone steak are easier still, done just the same way. If while cooking any of these pieces of meat a half-burnt log persists in sending up jets of flame to burn one point, and resists all prodding—then the large onion you were thoughtful enough to bring will come in handy. Cut thick slices and prop them beneath the vulnerable corner. The classic and simple oil-and-lemon mixture is suitable for all kinds of meat. It can have a little ground pepper added, but salt is best sprinkled on separately at the last moment, for salt toughens a grill. Paint everything frequently and lavishly. Any good-quality oil will do very well; walnut and olive oils are a luxury.

Much emboldened by these successful pleasures (he has quite forgotten all the cursing that went on, the blackened sausage and the cutlet which fell through the grill, the time it began to rain and when a sudden gust of wind blew ashes all over everything so that progress through the chicken was marked by a loud gritty crunching), the cook now wants to make a real parillada, inviting friends and showing off. This is pretty difficult, but there are ways of cheating without taking away pleasure.

Do not try to do a leg of lamb, a loin of beef, or any such thick and lengthy joint, which needs turnspit equipment, a great deal more trouble than it is worth. The joint used in a South American parillada which comes closest to what butchers in Europe can or will do is a rib or 'rack', the English 'best end', the French 'côtes premières'. In the Argentine it is propped up on sticks planted in an inverted V shape (the original meaning of 'barbecue' seems to be a wooden cage or framework) but it can be done too on a wire grill and, like the chicken, will take thirty minutes or so—remember that lamb must be rosy inside. The shoulder end, or côtes découvertes, is less suitable because it has no protecting band of fat, which can be sprinkled with any aromatic herb. But a shoulder-end or 'échine' of pork or veal does have plenty of protection: it needs, though, to be well cooked right through, and will take an hour. Since inside an hour the fire will need to be made up, which means not only lowered heat but a lot of smoke, this is the moment to cheat.

Take a rib of pork or veal, with, of course, its bones. Allow a really generous chop per person. Roast it in the oven in the ordinary way, the day before you wish to barbecue, but do this at a lower heat and for rather less time than you would ordinarily allow. This is best done in a thick, barely-oiled pot. Let the joint cool on a plate; pinkish juice will trickle from it and set to a jelly. When it is quite cool, bone it with a sharp butcher's knife. This is easy with cooked meat: begin at the top, where the flat rib-bones were sawed off, and slide the knife down and round the corner, keeping as near the bone as you can. At the corner the bones form knuckles and one loses some meat but this is of no consequence. These bones, cut at their joints, will be grilled too; each *convive* gets one, and they are the best pieces.

What you now have is a boned rib, not quite cooked, a little pale, underdone where the bones were removed. This grills very well. The whole joint is put on the grill for fifteen or twenty minutes, which heats it well through, finishes the cooking, and slightly chars—and seals—the pale places. This joint can be painted with a trickier and altogether more 'American' sauce. For a rib of pork, here is how you make it.

When the roasting was finished in the oven you were left with a hot pot containing browned 'gravy' traces and a little oil. Into this put a heaped tablespoon of Oxford marmalade (Mr. Cooper is a mainstay of the English kitchen) a tablespoon of brown sugar, and the juice of a lemon. Stir it all together, cook it enough to blend it, and transfer it to a little kitchen bowl. Stir in a sherry-glass of brandy and there is your sauce with which to paint the pork. If there is little fat and the joint seems dry, you can add a bit more oil. Instead of using marmalade, you can make the sauce of brandy, lemon and sugar only, roast apples whole (peeled and cored) on the grill with the meat, and anoint them with the sauce. The pink jelly from the meat is added to this sauce; it must on no account be lost.

Veal is better done with plain oil-and-lemon; its flavour is delicate and needs no emphasizing.

Naughty cooks use a lot more brandy, which will catch fire and draw attention to themselves. This is a waste of brandy but causes gaiety among young children.

Any grilled meat should have a good layer of fat. The present-day horror of fat and the consequent fashion for fillet steaks, which are tasteless as well as expensive, is a mistake. Nobody is obliged to eat fat, but meat grilled with all fat pared away will be dry, tough and unappetising. When I was a boy in the kitchen, a fillet was always sent from the larder accompanied by a thick slice of kidney suet, which was put to grill with the steak, and when the steak was turned was placed on top of it, protecting, moistening and impregnating it with flavour. This extremely simple trick, like buttering the inside of a casserole lid, has been forgotten. This is a pity. Well meaning but ignorant doctors, employed as dietetics experts by women's magazines, have engendered some really detestable eating habits.

7
'I LONG FOR MY PORRIDGE'

*Breakfasts, ducal and otherwise—Kedgeree—Grilled Kidneys—
Lamb Cutlet in Armour—Brains in butter—Grilled ham with banana
—Escargots—Eggs, scrambled, boiled, poached and en cocotte—
Persillade of ham*

Miss Nancy Mitford's frivolous dukes give us keen enjoyment
because they have such delight in life. They have, to be sure,
enormous amounts of money and are not in the least neurotic
about it, but much more than their extravagance it is their intelligence, their cultivated minds, and their amiability which
fills us with *allégresse*: they gild everybody's gingerbread with real
gold leaf. So many writers, good and less good, convey depression
in great moist swathes, whereas Charles-Edouard de Valhubert
digests well, never has liver attacks— he doesn't even cause them—
and makes everyone happy even when deceiving his wife, so
unlike all the other people we know.

Even at breakfast these dukes are good company. They get up
much too early, survey the empty table with horror, speak kindly
to the shy little girl who has made a gaffe, and take her instantly
out for a walk where she will not be oppressed by her embarrassment, which shows their niceness and their good manners.

'I too long for my porridge' he mutters zestfully, and we know
that he will fall upon breakfast—a brisk walk first, such a good
idea—with the same healthy appetite as upon pictures, women,
architecture, fast cars, and Louis XIV bronzes—'I do so love
them, so solid, so proof against housemaids'.

Since breakfast is a delight, a highly enjoyable prologue to a
delightful new day, why should it be so dank and uncomfortable a
moment, a thing nobody can take pleasure in? The menu is
scanty, dreary, surrounded by taboos, and utterly unimaginative.
French doctors, sensitive and sensible about most things, turn into
fiends at the bare mention of breakfast, and are forever trying to
stop me eating butter. Those ghastly biscottes, hatefully smeared

with jam; what could be nastier? French breakfast can be delicious when the coffee is really good, the croissants dark and crunchy, the brioche meltingly tender, the jam home-made and not over-sweetened; any one of these conditions is goodness knows hard to fulfil, and uniting all of them little short of a miracle.

Anyway, French breakfast is a bourgeois invention, designed to be eaten in the same twenty-four hours as a large early lunch (pawing with the hooves at midday precisely) and a large, late, lavish dinner: no time or energy left for making love, going to the opera, or any other civilized pursuit. If one is living this kind of existence—I must admit that it is agreeable occasionally—the rules are disregarded at one's peril. We must rest the digestion (not being dukes) and avoid inflaming and tormenting the liver by giving the whole system at least twelve hours to recover from those whopping great meals, or there is no hope at all of stuffing away with a clear conscience and a clean palate. We absolutely must have a good night's sleep, a large glass of Contrexeville and a fresh grapefruit at eight, a leisurely and luxurious toilet in complete calm, smelling the flowers from time to time while shaving—all this by preference at the Ritz in the Place Vendôme—and plenty of serious gymnastics on the balcony, silk dressing-gown thrown negligently upon the Empire chair. And finally, at the witching hour of nine a.m., the Limoges cup of black coffee and one croissant with Cooper's Oxford, just enough to stop the tummy flapping against our spine, and a mild claro cigar with the second cup, together with a glance at the headlines; but book reviews and murder trials only, nothing base and revolting like politics, the Bourse, or traffic accidents.

Fortunately, few of us lead this kind of existence at all often. We have to go to work, generally, and then it is madness to eat this kind of breakfast. French people have big bowls of coffee that is half milk and dip in huge crusts of fresh bread, and if they don't they get a frightful French disease which attacks them around ten, known as a *coup de pompe*. I do this, too, with individual variations like a perverted liking for very stale bread. I like to get up very early, because I work well then, have a dam' good lunch, and only a cup of soup-poached-egg sort of supper, but I rarely manage to keep this saintly routine intact for more than a week.

Lunch and dinner are much the same wherever one goes, with local eccentricities like the Spanish or Chilean habit of dinner at eleven at night, and apparently never going to bed at all except after lunch. But breakfast has several strong national character-istics and weird variations: thus the Dutch have cheese, cold ham and a currant bun, which sounds crass but isn't, as Ludwig Bemelmans said of the sweet spinach tart at the Arche, in the island of Porquerolles (I must admit I thought it horrid). The Germans eat *blutwurst* off a wooden plate, and the less said about this the better. Is it chauvinist to say that only the Anglo-Saxons understand breakfast? Why should breakfast and tea be sometimes so nice, and other meals often so nasty? *Sont fous ces Romains*, as Astérix says.

It could, of course, be utterly revolting. Chester Himes, marvellously malicious, drew a wicked picture of a Confederate Colonel eating a real Southern breakfast (his view of southern colonels is understandably pretty dim).

'He had a bowl of grits, swimming with butter; four fried eggs sunny side up; six fried home-made sausages; six down-home biscuits each an inch thick, with big slabs of butter stuck between the halves; and a pitcher of sorghum molasses. Alongside his heaping plate stood a tall bourbon whisky highball.'[1] This, of course, is propaganda, like the food in travel agency posters, but as with all really superior propaganda it needs only a retouch here or there to make it (distressingly) real. Grand stuff for any-one with a few thousand acres to ride around before breakfast (horseback riding as they say on the placards outside motels)—a few slaves to beat and a spot of rape to work up an appetite. But even in New York you can do better at breakfast than for the rest of the day, which sounds like faint praise and is too, rather.

English breakfast, preferably with *The Times* ironed by the club servants, can be super: my only real objection—apart from

[1] *Cotton comes to Harlem* by Chester Himes, one of the best thrillers ever written.

what an Irishman once described as eating stewed prunes by electric light in Bloomsbury—is that it has become unimaginative. One eats the bacon and eggs—marvellous—and next day the smoked haddock, equally so, and the day after that the sausages; alas, they are a sad fall from grace—and the fourth day the kippers, a disappointment generally; one's hopes were too high: and then suddenly there doesn't seem much choice left any more, a pity. I admit I am talking about hotels, and they notoriously never have any imagination about anything. Even the Ritz is apt to offer you the small pallid parsley omelette. Whereas I want fish-cakes, and mutton chop, and kedgeree, and kidneys. Obviously I should be making friends with English dukes.

Kipling, in *Captains Courageous*, says that the *morue* or salt cod, still to be found in Southern Europe and how I love it, in America went to make New England's breakfast, but he was talking about the turn of the century. The folks were robuster then.

I am not even scandalized by the big tall whisky highball. One of the conventions which bores me a lot is the ukase about not opening a bottle till the sun be over the yardarm. Well, this might have been all right for the Royal Navy; failing rum they had always buggery and the lash to be going on with, or so Churchill said and he should know. My trouble is that I feel on the whole lukewarm about these proposed diversions at breakfast time. I have a robust relative who fancies a bottle of Rioja: more fragile a flower, I like a glass of white, or perhaps a drop of the Special Old Pale, the Very one.

It could, I suppose, be a bad idea to drink at breakfast-time in the damp temperate climate of England, where the metabolism is slowed, but in a drier atmosphere, and it does not much matter whether it be warm or cold, I can't for the life of me see why one should not drink at breakfast time.

If as well as nothing to drink there is no fruit it—as Madeline found when catapulted by Pepito—

> *Causes pain and shocked surprise*
> *During morning exercise.*

—you must get up early and go for a walk or a swim or something. Everyone admits that this is nice, but I suspect that it is because they do it somewhat seldom.

Anyway, assume the getting up early, and assume the morning exercise, assume a bottle of plonk, and plenty of fruit, and I don't mean stewed prunes either, and a rough idea of breakfast begins to take shape. One should have a basket of fruit at a breakfast table, to look at, to smell, and even if not to eat every day to pick a few grapes before turning the bunch guiltily over so that the bad side does not show. Whatever we have done, we have now a good appetite. We are ready to consider, perhaps, a few suggestions.

Kedgeree—as nice as its name. The French call it 'Cadgery' which is not bad either. It is a left-over dish, of débris from fish or chicken, and if either was smoked the flavour is wonderfully improved. It is crumbled up with a cupful of cold cooked rice which is not sticky or clawky but which has cooked with the grains separate, and the mixture is seasoned with a very little curry powder. Add a hardboiled egg cut in quarters, make it very hot in a buttered dish of fireproof porcelain, and eat it with a fresh tomato.

Grilled lamb or pork kidneys. Must be done lightly and carefully, or they go dark, tough and leathery. Eaten with a little butter mixed with perhaps mustard, or lemon-juice, or a smashed anchovy fillet, or a pickled walnut, and with bread to mop the juice up.

Lamb cutlet in armour. The simplest method is to cut the rib rather large and then flatten it well out with a heavy object, egg-and-breadcrumb it, fry it gently in a little butter, and eat it as it is. Variations are to add a slice of ham cut to size and attached to the cutlet with a dot of mustard, and then pass through flour and egg. A thin slice of Gruyère cheese is also possible. There are too several kinds of stuffing, like *duxelles*, which is finely-chopped mushrooms and ham, but these are a bit heavy, and to my mind far too elaborate. A breakfast dish should be simple, and made of simple materials handled simply.

Fresh fish. Only possible, alack, if there is a fishmarket in the neighbourhood. Second condition is to go out and get it—

'morning exercise'. If neither of these conditions is overwhelmingly unthinkable the result is well worth the trouble. The classic fish is a fresh trout—several really, because the real ones are tiny, but they are hard to get, and if they can be found a market is the last place one would expect to see them. A farm trout is not much of a fish, but good for breakfast. A fresh herring is not to be sneered at. A lot of fish readily found, like dabs or lemon soles, not really serious fish, make a splendid breakfast none the less. They are fried simply in a walnut of butter with a squeeze of lemon-juice—as above, never in a complicated way or with a sauce.

Breakfast should be a foursquare honest meal eaten as near to the fresh air as one can get. Scrambled eggs with tricky little flavourings like sherry-and-grated-orange-peel do not taste nice, besides being too much work: they are dishes for night-time, with the curtains drawn.

Even so the variety of egg dishes is tremendous. They should either be very plain, with a scrap of butter or a thread of cream, or be accompanied by something with a firm texture and a pronounced flavour—an endy bit of smoked salmon, or a chicken liver, diced and stiffened in a dot of butter; a finger of stale cheese; a tiny left-over of braised meat; a *mirabeau* of a lemon slice with two anchovy fillets and four capers: one could easily go on and on. The point is made already that breakfast need not be dull.

Looking for fresh mushrooms before breakfast in autumn is perhaps the nicest morning exercise I know.

Brains make a good breakfast dish, but they are tiresomely fragile, and need work. If blanched the night before in salt water with vinegar, and rinsed under a thread of cold water they become less wobbly, and the bits of membrane are easily picked out with a tiny knife. Next morning they are halved, floured, and cooked in a hot pan with a nut of butter which is allowed to go brown, and a drop or two of red-wine vinegar added—the result is 'beurre noir' and very good.

Grilling a smallish but thickish piece of ham with a half banana is a well-known way of being promoted instantly to sales-manager or whatever the immediate ambition might be.

I like *escargots* for breakfast. If I were anxious about smelling of garlic I would neutralize it by chewing a sprig of fresh parsley. I do not bother about shells, and cunning little dishes and tweezers, since these are restaurant inventions, devices for putting the price up, which no sensible man bothers with. They are bought ready in a tin, and heated up in a little fireproof dish, with a pat of steak-butter. (Lemon-juice, garlic, parsley and a little black pepper.)

But the basic dish remains eggs; everyone falls back on eggs because almost everyone likes them, they are cheap, handy, and no trouble. Still, like anything else they need pains taken and above all the right cooking temperature. Everybody has suffered from eggs fried in over-heated oil—the unpleasant lace-curtain effect—or eggs slowly stewed in languid grease, which are nastier still. Eggs should be cooked only with their dairy companions, cream and butter—I know that lots of people use bacon fat but it is a heresy, really. It is better to take a little butter and either an omelette pan or little fireproof cocottes, which are a nuisance, and I compromise by using a French omelette pan of heavy cast iron with a close-fitting lid, which by enclosing and providing top heat makes turning eggs unnecessary and avoids all toughening. The sunny-side-up stuff can be forgotten, the eggs are tender and digestible—one wants a good breakfast, but no one wants a stomach-ache.

Scrambled eggs are cooked with a little butter and cream—or milk—and very gently, on a corner of the stove or over a water-bath. They cannot be hurried. They must be stopped while still a scrap liquid, because they go on scrambling in their own heat and quickly become hard, and nasty, and the same applies to an omelette. These two dishes, the simplest in the kitchen, are thus a trap—and a test: one can tell instantly whether the cook be good or bad.

Boiled eggs are tricky, because one cannot see inside, and the three-and-a-half minute rule of thumb is falsified if they have been kept in a fridge, as they generally are nowadays. Experience is needed in consequence, and they are tiresome things because everyone has a different notion of the degree of set wanted.

Poached eggs are hardest of all. The commonest and most horrible fallacy is to put vinegar in the water, which simply spoils the taste. The idea is to keep the egg from disintegrating— if stale it will in any case. Only real new-laid eggs can be poached, and the way to see is to crack each egg separately into a saucer, which all properly-trained cooks once did automatically, for any purpose. On the saucer a stale egg spreads out in a limp, flat, pusillanimous way. All bureaucratic eggs, thoughtfully provided with dates, little lions and tattoo-marks do this at once. A fresh egg is stiff, and the white forms a collar, as though heaped up. An egg like this can be poached in plain salted water just deep enough for the egg to swim—no, it is not easy. The water must not bubble, but have beaded bubbles winking at the brim—Ode to a Poached Egg. Surface just faintly quivering. Slide in off the saucer, bringing same up in a little vertical flip which folds the egg over upon itself. The white will then mask the yolk; the one firm, the other tender within.

A stale egg is best cooked in a little fireproof cocotte, buttered and sprinkled with salt and pepper; unless very stale it will pass muster.

Sometimes, on a summer morning, it is nice to have a cold breakfast, with no dam' cooking. One thinks at once of ham, of chicken, of asparagus—and why not of fresh tomatoes, cut in quarters, taken in the fingers, and dipped into a little bowl of vinaigrette that has fresh basil in it? But if you have guests—say— or want something a bit more splendid, here is a more elaborate, but simple, good egg dish.

The night before, in a little glass cocotte put a small circular slice of ham. On top, a cold poached egg. Fill the cocotte up with a nice blonde meat jelly after decorating the egg with a red ace cut from tomato or scarlet pimento. Restaurants use a black ace cut from truffle. This is *oeuf en gelée*; let set overnight and give two to each person: you will see your guests leap over the balcony like Tarzan.

Here is another dish, called *persillade of ham*—and both these dishes make good cold party hors d'oeuvres ... but are nicest for breakfast.

For each person take a slice of plain cooked ham, cut small but quite thick. Chop it coarsely into a dozen diamond-shaped morsels. Make a little pale, almost colourless meat jelly—simply done by cooking together a chicken carcase and a pig's trotter in default of a calf's foot. Strain this while hot into a bowl, and add a handful of fresh-chopped greenery; parsley, chervil, tarragon, deliberately not squeezed out over-much. Fresh mint is good, but not much of it. Stir this into the warm jelly until it takes on a pale green tint. For each guest now take a plain stemmed wine-glass, fill it one-third full of jelly and allow to set. Strew in the chopped ham together with the rest of the jelly when this is still liquid but beginning to set.

This party breakfast is, plainly, quite a bit of trouble, but does give a lovely summery effect and tastes delicious.

These cold dishes are eaten with a teaspoon and thin brown bread-and-butter.

I notice that about the only thing I have not expressed longing for at breakfast is porridge. Alack—I don't like it.

8

'FIE YOU GREASY LOUT—'

—'You Stink of the Kitchen'. I am quoting from memory and may not have the wording exact, but a crude phrase and an insulting tone there certainly was, and the quotation is accurate enough besides being part of an interesting story and a fascinating backstairs look at medieval habits. It is from Malory—the *Morte d'Arthur*.

It will be remembered that a young man appears at Arthur's court and asks to be made a knight. This is plainly impossible: he is a likely lad enough, being tall, well-built and of noble appearance, but he is of unknown family, and either can't or won't say anything of his background. But he begs to be allowed to stay, and half kindly, half contemptuously, he is given a job in the kitchen, where for a year he works humbly and courageously at scullion-turnspit tasks, which must in those days have been unpleasant indeed. After exactly a year, as in all correct stories, a damsel-in-distress turns up begging for help, with a lurid tale of a noble lady, Countess Whatnot, kidnapped and held in thrall by a whole gang of bandit knights, sinister rogues who do not sound at all easy nuts to crack; several gallant and romantic rovers have had a shot at rescuing her and come off extremely poorly. She begs the king in consequence to lend her a world-class boy, preferably the reigning heavyweight champion, Lancelot, for whom this job sounds made to measure; he is the complete James Bond of the period, only rather more of a gentleman: being the queen's titular lover he is quite scrupulous about who else he sleeps with.

In the middle of all the excited speculation the kitchen boy stands out suddenly with total assurance, and claims the task; it is, he says, his job by right, and belongs to him. Such is his dignity and simplicity that the king, much impressed by his noble manners, grants the request, despite a chorus of sniggers from Kay, who has a nasty tongue and for a whole year has teased the kitchen boy unmercifully, and much incredulous comment from everyone but Lancelot, who is not only nice, and sees the boy's steadfastness and fortitude, but also has a connoisseur's eye for muscles and footwork.

The lady however is furious; she wanted Lance, who is not only champion but a French prince, and has been presented with a scullion. She has no choice but to go with him, but gives him an awful time, both coldly sarcastic and very rude, until one is glad to say he not only polishes off all the bandits and rescues the countess, who turns out to be her sister, but beds the two of them with no more ado, and that settles her nonsense for her.

He turns out, of course, to be a prince, but the folklore does not concern us; we are occupied with the greasy knaves, and I was one for fifteen years, who Stink of the Kitchen. Because, by heaven, one did. I have sung the praises of old-fashioned equipment, and been snooty about modern technology, but the kitchen is nowadays less smelly than it used to be. The chemistry of fat—most cooking is done with one kind of fat or another—is such that kitchen air is charged with macro-molecules, amino-acids, and other unpleasant things, which cover everything in a brown greasy film and create that shrill pungent reek clinging like stale cigar-smoke, and even beastlier. Kitchen drains, too, are nobody's bed of violets, as anyone who ever had the army chore of 'cleaning the greasetraps' can testify.

No doubt of it; in all my experience this was the hardest thing to bear. The heat and cold, sweat and subsequent chills, confined atmosphere, endless hours on one's feet, burns and cuts, ghastly 'split duty' which meant a cook worked both early and late, worry and hurry, both chronic, and on top of all hard and often brutalizing work: all this was bearable but I never got used to the stink, which marked one down as a cook 'an hour in the wind' as the Dutch put it vividly. This of course was what Dame Linet meant when she kept her horse well ahead of poor Gareth's and held her nose so ostentatiously, although in medieval times even countesses were much more robust about stinks than we are now and everyone stank more or less; no toothbrush and no soap either till Moors or someone fiddling about with wood ash in efforts to keep clean made this useful discovery. Dogs everywhere, rushes on the

floor full of fleas, all that sweaty armour, and Dame Linet herself
can't have been a freshly blooming eglantine (one can almost
sympathize with Richard Coeur de Lion).

The trouble with modern technology, so-called, is that it is so
faint-hearted as well as feeble-minded (we are still stuck after
seventy years with the internal-combustion engine). Only very
recently has any real advance been made with kitchen equipment,
the French at last inventing a sealed-in deep fryer, and proper air-
conditioning equipment doing something about cabbage and
stale stockpots. Also, and this is sad, the cook is the better off for
these scraps of progress, but the food, decidedly, isn't. Organic
chemistry—change and decay in all around we see—means that
food has a smell, however hard supermarkets try to deny the fact
(the effort to suppress all sense of smell is a most interesting
modern neurosis).

Together with progress in kitchens goes a lamentable regression
in food products, which have no smell and consequently no taste—
hence the frantic over-use of herbs and spices as in medieval times,
when they were employed in an effort to conceal bad smells—and
are so impoverished into the bargain that we actually manage the
lunatic paradox of being overfed at the same time as having
deficiency diseases.

The push-pull effect realized means that a lot of confusion as
well as cant is brought into all discussion of food. The young
couple which fancies itself modern and is thinking of setting up
shop together tends nowadays to be quite uninterested in the
kitchen: having always eaten out in bad restaurants they intend
to go on doing so; they feel no sense of loss. This was neatly
demonstrated by a recent Sunday-supplement devoted to modern
architecture. This featured an apartment in womb-style such as
'modern' youth might be supposed to clamour for. No windows of
course—a camera flashing coloured pictures on the wall instead.
No furniture—a large divan in the shape of a hollow square. And
no kitchen. In a corner somewhere a small microwave oven was
built into the wall next the garbage disposer: one would have the
greatest difficulty in distinguishing between them. The designer

was most enthusiastic about this touch; think! no smell, no labour, no time used. And what would one cook? Well—er—he was a bit flummoxed: ah yes, a hamburger, and that in a few seconds. These poor people, eating the cornflakes of jargon instead of the hard bread of instruction, were, it was obvious, incapable of tasting, chewing or digesting any food whatever, whether mental or physical, and were perfectly happy with this state of affairs: at last they had got rid of all those nasty smells of earth, rain and sea, all that horrible matter. That mankind eats and defecates, what a ghastly state of affairs; it must be stopped instantly. One is re-minded of Thomas Beecham, who enjoyed life and when asked by proud Australians what he thought of the Sydney Harbour Bridge said 'It is far too big, and should be knocked down'.

One can argue, optimistically, that these people grow up. They can perhaps learn that the family unit is a necessity, and that small domestic servitudes are a satisfaction. Perhaps. . . .

A kitchen has an important role to play in society. It is only a technological development of the fireplace, and plenty of people have noticed that the decline of the fireplace has done interior design no good. A striking thing about all people who came from a 'working-class' home of before 1939 is the burning nostalgia with which they remember the kitchen—itself of course the living-room—full of washing, cooking, ironing stinks, permanently untidy, frequently filthy, fatally overcrowded from all the life that was in it. A sociologically-minded observer could make, and has probably made, a pretty thesis keying the decline in the traditional values, and the decay of European civilization, to the growth of the bourgeoisie who separated the living-room from the kitchen because they were ashamed of it. A palace can abolish a kitchen because a palace is a reflection of art and of artists, a place where civilization flowers. But a house where little people live is where the same civilization has its roots in the ground.

One can study the phenomenon in Parisians, who live in the most civilized and barbarous of cities, most beautiful and most bourgeois. They rush like lemmings to their country cottages, tiny peasant houses where the kitchen, directly entered from outside, is the central room in the building, probably the largest and certainly the most important. So that—manoeuvring a bit uneasily, disconcerted by the push-pull effect—we have to try and reconcile the ghastly twenty-second hamburger with the equally atrocious thought of the greasy lout: squalid flats in Warsaw, unbearably dark and poky, reeking of cabbage soup; coal-fired kitchens in pre-war Nottingham back-to-backs: have you mashed, Mam?

That we are still human enough to reject the hamburger there is no doubt. Why else are magazines packed with articles about food and full-page colour illustrations? What is more, we are human enough to reject the 'aseptic' kitchen, looking just like the bathroom and built side by side with it, so handy, hygienic ingurgitation and elimination in two economical footsteps. For the colour supplements are all solid folklore, featuring the rustic look; primitive earthenware pots, strings of onions, and reminders that you can still dispense with the automatic mixer and do things by hand—these illustrations invariably feature a pestle and mortar, and a big wooden salad-bowl. The recipes accompanying all this guff are nearly always ridiculous but that is irrelevant: the idea is to give people an illusion of food, a polite pretence not to know that in reality they are opening a foil packet of powdered soup. There are even advertisers brazen enough to pretend that the same powdered soup has been made with a pestle and mortar. . . . Analogous to the instant-coffee firms, whose illustrations tend to feature flowery coffee-pots in rococo silver, and in the background pretty black girls in turbans (hygienic!) grinningly cavorting on some lush Brazilian hillside.

This illusion of wonderful food, matched with the hideously arid reality, has quite a sadistic ring to it: in one of Edgar Rice Burroughs' Martian books (full of richly baroque imaginative effects) the hero is lowered into a torture-chamber and—after being tricked into eating a scrap of salt meat—left without food or drink. He is in total darkness but hidden lights suddenly glow, illuminating visions of fruit heaped up and beaded with condensation, crystal goblets of delicious drinks, and every variety of sophisticated culinary art. When he leaps forward to seize these he falls back stunned from a thick barrier of plate glass, while the lights go out with a snap, and 'mocking laughter rang in his ears'. The torture-chamber is called The Pit of Plenty.

There is, luckily, a brighter side to these horrors. Instead of buying powdered soup and cake mix, increasing numbers of people, especially men, teach themselves to cook. They actually like peeling onions and filling their eyes with stinging tears, mixing flour and butter with their fingertips, getting sticky and sweaty, even giving themselves a cut or a scorch once in a while. Cooking gives, in useful, accessible and relatively cheap form, a measure of relief from an existence with no activity (and no smells), a world in which one can work all day without once breathing real air, without once seeing daylight, without once walking up and down steps, a world in which the greatest muscular effort asked is initialling a piece of paper. In this world people drop dead suddenly, from horrible diseases for which the technicians have invented jargon names, which in more simple honest days would have been called grief and chagrin, passivity and boredom. If you go to Black Africa you will find neither lung cancer nor coronary heart disease. Ha, says the technician, but *we* do not have tuberculosis, yaws, ophthalmia—he is all set to give you the works but you can cut him off by saying that they had village idiots but no nervous depressions. It is the push-pull effect again, resulting in the very slow running-on-the-spot, with jerks and grimaces, which is our substitute for the Tritsch-Tratsch Polka. It should seem clear that bewildered children doing their own thing feel that they are being manipulated and played with. Cooking one's own dinner, however badly, is a simple and happy therapy. And what does it matter what you cook? Even with half a pound of sausages one can rediscover the pleasure of the past and be a greasy lout.

I am open, I suppose, to an accusation of reactionary sentimentalism, since I live in a country house in an isolated hilly district, and could play at Walden Pond to my heart's content should I feel so inclined. It is rather the opposite which is true. I place pathetic trust in technology, buy large, complex and expensive machines with an obstinate imbecility I fail totally to understand, and am an utter sucker for any sort of gadget. The house is eccentric and tends not to work, always at the worst possible moment.

> 'Though all the bathroom pipes are burst
> And the lavatory makes one fear the worst
> We're Proud of the Stately Homes of England'

lifting my hat in Mr. Coward's direction. These little shortcomings being aggravated by physical accidents, like a steep rocky terrain and occasional severe weather, and administrative difficulties like being several miles from shops and having to empty our own dustbin, I plunge frantically at any mechanical contrivance promising to simplify life and having of course exactly the opposite effect. We use gas, and electricity, and fuel oil, and coal, and wood, and we have had six cars in six years, are on our third washing machine, our third television set, and I still haven't learned a thing, except that a donkey and keeping-our-own-chickens would be even worse, if worse can be imagined.

Of course this is an inverted romanticism, quite as woolly-minded as making my own wine, creating a swimming-pool in the garden and several home-grown building projects, the planning of which keeps me happy for hours although remnants of sanity prevent me from actually attempting them. We live, in fact, in one of the most romanticized epochs there has ever been. Dreams of a world made happier and somehow more innocent by technology are dafter than any of the fantasies that overtake me, like pigging it in South America or going to live on a rather large sailing boat.

It is when intoxicated by some peculiarly witless notion that I find realities in the kitchen. Designing modern houses, full of technical improvements, which will form patterns to eliminate traffic problems, avoid all pollution and fit into landscaping with trees, all this on bits of greaseproof paper while waiting for the soup to boil, is a ravishing pastime, but peeling potatoes for seven's the necessary antidote.

9

THREE PARTY DISHES

There is nothing especially expensive about them, and only one is really elaborate. Extra pains?—extra trouble? Some. Original?—only in the sense that they are 'foreign' to both England and France. They come from the borders; from Holland, Belgium, and Alsace respectively. They share an attractive note of slight exoticism, and an unusual flavour.

The first, and by far the most complicated, is 'Nassi'; the proper name is *nassi goreng*, which is not Dutch at all but Indonesian, a dish brought back from Holland's one-time Far Eastern Empire and domiciled just like curry in Cheltenham. The recipe as I give it was taught me by an Amsterdammer, and keeps the light, crisp 'Chinese' character of the original. Anyone who enjoys Chinese food, and has a little experience of Chinese cookery will enjoy it, I promise.

Like all Chinese cookery it seems at first sight demanding and complicated, needing many ingredients, but it is worth the trouble. I give quantities, as usual, for four to five people.

The secret of this dish, as far as there is one, lies in preparing all the ingredients first, arranging them neatly on the table, having all the pots and pans lined up like horses at the starting line, and then working very rapidly for a short time. This is the familiar Chinese method. You can serve the finished dish either upon numerous small 'raviers' or oblong hors d'œvres dishes, ranged in a row and kept hot, in the oriental style, or upon one large dish if you prefer, but the basic ingredients of rice, meat, and vegetables must be kept separate and only mixed on the plate, or else there will be a soggy, unattractive mess.

The Meat: 500 gr. or a generous pound of lean, good quality pork, boned, like tenderloin or fillet. Cut it into regular cubes of handy size, that of a walnut. Larger than this takes too long, and smaller will dry out. These are either threaded six at a time on thin wooden skewers and grilled or left separate and shaken in a hot thick pan with a thread of oil. Either way they must be thoroughly but rapidly cooked, so that they remain juicy and tender.

These will be served masked in the following sauce. In the pan used for frying them put a little hot water to dissolve the coagulated juices, and enrich this with a meat cube, so as to have a decilitre or a quarter pint of strong gravy. Season this with a clove of garlic, crushed with the flat of a knife and chopped fine. Thicken to a sauce with a tablespoonful of peanut butter, whisking it in. Let it boil one minute, to blend and thicken to masking consistency. It will be poured over the meat at the last second.

The Rice: 500 gr. or a pound. It can be boiled, steamed or cooked as pilaff in twice its volume of water, to taste. All that matters is that the grains come out dry, unsticky, and a tiny bit underdone. For this a good-quality long-grain rice is indispensable. Do not flavour it, except for a little salt. When mixed at the last moment with small scraps of cooked chicken, or fish, or shrimps this gives a pleasant effect but is not at all necessary.

The vegetables: by far the most difficult and troublesome operation. Take two onions, two small leeks, and half a small savoy cabbage, which must be as fresh and crisp as possible. These vegetables are the equivalent in Europe of the bean-sprouts, bamboo-shoots, and other Chinese vegetables difficult to get fresh. They are sliced into fine shreds with a deep-bladed knife. They must be 'stir-fried' in the Chinese style. This can be done in a large deep frying-pan if you have one, or in a large pot if it has a rounded bottom. Heat it well with two tablespoons of vegetable oil—not olive oil—put in the shredded vegetables dry, and fry them while continually stirring, turning and mixing with a wooden spoon, so that they cook evenly. No liquid must be used, nor can they cook under cover: they would go damp and flabby. The whole point is that they stay dry, crisp, and underdone. In between five and ten minutes they will be ready. Season at the end with a pinch of salt.

The rice takes twenty minutes, roughly; the meat, and the vegetables, no more than ten. The rice, thus, must be started

first, and will finish the last. While waiting for it to be ready
there are two decorative additions to this dish. Each takes two
minutes.

First, *a banana* for each person, split and grilled or pan-fried
after being sprinkled with a little curry powder.

Second, *a tiny omelette*, taking one egg for two people, beaten
in a bowl the usual way, but cooked flat in the frying-pan, like a
pancake, instead of being rolled up. It can be spread out quite
thin. It is cut in strips generally, about 2 cm or an inch broad, and
these strips are often arranged in a lattice over the heaped dish of
rice.

As with all oriental rice dishes, little bowls of soya sauce are
served separately and, for those who like it, little bowls of 'sambal',
the familiar hot red peppers pounded to paste with a little oil.

The second dish is a famous Belgian classic: *Lapin à la bière*.
Like nassi, it is very good served with rice and with stir-fried
vegetables, but is excellent done in a traditional European way with
potatoes, boiled if they are good ones; and will stay whole, dry and
fluffy, mashed to a firm purée with a little milk if they are the
nasty kind that insist on disintegrating. A braised white cabbage is
good with this dish, or endive, or braised chicory, or sprouts; the
'Belgian' vegetables which are nowhere else as good.

A good-sized rabbit is enough for four to five persons. It is
easily cut in joints with a deep-bladed knife; the head, paws, and
small rib-bones are kept, for they make good soup. You also need
two large onions and about eight rashers of back bacon, not sliced
too thinly. Cut each onion into six neat quarters like the segments
of an orange, and roll the rashers up, narrow end first, into little
cigars.

To cook this you need a large fireproof dish, oblong or oval, of a
size to fit these ingredients comfortably side by side, so that they
are not packed or heaped, but remain touching, or nearly so. These
dishes have a lid, but you do not need it. They are often pretty
enough to serve in, and if this is the case so much the better; you
will be saved trouble. In this dish put a tablespoon of oil and a

walnut of butter, and heat over a medium flame till the butter is fizzling. Fry the joints of rabbit lightly on each side, so that they are just coloured. Some people dust them with flour first, like veal, but this is not necessary if you watch the heat and do not let the delicate meat frizzle or dry. A minute on each side is enough. Turn down the fire, or flame, and arrange the pieces of onion and bacon between and surrounding the joints of rabbit, until the dish is more or less full. The rabbit can be seasoned with a little salt and pepper, remembering that the bacon is salt. If you want a herb, a very small bayleaf can be crumbled up fine and strewn over, or a very little powdered thyme. The dish is now moistened with a bottle of beer—a half-pint is about right—most European bottles hold this quantity too. The Belgians have a very good, strong-flavoured beer called 'lambic' which they use (it makes a famous beef stew). Pilsener or lager beers are not quite right, being too blonde and a bit too bitter. The English 'brown ales' incline to be rather too sweet, and I think that perhaps Bass or Worthington would come nearest, or any well-hopped robust beer of good flavour; I am not at all an authority.

The beer may not cover the meat entirely, but this has no importance. You now strew a good tablespoon of dried seedless sultanas over the dish, allowing them to soak in the beer. The dish is then put in the oven, a medium oven, or even a bit on the slow side; it can be turned lower if it should appear to you that the dish is cooking too fast. The cooking method is easier to carry out than to describe, for the meat is not roasted, since there is a liquid, nor is it baked or braised, since the dish is not covered. Nor is it a stew, because it goes quite rapidly—hence the choice of a medium oven—and the liquid must reduce. What happens, as you will see if you try it out, is that the beer blends with the cooking oils and evaporates progressively until it forms a thin very strong sauce called a 'glaze', because it covers the meat with a film of shiny juices. The whole process takes around an hour, and during that time needs trouble and attention, because every quarter of an hour, say four times in all and one to finish up with, you should open the oven and with a spoon turn the joints around, basting them with spoonfuls of the juice, so that they are evenly, and in a sense continuously, moistened and impregnated with the cooking liquors. The onions and the bacon are thereby turned around too, but do not need stirring or shaking; you want to keep them whole and a nice shape, not to break them or they will be messy. The onions and the sultanas become perfectly tender; the bacon and the rabbit can be eaten with a spoon. I have said 'about an hour': this of course depends on the age of the rabbit, but they are nowadays reliable in this respect, for they are raised on farms, and sold skinned wrapped in cellophane by supermarkets, a thing I hate but wild rabbits are now a rarity. For a rather splendidly party dish one can sometimes get a leveret, which is a young hare.

Being without fat, these animals cannot be 'roasted' and it is a shame to stew them. Done in this way they are delicious. I realize that it is quite a lot of trouble.

If the liquid shows signs of reducing too quickly your oven is too hot. It must of course not dry out; there should be just enough glaze left at the end to bathe the joints with, as they are served.

The giblets (liver, heart and kidneys) are so tender and delicate that they cannot be cooked for so long. It is best if five minutes before serving time they are gently fried in a small pan with a dot of butter, and added to the rest at the last minute.

This is a splendid dish, but the basting process is troublesome; it is, I am afraid, indispensable.

The last dish is the rightly famous Alsatian 'Backeöffen'—this odd word can be spelt twenty ways, for the Alsatian dialect is a patois, spoken but not written, like Luxembourgeois, Schwyzer-dütsch or Belgian-German, and on paper one approximates. It is easily guessed that it means bake-in-the-oven. It is the least complex of the three dishes I describe, and can, thank heaven be forgotten about while cooking, a great relief after the last two. But it takes a bit of preliminary preparation. It is commonplace enough but for using three different kinds of meat, which gives the particular—and delicious—flavour, and for being cooked in dry white wine, traditionally an Alsace Riesling or Pinot.

You need, for four or five people, a pound and a half of meat, 250 gr. of each; beef, pork, and mutton. One takes braising pieces without bone, not too scraggy, like topside beef, shoulder of mutton and pork. No fat is needed, though I myself like always to have a thin layer; the meat is juicier and more tender thereby. Cut this meat into stew-size cubes, not too small, and put it in a deep fire-proof casserole. In Alsace these are of coarse earthenware, painted with peasant motifs and glazed; similar ones can be found in very many tourist districts. They break easily, but are cheap and attractive. The cooking and serving of this dish is done in them, but of course any glass or porcelain casserole does as well.

Sprinkle the meat with salt and pepper, add a sliced onion, two cloves of garlic (in Alsace it would be four or five), two cloves and a crumbled bayleaf. Moisten with enough white wine to cover the meat completely—nearly a whole bottle. A bottle is three-quarters of a litre, so that there may be a glass left, which is cook's perk. Stir the meat around a bit with a wooden spoon, so that it can soak well, and leave this marinade for twenty-four hours under the lid; ten minutes' work in all. The cooking is done next day. In Alsace it is 'Sunday dinner' and in bygone days the housewife gave it to the baker, to cook in his oven, before she went to Mass, just like the Auvergnat housewife with her leg of mutton: from this comes the classical 'boulangère' manner. This dish is very similar, being made with sliced onions and potatoes, but the manner is different, because of the earthenware pot.

Three and a quarter hours before dinner-time turn the marinade out into a bowl (how good it does smell!) and in the bottom of the casserole arrange a thick layer of potatoes sliced one centimetre thick (half an inch) and mixed with sliced onion and sliced white of leek—you will need in all two good-sized onions and two leeks. On top of this layer arrange the meat and the pot-herbs; your casserole should now be two-thirds full. Fill it up with another layer of potato and onion, sprinkle on a little more salt, and moisten the whole with the liquid from the marinade. Put on the lid of the casserole and you are ready to go. It cooks for three hours in a slow oven. But before putting it in, if you are ready to take a little extra trouble (and it is well worth it), you will seal the lid of your casserole with a strip of dough, simply made with flour, water and a thread of oil mixed to a soft unsticky paste. This cooks hard, will break cleanly off with no trouble at all, and will not mark or injure the casserole. What it will do is prevent all evaporation, seal in all the flavour of the dish, and produce a perfect meal which, I dare say, you will find unsurpassed anywhere. A French 'daube' of beef or mutton is done in the same way.

Since this dish is an 'eintopf' it needs no extra vegetable. But being rustic, heavy, and extremely solid, one might have a green salad after, and nothing to begin with.

The meat can be varied. Salt pork can be used in place of fresh, and delicious it is. Boiling chicken, and old braising duck can be used. The ubiquitous Alsatian goose pops up often. Veal could be used in place of mutton.

The drinks with these three dishes depend on taste. With nassi one traditionally drinks Pilsener beer. With the rabbit one could have the same beer as was used to cook with. Or Bordeaux. With the casserole again the same wine as went in.

None of these dishes needs anything much in the way of an introduction, though the Belgians, that robust race who eat more oysters than the rest of Europe put together, would not let the opportunity pass. ('Are there no oysters? Well, then, what about mussels?')

After nassi, one would, I think, eat pancakes, oriental ones with ginger. After backeöffen every true Alsatian would stow away a gigantic wedge of apple tart, but he does this whatever he has eaten. I don't think I could. More pancakes, with kirsch this time. And the Belgians? I feel sure that they would want one of their terrifying stinky cheeses, and I would settle for Stilton. And to digest these powerful meals—a marc distilled from grape-pressings. All districts have them, except Normans

who
have
Calva . . .

10

THREE WINTER CLASSICS AND SOME THOUGHTS ABOUT VEGETABLES

*Choucroute—Endives flamandes—Petits pois paysanne—Cabbages,
red, white and green*

The winter brings few joys to anyone. The cook, to be sure, rather
likes it; at last that hot kitchen and smell of soup have some point,
and his life is no longer so jarringly out of tune. These rather
pathetic comforts are hard-bought. But very few other people are
happy, and in England, by long tradition, misery becomes a
garment worn with a kind of sullen pride. This, I think, was
always so. Ivor Brown in a penetrating book on Shakespeare,
noticing that the month of April was fatal to many members of the
family, remarks that there is nothing unusual about that, considering how treacherous those raw east winds are after seven months
with no sun, and that the resistance was further much lowered by
the poor diet of Tudor England: even the rich, he points out,
relied too much on things like pigeon and ate hardly any vegetables.

Things have not changed all that much. English people still
hanker desperately for sunshine, complain of draughts and in-
adequate heating, and suffer from the monotony and poverty of
the available vegetables. To anyone who has lived for any length
of time in Continental Europe the pattern is clear enough, at
least in broad outline. The so-called continental climate is much
colder, but a great deal drier, and there is more sun, for the mari-
time drift, the unending westerly with rain and low cloud, is
checked and blocked by the big eastern and northern landmasses,
which send us the 'skaters' weather' of Holland and the ski weather
of the big central knot of mountains extending north to the
Ardennes and the German Taunus, and south to Jugoslavia and
Greece. The big stoves of central Europe keep houses warmer than
the traditional fire of coal-bearing England—and the food is more
varied. In Tudor times the poor people suffered, of course,
abominably, but perhaps more from war, pestilence and bandits
than from malnutrition.

I have already mentioned that many kinds of beans and peas still seem to be largely unknown in English cooking. Cabbage, though not available in so many varieties, is similarly neglected, so is the use of salt, not only for a winter vegetable like cabbage, but for autumn ones such as turnips and green beans.

Sour cabbage is the great winter stand-by of all central Europe, but in England it seems never to have been widely known, and is still thought of as something nasty liked only by Germans. In fact some people speak contemptuously of Germans as 'krauts', which is not very sensible if only because in England, for reasons which I do not always see clearly, vegetables are often of poor quality as well as lacking in variety. Visitors from abroad admire the wonderful milk and butter but wonder why the vegetables are so large, coarse, uninteresting and badly cooked. On the Continent, too, the products of the pig are handled with great ingenuity, economy, and much imagination, which is also a great help to the poor in the winter months, whereas in England charcuterie is a poor thing, spoken of contemptuously in my childhood as 'German sausage' and ignored. . . .

Alsace is an ideal terrain for studying winter food. It is in the heart of Europe, enclosed on all sides but the north by large mountain masses. It has a very cold but healthy winter climate. It is an extremely fertile alluvial plain. And sour cabbage, sauer kraut, has become French, is called 'choucroute' and is a way of life . . .

Geographically, the dismal area south of Strasbourg, where the Rhine overflows and logs the low-lying fields with water, is the ideal breeding-ground for this kind of cabbage, while ethnologically (a pompous word, but sour cabbage is a pompous thing) the German ingenuity for variations on pork has been lightened and refined by French civilization, which is Latin. And historically, like all French regional dishes, cabbage had titles of nobility conferred upon it by going to Paris. Pig-and-cabbage combinations, wonderful ones too, come from Lorraine, from Auvergne, and several other regions, but I should think (though I am subject to correction) that 'choucroute' did not become a by-word until the eighteen-eighties when Alsace was a national obsession after the German invasion. This, too, was the belle époque, highwater of bourgeois wealth and vulgarity: the two combined towards a golden age of brasseries. They have almost all disappeared: we mourn them, and the monstrous rococo welter of their furnishings, in magnificently execrable taste, is much sought after and devoured by antique shops as much as by junk dealers. To have a marble and cast-iron table or a copper gas chandelier from a brasserie on the Boulevard de Strasbourg in Paris is a powerful status symbol. To have drunk beer and eaten choucroute there is a poignant memory. One can still get it at Lipp at the Saint-Germain crossroads but it isn't the same. Those streets around the Gare de l'Est have great pathos: it was from here that so many thousands of train-loads left for the front before Verdun.

In Strasbourg itself one still eats choucroute served as in a temple—pompously—from consecrated dishes and according to rite, but first we have to get the proper atmosphere, as well as working up the proper appetite, by squelching through some muddy fields in gumboots.

Lots of little rivers guggle through the Alsace lowlands, overflowing frequently into little bogs full of stump and snag, tangles of alder and willow scrub gay in spring with kingcups. Everywhere under one's feet coarse reed-grass conceals runnels and overgrown ditches; little dams and rusty lock-gates everywhere illustrate the ingenuity of the farmer at draining and irrigating his fertile fields. There is almost certainly a heavy fog (Alsace in November, when the days are still warm and the nights cold, fairly sweats condensation) and there might easily be a chill drizzle. But it is not dreary; there are trees everywhere, and trees are happiness. Every verge is drained by fruit-trees (this is not real poplar country), fields are sheltered by oak and chestnut spinneys, and one even finds real woodland full of deer and spent cartridges cases, while everywhere is the bragging vanity, the quite unbearable stupidity of the pheasant, who is imbecile when alive and dull when dead, but goes very nicely, as we shall see, with sour cabbage.

In every field is the sight we came for; the farmer with a big crib-shaped wooden cart. Pulled, alas, by a tractor, now. He is filling it with the largest, firmest, roundest cabbages ever seen. He peels them to a pale silvery green which is pretty, and they are a fine sight travelling on the road with slow dignity (driving the motorist silly), piled extremely high in picturesque profusion and apparently never falling off. Should you follow them to the cabbage-factory you may, if interested by that sort of thing, see them seized by sharp rapid teeth which rend them into the familiar fine matted tangle, and men with pitchforks, waist deep in a foaming ocean of shredded cabbage: Alsace produces and exports the stuff in numbing amounts; the Chamber of Commerce has the figures, and not even West-African groundnuts could make duller reading.

They make sour cabbage at home too, of course: it is easy but, like wine, needs its own special primitive equipment. The shredded cabbage is put in a wooden tub with pickle spices and layers of coarse salt, covered with a wooden lid, and heavy weights are put on top. It ferments with the horrid smell of anything fermenting, oozing a ghastly liquid, but, again like wine, turns unexpectedly into delight—sour cabbage which is damp but not soggy, limp but nicely crunchy and chewable, with a pleasant invigorating smell, at once earthy and slightly musty, but nicely so, like a country wine-cellar. The note becomes a chord, for, married to the local Riesling, this forage, this nutriment, seeming to have been designed expressly for the stuffing of Stone Age mattresses, becomes simply paradisiacal.

The new season's sour cabbage is ready for the onset of winter. Since the supplies must last a year, to the end of the following autumn, becoming more sour the longer they are kept, the pungency of the flavour varies with the seasons. Before cooking it one must taste a little, and if it seems exaggeratedly or unpleasantly sour it should be rinsed under running cold water.

The essential mistake made in England with cabbage is to cook it with too much water. All fresh cabbage is cooked in the drops from the rinse, exactly like spinach: otherwise it will be soggy and tasteless, and will have shed most of its food value. Sour cabbage, having lost much of its natural moisture under pressure while fermenting, needs to have some of this lost liquid replaced. But not by water ... the Dutch have a bad habit of putting in water, and the result is sour cabbage, or rather baggage, in a bog; *à la flotte*, as the French say rudely. Fresh cabbage is braised in its own juice, and sour cabbage in a glass of white wine.

Enough talk; we are going to cook it, let's get on with it.

Take a heavy pot, round or oval, of enamelled iron or steel if you are going to cook on the fire, or a flameproof casserole if you prefer the oven. Put it on a fairly gentle flame, with a good table-spoonful of clean dripping from pork or duck or goose—bacon fat will do nicely, but beware of the salty sediment. Slice a large onion finely and throw it in, with six peppercorns and three juniper-berries. In Alsace they add plenty of garlic and so do I— this is a matter of taste.

When the onion begins to go transparent add the cabbage, a comfortable 500 gr., or 'a good pound', for four persons. Tease it out with a fork and let it fry gently for around ten minutes. Stir it with a wooden spoon, so that it cooks evenly. It must not, of course, burn or blacken, but can and should go a pale blonde colour, assisted by the onion doing the same. It will absorb all the dripping and may seem dry, but do not add more, or it will be greasy when the liquid is added.

When it starts to colour, and smells nice, moisten it with a wine-glass-full of any dry white wine of ordinary table quality, and add if needed a little water to bring the liquid barely to visibility-level. Add no herbs, and no salt. Cover and put on a gentle flame or in a slow oven to braise.

The cooking will take around two hours or rather more, depend-ing on how long the cabbage was in pickle. Some cabbages are eaten rather crisp and underdone, but this one must get really tender. It will not go sloshy or slimy even if overdone, so is better given a generous amount of time.

One now has the pleasant task of choosing what to cook with it. Pork of course in many forms. An old bird is delicious; a fowl or a duck, a goose (or piece of goose) and one of the nicest is pheasant, a dry bird which when roasted is a disappointment, but when braised with cabbage is—like an old partridge—splendid. These meats take an hour and a half or so to cook, and can be put in straight away: lift the lid, make a hollow nest in the cabbage with a wooden spoon and insert the bird deeply, so as to bury it. But if there is no bird, or not enough, you want some pork to go with it. A piece of smoked bacon, or salt pork, is always good. In a larger town there is a larger choice, and at the pork-butchers' you can choose anything that suits your fancy, including several kinds of sausage. The exception is the salami-cervelat type of dried smoked sausage: these are not cooked, and if one tries they just go tough.

All these things have different cooking times, and the dish must be dosed accordingly a longer or shorter time before dinner is planned. A piece of smoked or salted streaky needs an hour or more; a piece of ham or fresh pork less. A sausage takes about twenty minutes to braise or boil. One can also fry sausages separately, and add them at the last minute. Experience teaches one: thus after about an hour and a half, lift the lid and dabble about, to see whether anything put in at the start is yet ready. If the cabbage seems dry or over-reduced add a little more water—not wine, for wine needs long cooking. You could then add sausage, or small pieces of pork, and reckon on 'dinner in half an hour'.

In an Alsace restaurant one gets not only different kinds of choucroute, some very grand, cooked for instance in champagne, but traditionally several different kinds of meat—six, classically. To give an idea of the variety possible, besides the old game and poultry already mentioned, here is a list of what one might usually expect to find:

A braising sausage of finely minced smoked meat, and a frying sausage of coarser texture but more spiced: two kinds of bacon, salted or smoked, and often a piece of fresh pork as well, but more probably a cheap cut of streaky.

Different varieties, pink or white, of little tender boiling sausages made from pork or veal, called 'Frankfurter' or 'Münchener'.

Little dumplings of minced liver, also very Germanic these—called 'leberklose' ('*quenelles de foie*').

Wet-salted pork cutlets, or the smoked loin of pork, boned and rolled, called 'Kassler rib'—or a smoked palate, or tongue. The variations on charcuterie can appear infinite.

It is solid, earthy food—this book is full of country dishes, but this is perhaps the most 'countrified' of all. No vegetable is eaten with it, except a plain boiled potato—in Paris pushed disdainfully aside, and one stuffs with bread instead. Mustard is eaten with choucroute, and generally not the strong Dijon mustards, but much milder sorts of which one can eat a lot. In Alsace they have a way of filling up the table with all sorts of pickles. Well, contrary to what might be supposed, sour cabbage is not in the least indigestible, but pickles *are*.

Any white wine goes with it, as long as it is not sweet or over-perfumed. Also, of course, beer—'brasserie' means brewery. In Alsace as in England there are bewildering numbers of beers, and all one can say is that some are superb (the Germans, who ought to know, say better than theirs) and some are, to my taste at least, vile. Everyone has their own pets and hatreds about beer; it is most unsafe to dogmatize.

Sour cabbage is too dominating a dish to go with delicate meat, but it is amazing what can be done with it; a Jewish friend once boasted to me that she could make choucroute with any Christian, and I took her up on that, and she made one with salt beef and kosher sausage, and it was delectable. Up in Belgium they probably do it with horse.

One would not want to eat this dish very often—one might turn into a sour cabbage oneself, a frightful fate, overtaking many without their ever noticing. But on those shivery raw days between the New Year and May, to build up the lowered resistance—there really is nothing nicer.

Reverting to the question of British maltreatment of vegetables, I suppose that the biggest barrier to British enjoyment of something else than limp cabbage, woody carrots and whitened-sepulchres of cauliflower may well be the superabundance of very huge, very green peas. I cannot, with regret, do anything about this except to suggest they be put in concrete barrels together with the Mafia and radio-active wastes, and sunk.

A second barrier is a series of odd English assumptions, of which the oddest—nobody can explain it—is that chicory is called endive and endive is called chicory. This, which has led to tearful tourists tottering on to the car ferry sobbing 'Never Again', can be fixed. Or so one would think, but I should not like to be the one to try. And for a start here is the extremely simple recipe for *endives flamandes*—which turned up among friends under the jaunty title of Nik's Chik, and that tastes the same . . .

For four to five people, take about six heads of Belgian chicory, for that is the best. It should be very firm and crisp, the little yellow tips tightly overlapping, and with virtually no waste. Clip the root very slightly, not so much that the leaves disintegrate, and discard any bruised bits. Any very thick ones are cut in half lengthways, so that they are all roughly of even size. These are put in a large saucepan where they can lie in a flat bundle, are covered with lightly salted cold water, brought to the boil and simmered for about ten minutes or till they are cooked when tried with a fork, but still firm and underdone. Drain them thoroughly.

For each piece of chicory you have bought a thin slice of ham. Shoulder ham, which is boned and pressed, and comes out a neat rectangular shape, is perfect for this dish. Roll each piece up in a slice like a cigar, and arrange them in a shallow oblong gratin dish which you have greased with a bit of butter-paper. You need now enough cream sauce, made of flour, butter and milk, to mask them: that is a tablespoon of butter, a good tablespoon— meaning heaped up a little—of flour, and around three-quarters of a pint, or four decilitres, of milk. It can be seasoned with salt and a little pepper, and perhaps a grate of nutmeg.

With a little practice anyone can make good cream sauce. I do not give proportions intended to be exact: experience is a better guide. There is no secret involved, and only one simple trick, which is to use a wooden spoon and not have the milk too hot, nor

add too much at a time. Always use a thick enamelled saucepan
and never aluminium. If the milk, by the sort of hazard which is
frequent, *has* got too hot, then take the pan with the butter and
flour mixture right off the fire before adding it: lumps will be the
less likely to form. Let a sauce like this boil for a few minutes
gently: to see if it is the right thickness dip in the wooden spoon
and hold it up, to judge how the sauce trickles off. A well-made
cream sauce is shiny.

The chicory-ham cigars are masked with this, a little fine brown
breadcrumb, grated parmesan, (or a mixture of both), is scattered
over, and the dish is put to *gratiner* in a medium-to-fast oven for
ten minutes, or till nicely brown and very hot all through. The
rich flavour of ham in cream sauce balances perfectly against the
clean and slightly bitter taste and crisp texture of the chicory.

These vegetable dishes, very frequent in a French kitchen, are
simple, economical and satisfying: they are generally a supper dish
but for anyone wishing a light lunch they are well adapted. One
does not need potatoes; a little bread suffices. Here is another
which is very quick.

Petits pois paysanne: for four to five people take a litre tin of
French peas, the 'fin' or 'très fin' grade—or 'extra fin' if there are
guests. For each person a thickly cut slice of back bacon. Slice
these across to the length of a matchstick and the width of a
pencil; put them in a heavy saucepan without fat, upon a medium
flame. When they begin to fry stir them so that they cook evenly.
When they start to produce a little melted fat add a coarsely
chopped onion, turn the flame low and let the mixture simmer
until pale blonde. Add the peas, obeying the instructions on the
tin. Some peas are 'au naturel'—so-called—and the juice they
contain must be drained, and the peas rinsed before use. Others
can be used juice and all, and this is the type to get. Otherwise
one must add a little water. The peas need no seasoning, but a
little tarragon can be added.

Wash out the leaves of a lettuce, squeeze them slightly, roll
them into a cigar-like bundle under your hand, and slice them
across, the width of a grass-blade; add this to the peas. This dish

needs scarcely any cooking, unless of course you have the luck to have fresh peas, which must be simmered gently till done. The dish is finished by binding the juice with a hazelnut of butter mixed with a teaspoon of flour: not a 'sauce' but enough to give the juice a creamy consistency. I have no opinion at all of deep-frozen peas.

The worst mistakes which can be made with vegetables is to cook them with too much water. Very few types are cooked 'swimming'. Artichokes of course, and asparagus, and boiled potatoes. As a general rule, they need just enough to cover them and no more. If they are cooked gently with a tightly-fitting lid to the saucepan they will keep more of their flavour and their food value. They then need only very light salting. What stock is left can in most cases be used for a sauce or a soup. With root vegetables like carrots one can thicken the stock to a sauce, adding a little cream and serving them in their own juice. Fresh summer carrots and turnips are cooked with so little water that by the time they are ready it has reduced to a few drops. A hazelnut of butter and a tiny pinch of sugar are added.

Brassica vegetables, like cauliflower, brussels sprouts and the small summery cabbages, have to be kept very crisp and decidedly underdone. Their stock is not good for soup and is thrown away.

An extraordinary myth, perpetrated by many books, states that green vegetables should be boiled hard in lots of water without a lid. The notion appears to be 'to keep the pretty colour'. This advice is wrong on all three counts. If you want very badly to eat bright green things, then your best bet is watercress which is not cooked at all.

The big winter cabbages are braised, because they are hard and fibrous, and need slow cooking which sometimes takes a long time. The extreme case is a red cabbage, a thing needing around three hours; it must be very tender. There is only one basic recipe for it, but it is a very good one. This, along with sour cabbage, belongs with our 'winter classics'.

In a large braising pot, for the cabbage when raw takes up a lot of space, put a spoonful of beef or pork dripping, or oil: butter can be used. On a very gentle fire put in a large onion, finely sliced, to melt slowly. Meanwhile quarter the cabbage, take off bruised or gnawed outer leaves, cut out the stalk, and slice it fine with a deep-bladed knife. Rinse it rapidly in a sink full of cold water. Pick it out with a strainer, and add it to the pot, filling this about half full and reserving the rest for a moment. Make a nest in the middle of the pot for a piece of meat, which can be smoked, salted or fresh pork. You do not need much; half a pound will do. Around the meat strew a peeled, cored, sliced cooking apple. Sprinkle all this quite generously with powdered cinnamon. Add if you like a clove or two. Season with salt, never much, and if you have salted meat rather little. Add the rest of the cabbage. The drops of water clinging to it give enough liquid. Cover the pot with the lid and let it braise very very gently for two hours. You then give it a thorough stir, fish out the piece of meat which will by now be quite cooked, and taste the cabbage. It will almost certainly still be hard. It may need a little more salt. It should not be dry, but if by hazard it is add a glass of red wine or of water. In all probability it needs another hour's very gentle cooking. The trimmed finely sliced meat is put back at the last minute and the dish is served with purée potatoes.

If one wants to make a party dish of this it is very good with grilled gammon ham. You then need to cook no meat with the cabbage, but a pork rind and a few bones will make it juicier.

A white cabbage sounds much the same thing, but is in fact different in many respects. The same method is used, but without meat. A glass of dry white wine can be used. Instead of being cooked very slowly till quite tender it is kept more crisp, and should not take much more than an hour and a half. It is seasoned with a few caraway seeds instead of cinnamon. Its flavour is lighter and more delicate than that of red cabbage, and it is altogether less rustic a dish. Instead of eating it with gammon, which has a crude hearty flavour, one would choose to grill a pork chop, or a nice variation would be a pork tenderloin, which can be grilled or roasted but since it has not fat is better *poêlé*, like veal, flavoured with nothing but salt and pepper and cooked in around thirty minutes, in a closed pan with a nut of butter.

A green or 'savoy' type cabbage has a delicate flavour, and while it is done in the same way it needs no onion, no bacon, and no seasoning beyond salt and a couple of juniper berries. It melts away much more than the other two, will not need much over an hour's cooking, and care must be taken to cook it very gently, for it is fragile and easily goes brown. It does not need to be sliced fine, and many people like it kept in large chunks: a small one quartered in four, a larger in six or eight. It is good with fresh pork, but better still with beef. With beef à la mode for instance, or with a *pot au feu*, when it should to my mind be kept separate in its own casserole, rather than cooked with the beef: a little of the beef stock can be added to it.

I have tried to show while writing this book a number of truths which I think have become forgotten or obscured in the years since the last great war. Other points are more contestable, and I have not wished to be dogmatic, where matters of taste or opinion are concerned. Quite often I have gone against accepted currents of opinion. This need not worry anyone—we have seen too many examples of ideas which because they were new and modish caught on very rapidly with the majority of populations, were regarded as sacred dogmas and often as universal panaceas, and have since been found utterly untrustworthy. DDT insecticides are a classic example. So to my mind is deep-frozen food. A deep-freeze has a good deal of use in the home, especially for things which are superabundant during a short season, or extremely cheap because of a glut, but the commercial use of the method is to my mind a complete failure.

One idea which is at the present very modish in 'over-developed' countries is that we eat too much, especially proteins. I think that worrying about our cholesterol level is also likely to be a passing phase, but that the immediate effect of this idea will be to make food even nastier and drearier than it now is. I am convinced that a little more thought about food, understanding of food chemistry, and willingness to take more trouble would put many of these ideas back into their proper proportion. There is no need to have fads about food, and the averagely-constituted person, who has no unusual glandular or physiological imbalance, and takes a reasonable amount of physical exercise, can learn to digest his food properly and can eat anything. The fashion for very slim women is only a passing phase. One gets into a habit of dieting, just as one gets into a habit of eating too much or being constipated. In Western Europe or America we can get a very large variety of food and we should try to renew and rethink out eating habits. Cookery books, as I have so often said, are not very good guides to good cooking, but they do at least spur the imagination and encourage us to alter our little ways. I do not wish—once more —to be dogmatic, but if we eat too much meat it is easy on one day in the week to eat only vegetables and fruit. If the cholesterol is too high one can have meals almost without fat, with braised meat, poached chickens and raw vegetables. One can learn to balance different kinds of food. It is not very difficult if one enjoys food and enjoys the kitchen. . . .

To get the best out of vegetables—and avoid the burden of buying huge quantities of Vitamin C capsules—they should be peeled as little as possible, washed as little as possible (we absorb anyway huge amounts of very vile and doubtless dangerous insecticides and artificial fertilisers, but luckily we are very adaptable) and cooked as little as possible. One can eat two vegetables or more instead of meat without being a food-faddist. Vegetables, even the commonest and most banal, have considerable therapeutic value. This cannot replace synthesized pharmaceutical chemicals, but can go a long way towards having fewer pills in the bathroom cupboard. Thus a digestive upset, such as cramps or diarrhoea, can be relieved and often cured by going without a meal and having a large salad of raw carrots instead, with lemon juice and a little oil. Onions, boiled or braised, give great relief from rheumatism. Lemon juice is an excellent disinfectant. One could go on for some time: herbal remedies are not to be sneezed at. Lastly, it never did anybody any harm to eat a lot of fruit, stale crusts of bread, and green salad, and to drink lots of water. One can drink a lot of alcohol if one takes a day now and then on Evian and fruit juice. This is all labouring the obvious, like walking instead of taking a taxi. I'm not going on; it begins to sound like Ian Fleming teaching everyone how to make coffee.

II

THREE OLD-FASHIONED
VEAL DISHES

Roast Loin Meran—Osso bucco—Pommes Anna—Risotto
Fricandeau à l'Oseille

The human being is such a creature of habit that he falls easily into laziness and monotony. He dislikes both the effort of altering his basic conceptions and the need for concentration in carrying out new or at least unaccustomed movements, and this applies to cooking and cooks as much as to musicians, politicians, or physicians. The cook falls easily into narrow and hidebound ways, and while the strength of regional cooking lies in doing the same thing over and over again until it is perfect, the weakness is that standards are blunted by repetition and rigidity. A country restaurant loses its reputation, often very quickly, when work on the three or four dishes in which it specializes becomes listless and mechanical.

Exactly the converse process takes over in 'international' restaurants, where the menu is far too big and varied, where there is a high turnover of staff, and where there is great pressure to allow vulgar, luxurious and flashy presentation to compensate for lacklustre food cooked in a slipshod way. The cook at home has the same problems. Living in the country, as I know by experience, one becomes too easily resigned to a butcher who does only a few things at all well, to never seeing some kinds of vegetable at all, and to work of a plodding, rustic sort with little virtue in it because imagination and enterprise have become dulled. Whereas the cook who lives in the town, with an immense choice, is tempted to chase after novelties, to be in too much of a hurry and work badly, and excuse the one on the ground of the other. Supermarkets with too much choice are as bad as village shops with no choice at all. Gigantic cookery books with five thousand recipes are bad, because nine-tenths of the stuff is there just for show. The famous master Monsieur Pellaprat wrote an excellent simple handbook for pastrycooks, serious and professional and beautifully lucid; he also wrote a monstrous encyclopedia which is frankly very bad.

I wanted this book to have only a few recipes, but if they dealt with nothing but pea-soup and cabbage it would be very boring. After considering pork and beans at some length the reader as well as the writer wants something lighter and more delicate to clear his palate.

Traditionally veal was bad in England, where the farmer did not know how to produce it, the butcher did not know how to cut it, and the housewife had no experience of preparing it. But in Austria and Italy, where one is flooded with veal, it can be just as bad because of the slipshod habits I have been going on about. Here then are three recipes for veal, one Austrian, one Italian and one French; all of them can be horrors, so that to enjoy them it is necessary to remember again what they were like when they were new. I think of my first glimpse of Italy—Como, from the train—and of Austria; not so much the sight as the smell of a ski-village in the Arlberg.

A *roast loin of veal Meran*, or Meraner Art as it is properly called, is a big party dish for several people. The loin can of course be cut to any size beginning with a single chop, but the one indispensable thing in this dish is the kidney which goes with it, and no butcher will give you a veal kidney, which to him is equivalent to a Nobel Prize, unless you take the whole loin, which few people can cope with. So that we have to cheat a little. Take a pork kidney—itself an excellent thing—and enough suet to wrap it up in. For up to six persons you want 1200 gr., or nearly three pounds, of loin, which when boned will give you just under a kilo. This you can do quite easily at home.

Put the meat hollow side up and narrow end towards you so that the thick ridge of spine is on the far side. If the joint has a piece of filet mignon you can now see it, and detach it easily with a sharp boning knife. This will expose the short flat rib-bones. If you now stand the joint up and bend the meat back with one hand you can cut along the line at the top of them, slide the knife down the flat surface behind and along the serpentine curve of the backbone: it is much easier to do than to describe. Holding and pushing the meat away from the bone it is now quite simple to scrape and detach it from the spine, keeping the knife as close to the bone as you can and not allowing the blade to cut into the meat. Beef or mutton are hard to bone without training and practice, but veal is easy, or else I would not suggest this. The firm, pink, elastic meat has little sinew and no heavy fat, and the contours of the bones are smooth, round, easy to feel for and follow. Instead of being a squarish block the joint now opens out and lies flat. Turn it skin side up and you will see that where the meat joined the spine there is a strong band of sinew which ran, originally, all along the spinal column. Cut this off, along the length of the joint and to about 2 cm. or an inch wide: it is easy to do since the sinew is right on the corner.

Now turn the joint again flesh side uppermost and sprinkle it with the finely grated peel of one lemon, spreading this and working it in with your finger. Dust the same surface with paprika, finely and evenly. Arrange the kidney, wrapped in its suet, lengthwise in the hollow, with the piece of filet mignon if there was one, roll the joint up tightly to a neat sausage shape, and tie it with six lengths of string. Your heart has already failed you, just reading all this. I quite agree; it is infinitely tiresome work. I have also said that a proper joint had the bones left on and needed no string. I still say this. But a 'rognonade' (technical word for this joint) is so delicious that it is worth the trouble for once. If you do not feel able to do the boning you can ask the butcher to do so.

Chop the bones up into inch-long lengths, or three centimetres. Arrange them in an oval or oblong fireproof dish. Add a sliced carrot and onion, a little branch of fresh marjolaine or a tiny pinch of dried, and arrange the rolled loin on top. With a table-knife, butter the inside of the dish's lid thickly, as though it were a crust of fresh bread. Cover the dish and let the joint cook lengthily and thoroughly in a medium oven. For this type of cooking no English word exists. It is not a roast, since you are cooking with the lid on. It is not a braise, for you have added no liquid. In French it is called to *poêler*: it is an excellent, simple and delicious method but can only be done with fine cuts of good quality meat, and is particularly suitable for veal and chickens. You are simply cooking in the natural juice and fat of the piece in question. Since neither veal nor chickens have quite enough fat of their own you butter the dish as I describe.

A piece of veal of this size will take to up an hour and a half. Around half-way you should look at it, turn it top to bottom, baste it with the juice, and assure yourself the oven is neither too fast—the meat too brown and dry—nor too slow—the meat colourless and stewing languidly. It should go a good honey-blonde colour. The outside will not go crisp because of the steam, but will form a delicate brown crust. When you feel that it must be nearly ready, after an hour and a quarter, prick deeply with a fork into the centre. Remember that both veal and kidney must be thoroughly cooked. The juice which comes out must be quite colourless. If this is the case, lift the joint out to a carving board and let it rest. Put the pot, without its lid, on a medium flame. When the bones begin to brown and sizzle add a pound of fresh tomatoes, preferably sloshy, and season with salt; salt the joint also at the same time. Cover the pot and let this tomato sauce cook well out for ten minutes before straining it. At the last moment cut the strings of the joint and slice it not too thinly with a sharp steak knife.

This extremely fine dish deserves a good wine, like a Burgundy, and a simple but carefully done accompaniment, for instance potatoes baked in their jackets (done in the oven at the same time as the meat) and fresh French beans cooked in as little water as possible, left a scrap underdone, and finished with a good walnut of butter and plenty of chopped parsley.

Since this is a meal of very delicate flavour do not spoil your palate or your appetite beforehand. No whisky or highly flavoured apéritif, or pickles. A bowl of beef consommé, a glass of wine, and a piece of bread. And to follow, a nice light apple tart or turnover, or charlotte.

The second dish is *osso bucco*, or rather *ossi bucchi*, but my Italian is that of a Spanish cow. Everybody has had this done badly, with a slovenly Milanese mess of overcooked spaghetti and over-flavoured tomato sauce. But it is a dish worth taking trouble over, for all its banality. Here are two versions, one Basquaise, the other Piedmontaise.

It is a shin of veal, whole but sawed into sections three centimetres broad (an inch) and this is best done by the butcher, because it needs a meat saw and also one has to know the trick. You now have four or five medallions, each large enough for one person, of firm meat with no waste, with at the centre a hollow bone (osso bucco) containing veal marrow. .

Take a shallow fireproof dish large enough for all the pieces to fit flat on the bottom. Put it on a medium flame with a spoonful of oil and a small nut of butter. Fry the medallions of meat for a minute on each side, enough to stiffen them and brown them lightly. Lift them out on to a plate. In the now browned oil put a large onion sliced fine, a good green pepper with the core, pith and pips taken out, also finely sliced (this is the 'basquaise' version), two good cloves of garlic, peeled and sliced, salt and pepper, and a little branch of fresh rosemary. Do not let the vegetables go brown, but pale blonde. When they have cooked down moisten them with a good glass of dry white wine—it does not really matter if this is not from the Pyrenean region. Fit the meat back into the pot, and if needed add just enough water barely to cover the medallions. Put the lid on the pot and simmer for an hour very gently indeed. Lift the lid and add four fresh tomatoes, each cut in eight sections. Put the lid back and simmer another fifteen minutes, when all should be perfectly done and the meat very tender, but do not hesitate to cook it for longer if needed. Sprinkle the stew with plenty of chopped parsley and eat it out of the same dish, because the medallions are fragile, and if heaved about the little 'hearts' of marrow may get lost.

The Piedmontaise version is done in exactly the same way, but instead of green pepper, use the peel of a lemon—only the yellow; cut off the white pith—sliced fine. The wine is Alpine instead of Pyrenean, and for a variation a tiny branch of sage is used instead of rosemary. Since this dish, like most stews, already has vegetables with it no further vegetable is needed. Instead, green salad afterwards. The accompaniment could be potatoes, or rice. In the Pyrenees country one would probably be offered potatoes finely sliced and cooked in oil, in a shallow metal pan in the oven, until they got a nice brown crust above and below, one of the innumerable varieties of '*Pommes Anna*'. In the French Alps you might get offered a *gratin dauphinois* or *savoyard* (they are much the same) which is similar but the sliced potatoes are cooked in thin cream or top-milk mixed with a beaten-up egg: the pan containing this mixture is put in the oven until crisp and brown on top and tender inside; it should not be too dry.

In the Italian Alps you would get *risotto*. This is very easy. For four people take a soup-bowl of raw long-grain rice. In a good thick saucepan melt a finely chopped onion over a gentle flame, with a spoonful of oil and a hazel-nut of butter. Add a crushed clove of garlic. Add the rice, and let it slowly absorb all the fat: it will take on a transparent look. Stir it with a wooden spoon. Add, gradually, half a bowl at a time, two soup-bowls (double the amount of rice) of water or clean white stock. Each time this boils stir the mixture with a fork, to loosen it and cook it evenly, and add another half-bowl-full. The total cooking time will be twenty minutes, about. With the last shot of water do not stir but give the pot a gentle shake. When the rice is cooked (it is not dry like a pilaff but moist and a bit creamy) take it off the flame, taste it for seasoning, and add more salt if needed, a turn of the pepper-mill, another nut of butter and a tablespoonful of finely grated parmesan cheese. Stir this well through with the fork and eat it at once. If left it will go on cooking, and become clawky.

The last dish—and none the worse for that—is *Fricandeau à l'Oseille*, once one of the most commonplace dishes of the French bourgeois kitchen but now (the French bourgeoisie is not what it was) it is a weekend dish, almost a party dish, along with beef à la mode and stuffed shoulder of mutton and even pot au feu, since the French housewife is as much in a hurry as anyone, and slaps you out those boring escalopes without a tremor.

When the hindquarter of beef is butchered, you have topside

and silverside and the rest, but for the quarter of veal no names that I know exist in English. Luckily it does not matter much, because if the veal is of good quality the thick joints of the hind-quarter can be cooked in the way described for the loin—they are all cut for escalopes. But, as everyone knows, the 'topside' of beef is finer-grained and at a pinch can be roasted, whereas the bigger, coarser silverside is a braising piece. So with veal: the topside, called in France the 'noix' cooks very well when *poêlé*, and if wrapped in a sheet of thin pork fat as a French butcher does it, will roast perfectly. To *poêler* a silverside may take more time, and it will not be quite as tender, but with modern veal it is perfectly possible. The *fricandeau*, as this piece is called, used to be braised in traditional recipes, and the old-fashioned French *fricandeau* was a piece cut like a very thick escalope and larded through with fat pork. Nowadays it can be left in one piece, in the size wanted. For four to five people allow a piece of 800 gr. or rather over a pound and a half. Tell the butcher you want half a pound of veal bones chopped small. This piece can be cooked on the bones, with a carrot and an onion, in a buttered pot rather than a fireproof dish, for to get it nice it needs enough heat to get it well browned, and some casseroles do not take kindly to anything hotter than a slow oven. The piece is thinner than a rolled loin, and will be cooked quicker, in about an hour or a few minutes over, and since it is a poorer, drier piece it can be snuggled down to the bottom of the pot with the bones on top and the vegetables surrounding. Done in this way it stays moist. Salt it when it comes out of the oven, and add a teaspoon of tomato purée and two cups of white stock to the bones. If this is boiled down to half you will have a very good strong gravy called *fonds* when it is strained and thickened with a little potato starch (one teaspoonful, stirred with two of sherry, added to the boiling liquid).

Oseille, or sorrel, except in Italy or a few country markets of the French backwoods, is now rarely seen. The modern equivalent is to use spinach, which both looks and tastes very similar. This is cooked in a saucepan greased with a drop or two of oil, in no more than the few drops of water left hanging on the leaves after washing, with the lid on: it cooks quickly. Strain it into a wire sieve and allow the liquid to drain away naturally for five minutes. Unless very old and huge it is a pity to chop or mince spinach. The sharp metallic accent of this vegetable is the right accompaniment for the bland texture and delicate flavour of *fricandeau*. Deep-fried potatoes, *pont-neuf* or *allumette*, go well as the third note of the chord, and a good full white wine, an Auxerrois or a Sancerre of respectable family, would add a flourish.

12

TWO FLOURISHES AND
AN EPIGRAM

Cinnamon lamb stew—Lamb 'Epigrams'—Moussaka

The chief difficulty with lamb, or mutton—we need a new name really since what is sold nowadays is neither the one nor the other —is the nasty flavour of the fat. Fat—I have said this before—is indispensable to a successful dish containing meat, which becomes cardboardy if cooked without it. If properly cooked the flavour added is another advantage. But surplus fat is a horrible thing, especially melted and floating about, and few things are nastier than the Dutch version of chicken soup with a thick yellow layer upon it, except perhaps the notion of Tibetan tea as it is generally described, with rancid butter added. . . .

Mutton fat has a peculiarly stale flavour which seems to accentuate the greasiness, and to work in consequence with anything but a leg of lamb, or with the little grills and roasts from the ribs and loin, poses this problem in acute form. And yet the forequarter exists and cannot be just disregarded. It is cheap too, which can be of great importance. It can be made delicious. But no doubt of it that those necks and shoulders with their seemingly indecipherable mixtures of fat and bones are nasty complicated things. Alexander Dumas, passionately interested in food, a perfect goldmine—and occasionally a rubbish-heap—of kitchen folklore, suggested that the only way was to grill the pieces fiercely first before stewing them. This he says gets rid of the taste of *suif*. The method works well with some classical dishes like *navarin*, though this is a stew with spring vegetables, and at its best is made with the scraggy bits of a spring lamb, which has of course hardly any fat. . . . Like many of his notions it is only half thought out; the flavour of burned *suif* is in no way pleasanter than that of boiled suif. A French *Champvallon* can taste quite as beastly as a bad Irish stew.

There are two ways of turning the difficulty, and here is a recipe for each of them. The first is to perfume the meat with added flavours of a pungent kind, and the obvious example is curry: few things could be nicer than good mutton curry with coconut milk and sour tamarind pickles and all those other delectable whatnots. But it is a lot of trouble, few people now can be bothered to do it at home properly, and in England, which used to be a temple of curry, the Imperial traditions seem to have been transferred to specialized Indian, Pakistani and recently Indonesian restaurants. But one doesn't have to use curry: there are other oriental spices besides that rather revolting-sounding turmeric. In fact the whole middle East is full of mutton dishes which are marvellous to eat when travelling about in the Lebanon or wherever, but when taken to pieces for examination sound forbidding and dreadfully complex. As anybody who has tried to make cous-cous, classic standby of North Africa, will confirm, fidgeting round with semolina is enough to turn the most enthusiastic cook into Saint Simon Stylites pillar and all, and what on earth is harissa anyway? And all those dishes full of yoghourt, so ominously Saddle of Camel Bulgarian Style . . . oh dear.

As a child reading Kipling I became fascinated with his phrase about the cinnamon stew of the fat-tailed sheep. Sounds ominous; plainly there's a lot of *suif* about, but he shouts about it with such noisy enthusiasm that I wanted to know more. There are a myriad versions— every little valley from Tangier to Afghanistan has its own notion of cinnamon stew and this is a simplified, Europeanized version. For four to five people, allow a kilo or two pounds of cheap forequarter *lambton*—by which I mean of either lamb or mutton. This sounds a lot but the price is low and the loss with bones immense. Chop it into manageable pieces, and trim excess bits of fat and bone—beware of splinters—as well as you can. In a good-sized heavy pot, for it takes up a lot of room, brown these pieces rapidly in a tablespoonful of vegetable oil: it is probable that this must be done in two stages. Take them all out, keep them on a plate, and turn the flame down.

In the pot you put two onions chopped fairly fine and stir them about with a wooden spoon till they are pale blonde. Add two teaspoonfuls of tomato purée and about the same of powdered cinnamon, stirring it to a paste, much as you would do with curry. Add a small amount, about a coffeespoonful, of powdered ginger: the amounts used of these spices depend on their freshness. The little jars sold in the shops are invariably stale, and need to be used more generously. Thicken this paste further still with a teaspoonful or more of flour; the sauce must not be over-thick, but one needs a good deal to cook all that meat. The sauce is made in the ordinary way with cold water, adding it little by little and stirring vigorously to get a smooth mixture. Season the sauce with salt and a little piece of bayleaf. When it boils up you put in the meat, turn it down to a simmer, and cook it as a stew for about an hour and a half or till very tender indeed. Lift out the meat carefully and keep it on a plate. Let the sauce go off the boil. After a few minutes you will find a layer of melted fat on the surface which must be scrupulously skimmed. Allow to stand and repeat this after another two minutes. You have now rather too much of rather too thin a sauce, which can be reduced by boiling it on a medium flame with the lid off, stirring it frequently with a wooden spoon to avoid sticking. This sauce can be flavoured now with the various traditional relishes, generally dried fruit and nuts. Sultanas can be used, but dried apricots are much better, having a tart flavour which marries well. These must cook enough to swell them and make them tender. Almonds or better hazelnuts, salted and grilled, can be added or kept separate. Exotic things like cardamoms and pine-kernels can be found in speciality shops. They are not necessary. Imagination and enterprise will suggest other variations. Sweet pickles and so on.

While the sauce is cooking down, prepare a large heap of boiled rice as dry and fluffy as you can get it. You take as many bones as you can out of the meat and either add it to the rice or keep it separate: the sauce is always kept apart.

If when you boil rice you add the peel of a lemon to the water you will find the flavour much improved. Some people put it in the sauce but I think that the mingling of too many spices leads to confusion, and to tasting none of them properly.

The second dish concerns the other way of avoiding the *suif* flavour, which is to grill the meat after it has been cooked instead of before. Even more than the cinnamon stew, it shows that the cheapest and most despised scraps of meat there are can be wonderful if one is prepared to take trouble. This dish belongs to the 'two-day' category because it needs little cooking but a lot of preparation: it is a very old-fashioned French country recipe called Sainte-Menehould, and in restaurants—when found; it is now a rarity!—is given the poetic name of 'Epigrams'.

For four to five persons, ask the butcher for two breasts of lamb, whole. Nobody buys them now; they cost about sixpence. . . . In a wide pot, season enough water to cover them with carrot, onion, celery, peppercorns, salt, and tarragon. Cook this stock for twenty minutes, enough to flavour and perfume it, and poach the breasts of lamb gently for thirty to forty minutes or until a fork slips effortlessly in and out of the meat. Fish them out, put them on a flat dish, put a plate on top, and weight this with a heavy object, such as one of those large impressive cookery books—a use found for them. . . .

Do not throw away the stock; it will make excellent Scotch broth or any other mutton-based soup. Put the breasts of lamb in a cool place and forget about them till next day, when they will be found in rigor mortis which is just the way you want them. Bone them as much as possible—the flat rib-bones slide out easily and the knobbly bits at the breast can be cut out with little effort, together with the skin and surplus fat. This job, impossible with raw or hot meat, is no trouble with cold cooked meat. You have now two largish pieces of boned meat about an inch thick. Trim any ragged edges and cut neat domino-shaped pieces about four inches long and two wide: 10 cm. by 5. Cut across the breasts, in their width, so that the epigrams follow the grain, as the fibre is called. The meat is tender but firm, and cuts easily into these sharp right-angled pieces. Dust them with flour, dip them in egg beaten up with salt, pepper, and a little cold water, and pass them through fresh white breadcrumbs: press the crumbs well in to the meat and pat off any excess.

The whole success of this meal, and it can be superb, depends on what you now do. Consider:—egg-and-breadcrumbed pieces are fried in butter, which is fine for escalopes, chickens and such-like dry pieces, but would be unbearable with greasy bits of lambton. You need a grill, but an ordinary grill would simply burn the breadcrumbs. . . . The compromise, and the technical trick or *tour de main* of this dish is to use your heaviest cast-iron pot. The bottom of this is probably not wide enough or flat enough to grill all the epigrams together, but no matter: they don't take more than a minute or two, since they are already cooked. All they need is a short time on a very hot surface, to grill the outside and heat the inside through.

To do the job you heat the pot till it is very hot indeed, and you put in very little oil, a teaspoonful. One generally allows about three epigrams to each person, and two breasts will afford sixteen. They can thus be handily grilled four at a time. When the oil is really smoking hot put the pieces in, turn them rapidly, grill them till dark brown—and they can be a bit blackened at the edges—and lift them on to a warmed dish. The seared and almost blackened breadcrumb, with its flavour of grilled meat and slightly scorched toast, gives this 'poor man's feast' a unique and marvellous flavour.

I think that perhaps one could eat a purée of potatoes with epigrams, but I am not sure whether it might not be one of those dishes that are best eaten with the fingers, together with bread, an earthenware pot of Beaujolais, and a big bowl of one of those jumble-sale salads which are made of all the things in the kitchen 'there wasn't enough of to be worth keeping': dandelion, watercress, a tomato or two, that rather limp small lettuce, a few olives on a saucer, a piece of green pepper left over from the soup.

Last offering in the mutton line is a great change and a vast relief, being neither greasy nor bony, Gott sei dank, and great sighs of content go up inevitably at that thought, no matter how much other work is involved, and in truth there isn't much.

The dish is called Moussaka. Cookery books frequently contain some very fancy versions of this, swaggering under the Greek or Turk flag, all suspiciously like that dread saddle of camel and no wonder Othello got so upset when he went to Cyprus. This variation is in French kitchens called Moussaka Moldava, which has a homely farmyard sound and if a bit more French than Czech that is just kitchen folklore, much like strewing bits of pineapple about and calling the result Hawaiian.

It is not made with raw meat, nor mercifully with the wreck of neck, but with a left-over roast, generally a leg. It happens very frequently that a roast leg is not all eaten the first day, and fairly often there is a good deal, quite enough for another meal with a bit of padding-out, and that is the purpose of this dish.

With a sharp boning-knife, take the meat in as large pieces as you can manage off the bone; you will, very likely, have two or three good-sized chunks and some scraps. Trim off any burned or hardened edges; put these together with the bones in a small saucepan and simmer them with any gravy you have left over and any vegetable scraps like onion skins, to make about half a litre, or around a pint, of brown stock with a muttony flavour. This stock can be enriched with a spoonful of tomato purée, and darkened with a drop of caramel blackjack. About an hour's cooking will pull the flavour out of the bone and reduce the stock. Meanwhile you can blanch six firm tomatoes for ten seconds in boiling water, which is enough to loosen their skins (add tomato skins and cores to the stock) and cut your meat into thick slices, and from there into small cubes. Working with left-overs does always, I am afraid, involve one in these fiddling jobs, which eat up a lot of time, but this work could easily enough be done the evening before, saving trouble and time next day.

When the stock is well cooked out, chop an onion coarsely, fry it in a small spoonful of oil, using a thick pot, and when it is just beginning to brown add the finely diced meat and two cloves of peeled garlic. Turn the flame down, stir all together, let it fry gently for a few seconds, and thicken the mixture with a spoonful of flour—as you notice, this is all very similar to the method for shepherd's pie, and that is just what Moussaka is. In your rôle as Czech shepherd you now strain in the stock, stirring regularly that it should not be lumpy, and bring the whole gently to the boil. In your pot you now have a fairly slack sauce, containing diced meat, with a good smell and a nice flavour, which you improve with a little salt and a scrap of thyme or marjoram, or, if preferred, tarragon.

This meat, being roasted, will toughen as soon as it meets the boiling stock, and will need an hour's simmering in the sauce to get it really good and tender again. While this is going on take three nice aubergines (I am assuming throughout that as usual you are working for four or five persons), cut off their stalks, and peel the shiny black skin finely. Cut each aubergine lengthways into about four thick slices—or if you prefer crossways into ten or more rounds, each slice to be two centimetres thick or about three quarters of an inch, dust them in flour, and fry them rapidly in a large shallow pan as though they were fish, seasoning them like fish with salt and a squeeze of lemon juice. Two minutes each side in a hot pan is plenty. You will notice that they absorb a lot of oil; do not let this worry you, for the meat is lean and your sauce is not greasy. The aubergines need not cook right through, and should on no account be allowed to shrivel up or dry out. To fry them to a light brown is quite sufficient.

You now take a shallow oblong gratin dish, just as for shepherd's pie, and fill it half to two-thirds full of the cooked sauce mixture. Lay the aubergines in rows over this, alternating and overlapping with slices of the skinned raw tomatoes. When the pot is full, or nearly so, sprinkle fine brown breadcrumbs evenly over the top to make a crisp crust and put the dish in a hot gratin oven, near the top, for ten minutes or enough time for the dish to become very hot and crunchily brown on the surface. Plain boiled potatoes—or baked in their jackets, but cooked in any case without fat—go well with this dish: no other vegetable is needed except plenty of fresh chopped parsley for greenery. If you feel like it you could always eat some salad—for example of French beans—either before or after. It is a rich but quite a light dish, there is often not a great deal of it, and one could very well decide to top up with a steamed or baked sponge pud. Almost any wine, red, white or rosé. This dish is so good that the shepherd's existence, which sounds excruciating enough as a rule, appears in quite a rosy light.

13

THREE SIMPLE CHICKEN DISHES

A chicken—not at all long ago—was a party dish, something fit to be offered to the most exacting guest and at home a feast. Rarely can there have been so total a déclassement, so sudden and dramatic a collapse in social standing and consequence: it is like Horatio Bottomley the People's Friend, disgraced and flung in jail. All this is the fault of those revolting deep-freeze chickens, or rather blobs of vile protoplasm for they deserve no name, those musty, slimy, tasteless, diseased things, foully distorted and perverted in their miserable chicken Auschwitz, soaked in water and then frozen, cheating us to the very end. The poor devils imprisoned in Alcatraz—as though that was not enough—went on hunger strike against these objects, and one is not remotely surprised. The one advantage that they have brought about is to have made other, real chickens so cheap, by a mercy and a dispensation of loving providence, that we can buy the very best chickens there are and still congratulate ourselves on being economical. It is long since I bought them in England, but in France there are more than a dozen kinds of good ones from varying regions, culminating in the famous birds of la Bresse, each stamped and guaranteed by the local Syndicate as hand-reared and healthily fed, and something of the sort must surely exist in other lands.

Buy your chicken fresh and examine it carefully, for paws which have walked upon real ground with worn healthy nails, for straight healthy limbs, a clean healthy skin, a bright eye, and above all for a large, firm, healthy, milk-chocolate-coloured liver, which is the most telling sign of all that this bird has nourished itself upon honest maize and no ghastly hormones.

The first chicken and the best chicken is a *roast* chicken. Indeed we are back with Proust. We may have got a bit bored with tiresome Odette or frightful Madame Verdurin, but we have that

unique physical apprehension of colour, sound, smell and form—
Proust's roast chicken, cooked of course by Françoise and
magnetizing us utterly from the moment she horrified poor
Marcel, chasing it around the yard, roaring out 'Sale bête'.

It is the nicest of all poultry; flesh firm but tender, not dry, of
marvellously delicate flavour. Its proportion of fat is perfectly
balanced, anyone can digest it, and it is splendidly docile, lending
itself to a thousand accompaniments. In the classical repertoire,
there are as many different recipes for chicken as for all other
kinds of meat put together. It is extremely simple to cook. A roast
chicken, perfectly plain, the simplest of all, is to my mind the best
of all.

In England, I am sorry to say, as the lawyers put it, 'I am
instructed there is a notoriety.' People will cook the poor bird too
long and too slowly, and it dries out, can't help it. Wicked cookery
books must bear much blame.

Françoise began by 'Sorry, Madame Octave, but I have to poke
my fire' and the best roast is done in an old coal range. We have to
put up with shiny but inferior modern stoves (the most 'hygienic'
kitchens generally produce the worst food, as Mr. Christopher
Driver sensibly puts it in a recent article in *The Times*) which have a
thermostat, and since a chicken needs a lower temperature than
other roasting meats, and is best cooked in butter, a fat which
burns easily, this needs careful setting. As a general rule, the
smaller the bird the hotter the oven should be, but for a bird of a
kilo and a half, or about three pounds, which is right for four or
five people, I would set the temperature half-way up the thermostat or a little over, but not more than 'six out of ten'. I would
cook it in an enamelled iron pot, just big enough for the bird to sit
in, or a heavy fireproof dish, not too shallow.

Chickens are often sold 'oven-ready', meaning cleaned: they
are no such thing but must be singed on a sharp flame, burning off
all fluff and feather, leaving the skin dry and feeling floury. It is
quite unnecessary to pat flour on the skin; indeed it is silly. If the
chicken has been cleaned you should have the giblets left you: the
neck, heart, liver and the skinned stomach. If you want to make

gravy this is all put into the pot underneath the chicken where it will brown. Otherwise it is put in a saucepan with cold water, boiled up, skimmed two or three times over as many minutes, and left to simmer on a slow fire. The chicken bones can be added later.

A chicken in a pot needs no tying with string, but it must first be arranged as though for tying, the kneejoints together closing the fundament, the little winglets trimmed off (stockpot) and the wings not wrenched back but arranged naturally on either side of the thoracic opening.

A properly nourished chicken has not only plump flesh but quite a lot of fat inside, firm, and if maize-fed a butter colour. If this has not carelessly been removed it should be left where it is. If there is no fat then a hazel-nut of butter can be put inside. For the outside, a walnut of butter is enough. It can be rubbed over the skin, or used to butter the inside of a deep round pot that just fits the bird, which comes to much the same thing. Sprinkle the bird lightly with salt and grind a very little pepper into the bottom of the pot, over the giblets if used.

A roast chicken needs no herbs whatever. A little sliced onion at the most, Françoise would have peeled a single shallot, split it, and tucked it into the tail opening.

Recipes frequently tell you to place the bird on its back. This is as good a formula as I know for changing gold into dross. There is also much clotted nonsense spoken about 'twenty minutes to the pound and twenty over'. This could be possible for a stuffed chicken, but will dry a plain bird fatally. A bird weighing 1,200 gr. or two and a half pounds, will take three quarters of an hour. It is laid in the pot on its side, resting on the thigh joint. After a quarter of an hour it is turned on to the other thigh, and for the last quarter it is put on its back to colour the breast crisp and gold.

With a thermostat there is no difficulty. Even without one it is easy to judge. When you open the oven after the first quarter the butter will be brown and sizzling. The top thigh will be just starting to colour. If the butter is blackening, or the skin of the bird scorching, the oven is too high and must be reduced at once.

If everything seems pale and languid, plainly the fire is too low.

The bird is turned with a sharp fork, pronged well in under the thigh and next the backbone. Do not prick thigh or breast. You would not with a woman either. The undermost thigh, now on top, is already a nice colour, and if with a half-lemon you trickle a few drops of juice upon it, and upon the exposed wing, you will be having a very pleasant meal rather soon.

If, when turned on its back for the last quarter, the breast already seems brown it can be protected with the foil off a butter-packet. The often-advised wrapping of the whole bird in kitchen foil is simply nonsense: such a process is suitable for very dry nasty birds like pheasants and guinea-hens.

When taking the bird out, check that it is really cooked. A chicken must be 'only barely' done, but must not be pink. When well pronged upon its fork hold it up tail downward: the juice which trickles should be quite colourless. If it is pink, as happens sometimes with heavy-boned birds, give it another five minutes.

Leave the bird—like all roasts—ten minutes to settle on the carving board before cutting it.

The buttery juices from the pot are poured into a little bowl, and the sticky bits which have coagulated are dissolved by pouring in a sherry glass of water, rinsing it round, and boiling it up. All this does not produce much 'gravy', but a properly roast chicken is very juicy anyhow, and is also served traditionally with deep-fried potatoes and a green salad of watercress, or iceberg or batavie lettuce, or cos lettuce (and I wonder why cos and what it means).

If gravy is insisted upon, as in Mrs. Todgers' household, the pot is left upon a gentle flame until the giblets have gone properly brown and the fat has clarified: it can then be poured off, and the pot rinsed with half a pint of water or white stock, which has to be simmered under cover for ten minutes to bring out the flavour and the colour, and seasoned with a pinch of salt before it is strained. Potatoes baked in their jackets are then perhaps a better choice than fried, and a vegetable could replace the salad, for preference a fresh summer vegetable like peas, French or runner beans, or endive.

I know that in England it is the custom to cook bacon or sausages with a roast chicken. These things are all good in their way, but it seems to me a pity to combine the delicate taste of chicken with the crude flavours of smoked, salted or spiced pork. I like things to taste of themselves and to be simple—Curnonsky, the gastronome who was a kind of twentieth-century Brillat-Savarin, went so far as to say that this was a prerequisite of any good cooking, in which I think he showed sound judgement. Bread sauce, though, is surely a brilliant invention. Red wine, wherever it comes from, will go with roast chicken as long as it is light, unaggressive and in no way harsh.

One could begin this meal with a vegetable soup, or with paté, or indeed with anything that does not have too overpowering a taste. Since this makes a very light and digestible meal, one might be tempted into having a massive pud afterwards, that is if one were as greedy about suet roly-poly as I am.

The second dish is *chicken risotto*. Hereabouts it is easy to fall into a tangle of pedantry concerning nomenclature. French cookery books call any kind of chicken stew a fricassée, and there are two kinds: brown ones and white ones. I suppose that this would be clear enough were it not that 'chicken sauté' is very similar. It is cooked in a different manner, but the result looks the same because the pieces of chicken end up, too, in a sauce. It is a more sophisticated dish. Trying, perhaps incompetently, to express the difference in simple terms I will say that chicken can be cooked in a liquid—and this recipe illustrates one way of doing so—or it can be cooked in its own juice, which is a true chicken sauté and we'll have a shot by and by. For the moment we'll stick to risotto (quite a good choice of verb, that) and start by saying that the principal element is a chopping knife, because a raw chicken is cut into small pieces. It is quite easy. With a boning-knife cut through the skin which binds the thigh to the carcase, below the wing. You can now double the thigh back towards the tail, pressing it out and cutting along the backbone. As you come down towards the tail you meet a ball-and-socket joint which was the bird's hip: it is only held by a little tendon easily snicked through. Once this is done the whole thigh peels off in your hand. Repeat on the other side. With the deep-bladed knife you cut through the joint between thigh and drumstick, and cut the thigh in two with a light chop, only a tap, through the bone, Two more taps cut the knuckles off the top and bottom of the drumstick. Each leg has made three neat pieces.

The carcase now shows up in a triangular shape, like a wedge of cheese. The wings form the broad end. Holding the carcase with this towards you, first cut off the winglets and then the two wing corners; since this is not at all lucid here are some little drawings. The wedge is now a thick slice, with the breast on top and the back below, held together by the rib-bones and by membrane. Separate the whole back with one good chop, and cut the breast into three or four regular pieces. Since this whole section is a technical description it can be skipped if it bores you. But it is worth the trouble, because these technicalities can be interesting, and skipping deprives you of a good dish.

Chop up the carcase, and put all the bones into a small saucepan with vegetable trimmings, to make nearly a pint, or about four decilitres, of strong stock, by adding cold water and simmering for

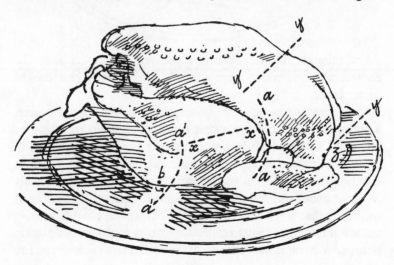

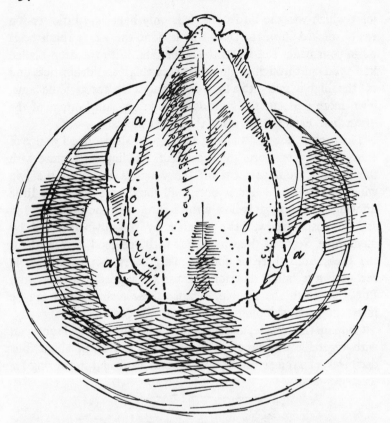

thirty minutes. In the meantime you are getting on with the risotto, which is really more a pilaff, because it is best cooked under cover.

Put a large fireproof dish, quite a shallow one (or, of course, a pot) on a medium flame with a spoonful of oil and a walnut of butter. When this goes brown and sizzles drop in your pieces of chicken. Stir them about with a wooden spoon, so that they brown lightly all round. When they begin to go blonde add a coarsely chopped onion and the white of two small leeks cut in one centimetre lengths. When this, too, starts to blonde add a soupbowlful— we are thinking as usual of four or five persons—of long-grain rice, and a pinch of raw saffron. Make the flame as low as you can get it and leave this, giving it a stir occasionally, until the stock is ready. The rice will absorb any surplus fat there is, and take on a transparent look.

Strain the stock into the rice, measuring two soup-bowls of liquid but no more; if over-reduced make up the quantity with water. Stir the dish so that everything is settled evenly, and the chicken pieces covered by stock. Cover and simmer for twenty minutes, after seasoning with salt and nothing else. That is all. By that time the rice and the chicken will have cooked tender, all the liquid has been absorbed, and all the ingredients have taken on the buttercup colour and delicate flavour of the saffron. Transfer to a serving dish if you like, and sprinkle the whole with chopped chives, or chervil, or parsley. Garlic can be added to this dish if you like it. If you have a party, or if you wish to stretch this dish for extra persons, shellfish of any kind can be added as well as more rice. You then have the well-known Valencia rice. Chicken with pretty well any shellfish or such things as baby octopus forms a classic and very successful combination. Other vegetables, such as green peas or beans, baby artichokes, courgettes, fennel (all 'Italian' vegetables as well as Spanish) can be added, though they are best cooked separately and mixed in at the end. So can bits of raw or cooked ham. Bits of Spanish sausage I am less keen about, since I think they spoil the flavour, for they are as a rule highly seasoned with fresh paprika. I like the chicken by itself, when it tastes wonderful, and this although I adore shellfish.

Cold lager beer is good with rice dishes. Some kinds are awful. The nicest, strong but very delicate, comes from Pilsen in Czechoslovakia.

As I tried—badly—to explain, *chicken sauté* is not stewed, but comes out with the texture and flavour of a roast chicken. For this effect it is 'poêlé', a cooking method I described when talking about veal, but a chicken is much easier, and does not take as long.

The chicken is cut as for risotto, but in larger pieces; eight for a bird of 12-1,300 gr. or two and a half pounds—two thighs, two drumsticks, two wings and two pieces of breast. These are turned and stiffened in hot butter, in a pot or dish large enough for them to fit comfortably close together. They can be allowed to colour or not, according to whether the sauce to be made afterwards is designed to be white or brown. Quite often the pieces are sprinkled with alcohol and set afire at this stage. The pot is then covered and allowed to cook on a gentle fire or in a slow oven for twenty minutes. The 'white' pieces (wings and breasts) will now be cooked, but the dark meat generally takes another five to ten minutes before becoming quite tender. The meat should leave the bone effortlessly. A chicken which was slightly too fresh may take up to thirty minutes in all. The carcase is cooked in with the meat for flavour: all meat needs bones cooked with it in order to be at its best. Those oh-so-handy pieces of boned turkey or veal sold by eager supermarkets are always notorious for having no taste whatever, even if you have shovelled in enough brandy to give the wretched animal delirium tremens.

The sauce is made in the pot after the chicken is taken out (and kept warm, not hot, between two soup-plates). A cream sauce with wine or white stock, or a brown sauce: there are literally hundreds of recipes of this kind. But what I myself—for what that is worth—like best is to have a vegetable which will braise quickly in the pot, and to serve it simply with the chicken, along with noodles, or potatoes, or boiled rice. Tomatoes for instance, cut in quarters after being blanched and peeled, with a little basil. Celery or fennel, cut in quarters lengthwise. White turnips cut in fingers. Courgettes. Everybody has different likes. One can of course combine two or more vegetables; as a suggestion the Provençal 'Mireille', which is aubergine cut in slices and mixed with quarters of tomato and perhaps a few black olives, or ratatouille, which is aubergine, tomato, courgette and fennel with onion and garlic in any proportion you fancy.

The general method is to sprinkle finely chopped onion in the pot, add the vegetables in neat sections or slices, put the lid back on, and braise in the chicken juices for ten, fifteen or twenty minutes as the case may be. The pieces of chicken are put back in for a minute at the end to reheat, taking care not to boil them or steam them for any length of time. The most classical, and deservedly famous, of all these dishes is the Côte d'Or 'coq au vin' with a sauce made of diced bacon, whole tiny onions and mushrooms —or larger ones in quarters—and a half-bottle of good burgundy like a Volnay or a Chambertin, thickened at the end with a walnut of butter mixed thoroughly with a tablespoon of flour and whisked into the simmering liquid. It is not possible to use cheap cooking wine for this dish; the burgundy will cook out quite quickly and have no trace of acidity. The chicken is generally set alight at the start with a tablespoon of cognac.

AN EDWARDIAN DINNER PARTY

One can only have a sense of satisfaction in coming to the end of a book, like that of the workman who tidies up his bench, puts his tools away, throws out a dustbin full of rubbish and is then struck by the notion—belatedly—that it might be an idea to get the broom and give the floor a sweep. This satisfaction, a humble enough affair since it is no more than the mutter 'that job's done, anyhow', itself a reminder that the work is never done and that this is the merest pause, is not self-satisfaction. It is only the youngest and greenest apprentice who would congratulate himself. 'Made a good job of that' he chuckles, and is quickly damped by a resounding snub from his elders. The journeyman will say no more than 'Well, it was a job. It's done. May not be very well done but it's too late to think of that. It's done as well as I could do it, and if they're not content with that, well—sorry.' The master craftsman, who has more imagination as well as more talent, is likely to simplify further still: looking at his work he thinks that he could have done it better, asks himself why he did not do it better, and, immediately making the imaginative link, forces himself to look deliberately, with detachment, and observe how he could have done it better, for this will be of value in the future.

One thing they all have in common, which is to stand back and take a long look, before reaching for a piece of sandpaper, an oily rag, or a brush dipped in the varnish-tin. The act of 'standing back', to distance the object and get it in perspective, is common to every workman: it is an instinctive gesture. So do we all and it was in so doing that it came into my head that an 'afterword' would not alleviate or correct the defects in my work—daylight and champagne could not be clearer—but that it might be used to put our collective notion of food, of cooking, of the kitchen in these days into perspective, so that some idea might be formed of progress made, if any. Conceivably regress, or neither the one nor the other, since my private opinion is that the human being, running very hard indeed, remains invariably in the same place, which is one reason why such things as men walking on the moon appear more pathetic and touching than anything else: none but the most superficial could talk seriously of 'progress'—or none, perhaps, but the most innocent; Americans as a whole, and we too, having only so recently noticed that the gate to the Garden of Eden is barred.

The point at which we have in our turn said

> 'Brightness falls from the air.
> We are sick: we must die'

may vary individually but most Europeans of over forty would I suppose agree that the point of no return for European civilization came in the doomed brightness of the golden summer in 1914, and that the decorative arts of the belle époque, which we now admire with such nostalgia, cherish as 'antiques' and view as a final decadent flowering of the Renaissance rosebushes, were our last, already tainted moments of innocence. Good, let art-historians judge: I am not one of them, nor is this my theme. For the cook it is a well-chosen moment for looking at the kitchen. A cook wishing to get a distancing effect for his kitchen work need only glance at the files of menus preserved in, let us say, the Connaught Hotel. But I am no more than the outline of a cook; my juices have passed by a commonplace osmosis into letters, so that my fingers now sort through sacks of words instead of onions. Looking for an Edwardian dinner party I did not search the desk in the chef's office but the desk of a writer who was a witness to these times.

My dinner party is post-Edwardian, because we are in 1915. This has no importance, because the menu is perfectly Edwardian in feeling, and because the characters are harking back with nostalgia to the days they have known. The story unfolded during this dinner party is a nasty one, of a change in men's souls, of minds perverted, generosity soured, ideals as things a combatant can no longer afford—and a strong suspicion of self-respect lost. These men are unhappy. Brightness has fallen from the air. They attack their food in a pathetic endeavour to recapture health and life. They are sick; they know that they are about to die. We are in a Rudyard Kipling story called *Sea Constables* and much more might be said, but we have to close our eyes to all but the immediately relevant details—the Edwardian kitchen, table, and eating habits, in all their staggering vulgarity and luxury. King George has been on the throne five years, and what is more King George is about to kill this kitchen stone dead, by instituting austerity in the palace, but this is still the moment before hotel-keepers noticed such things. Kipling, expert journalist and superlative craftsman as well as writer of uncommon gifts and power, gives it us in exact details and with lovely economy.

We know all the circumstances. We are in an expensive and snobbish West-End hotel where there are 'rose-frilled electrics'—and rose-pink candles into the bargain, a lavishness which would have been unthinkable in 1939. The waiters are French; the food is the best.

It is a bachelor party, which makes no difference to the menu but the point is interesting, for it accentuates still further the insolent vulgarity of the proceedings—a turn of the screw. The party is for four officers of the Royal Navy Volunteer Reserve. They have in civil life been prosperous London business men; one a stockbroker, another a lawyer. It is noticeable that we are far from the gay and gentle cavaliers of *The Riddle of the Sands*. They gulp, they gobble, they speak with their mouths full and have lamentable manners. They are on leave from the hardships of coastal patrol in converted yachts: by definition nothing is too good for them. What is more, we are told that the headwaiter is under considerable obligation to the host, and that he has in consequence made a special effort. Whatever these men, they are going to eat the high crown of Edwardian food.

I think that to get the full impact one must give the menu all together in a breath as Kipling gives it (read aloud, with lamentable manners, by one of the characters) before examining it in any detail. Here it is. Oysters; Vesiga soup, Sole Colbert, Suprême of Chicken (manner unspecified), Filet Béarnaise, Woodcock, Pêches Melba, Croûtes Baron. There are only two wines—but what wines.

With the soup arrives a Pol Roger '04. This marque was with the 'Widow' the favourite English brand, and has maintained its reputation to this day. 1904 was an outstanding year for many wines, notably port. It was certainly 'millésime' in the Champagne, where only exceptional years are given a date at all, and must in '15 have been superb. They went on with this (so that there must have been at least two bottles) till the woodcock, when one of the most monumental of Edwardian Burgundies makes its appearance—a Richebourg '74. Wine purists might raise an eyebrow at this and wonder whether in '15 the stuff would still be drinkable. It may be a mistake of Kipling's, who might have thought it a claret, but this would be unlike him; he was extremely conscientious in researching details, but this is relatively unimportant: what is meant was that this should have been the grandest bottle in a very well-stocked cellar! The food has to be worthy of this; let us take a closer look.

One last introductory detail. The headwaiter says, and with some vanity, that 'he has composed the menu himself'. We may take it then that this represents the absolute top, not only in the treatment of the materials, and the method chosen for each dish, but in their juxtaposition. The point is the more important because there is such a staggering amount to eat. It is emphasized by Kipling that both the host and his guests are delighted by the choice. 'I couldn't have done better myself' the host says, with we may think some self-satisfaction, adding portentously, to show his worldly wisdom (a thing the men in *The Riddle of the Sands* would never dream of doing) 'though one *might* have substituted quails en casserole for the woodcock'. But then, argues a friend, playing the same card of self-content, there would have been no reason for the burgundy. (Aha, no, Kipling did not think it a Bordeaux.) They all nod solemnly in agreement.

The oysters are passed in silence. The men are hungry, they only want to give themselves an appetite, and these things are of no importance. Indeed oysters were then thought of as frivolities, hardly worth mentioning—like the modern saucers of olives and potato chips served with the apéritif. Yet these were for a certainty the best of native Whitstables, massive in size and at least a dozen each. There would be a great fuss made about them now. Only a few years later, in the early twenties, Galsworthy shows us Michael Mont and Bicket 'going into a fish place' for lunch. 'Two dozen oysters and two soles, and a bottle of Chablis' says Michael —then as now this was thought quite enough for lunch. We are also told that Michael bearded them, which we would not do. Michael was a very gentlemanly boy, and highly sensitive; he would not have embarrassed Bicket, and indeed the Cockney shop clerk polishes them off. Things have changed since!

Vesiga soup: I wonder if it is still to be found. I have never eaten or ever seen it, though when I was a boy in good restaurants I heard it spoken of, and it was in the classical repertory: it went I think also into salmon coulibiac, a kind of grand pie. It would not often have been seen, for it came like caviar from Russia, and had to do with the spine of the sturgeon. I am vague as to what it actually was: a half-recalled memory (can I have after all seen it?) tells me that it was gelatinous and swelled up like Chinese birds' nests, but I cannot guarantee that. It must have been the spinal marrow. What seems clear is that the soup was a very strong, good consommé with goodies therein—and that not just tapioca!

Still, oysters and a clear soup: that seems so far reasonably light. But wait!

Sole Colbert needs little comment. It is to this day one of the most familiar of French classics. An English speciality; Ludwig Bemelmans, writing in Brussels about the late twenties just before the stock-market collapsed says that anywhere near the Channel it was the best dish on the menu. These 'Dover' soles are much devalued objects. In 1915 the speed of trains and fish deliveries to London was faster by far than it is now: the sole would have been absolutely fresh, and what is more it was fried in butter. A fried sole was then thought of as a very light simple dish, suitable for invalids—convalescents got a mutton chop—to fortify. It is an arresting thought that a business man nowadays who had consommé and a sole Colbert would be anxious about his figure and would hurry on to cheese. These four villains are not properly

started yet. An entrée—two if we count the grill—and a roast are
to come. We will assume charitably that it was a small sole, and
recall that these four heroes have not had a decent meal in weeks—
but none the less . . .

The suprême of chicken—alas, we are told nothing about it. It
must have been polished off very rapidly, judging by the length of
the conversation before the fillet appears—and Kipling was
scrupulous about such details, but he was a ferocious cutter of
his manuscripts, and though his narrative unfolds in pace with
the menu he may have decided that too much introduction would
upset his artistic balance if not his characters' digestion! By
definition though, it was more than a mouthful. A suprême is a
whole boned wing, and not from a poussin or baby chick! Indeed
we can guess a good deal about it with accuracy. It was cooked in
a pan with butter, and served with a vegetable accompaniment,
artichoke bottoms, asparagus tips, or mushrooms, and of course
a sauce (we feel instinctively that tomatoes or peas would not have
been thought sufficiently festive.)

Observe the concentration of protein food that has appeared so
far. Being English, they would not have eaten much bread.

The fillet—another familiar classic. We might have assumed that
these were little individual 'tournedos' steaks were it not that
Kipling specifically gives us a man saying 'I'm going to have a
little more': it was therefore a whole fillet, roast rather than
grilled. This would be served with the sauceboat of béarnaise
separate, and would not have been alone on the dish. Baby vegetables, probably potatoes too, in a 'bouquetière' we can feel sure.
Notice too that béarnaise is yet more butter, and plenty of it too.

The woodcock . . . we are at the high point of the meal and must
be careful. They would have had one each and plainly done, but
think of the sole, the chicken, and the beef which have already been
guzzled. Because it is described in English, simply as 'Woodcock'
it would certainly have been served 'à l'Anglaise' meaning plain
roast, nicely underdone, served upon a canapé of fried bread with
a bunch of watercress and a little sauceboat of gravy. Any vegetable or other accompaniment would, it was felt, spoil this magni-

ficent dish, and quite right too, Suvarov or no Suvarov (a complex French dish of birds stuffed with foie gras). A woodcock is beyond question the finest of all game birds; a pheasant is rubbish in comparison, and the remark about quails en casserole pure nonsense. A woodcock has no gall, and is not cleaned; the creamy parts inside are spread upon the canapé in lieu of stuffing, and no Edwardian man would have resisted this delicious goody for an instant.

What is at this moment remarkable is that one guest refuses the burgundy and sticks to 'the Jolly Roger'. He is within his rights, since champagne can be drunk throughout any meal, and does not give one a hangover, but it is hard to imagine anyone turning down that burgundy—with woodcock too!

It is reasonable to comment that there is no salad, but these *convives* are not French. Nor is there any nonsense about sorbet: no, course upon course of solid stuffing! And they polished it all off. By this time the narrative is at its height, and neither Kipling nor his characters have anything further to say about food, except for the curious and suggestive detail that one looks lecherously at an actress who sits near by, remarking vulgarly that 'That's a peach melba too': hm; the evening is by no means finished.

Peach Melba sounds nowadays very lowly-Lyons. One must remember that then it was quite the contrary. Dame Nellie was the great star of the era, and this dessert was composed for her in person by Escoffier in person. Vanilla ice, and that made of fresh cream, a whole fresh peach poached in sugar syrup, a purée of fresh raspberries (by no means the jam-and-water of today) and snippers of fresh grilled almonds. There was not chantilly cream as well, I think—but I am open to correction.

Lastly—even now we have not yet finished—there was that essentially English and Edwardian invention the Savoury. I do not know what 'Croûte Baron' was, but with a name like that it was probably a tartlet, or a 'bouchée' if made of leafy pastry. What went in it? Well, the Edwardians had a passion for things like sweetbreads and cockscombs, with little piquant whatnots—the famous 'Financière' has stoned olives and pieces of gherkin.

One well-known savoury of the period, much appreciated at Elysée or Matignon banquets and carrying the dignified name of Canapé MacMahon, is a short-paste tartlet filled with slices of chicken-liver, mushrooms, and beef marrow, rolled in meat-glaze: no more need be said except that yet another, famous to this day (I have myself made both these many times for pompous banquets such as the annual beanfeast of the Lower Limousin Cattle Dealers) is 'Beurreck', and my purpose is only to show how richly buttery these things could be even after the gigantesque meal described. Beurreck is an oblong slice of firm cheese, a Gruyère or such-like, about the size of a packet of twenty cigarettes but of course thinner, around which a pancake is wrapped, envelope wise, stuck down with raw egg. This envelope is then itself egg-and-breadcrumbed and fried ... words fail me.

They do not finish up with a handful of walnuts—or maybe they did, but we are not told. Nor is anything said about coffee, brandy, or port, to do them justice. But what is said is that before leaving one remarks that 'There's a glass left all round' which means that for the four of them—no, three, but there are four glasses—there were at least two bottles of Burgundy.

And quite in character they drink it happily off.

'The usual I suppose—damnation to all neutrals.'

For the first time, the destruction of the world is a patriotic objective.

INDEX